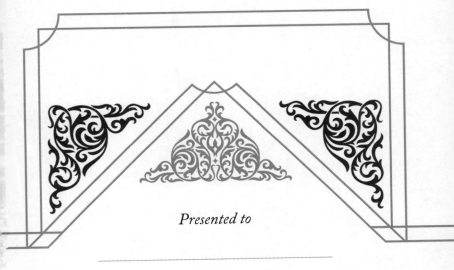

Presented to

....

From

....

On date

....

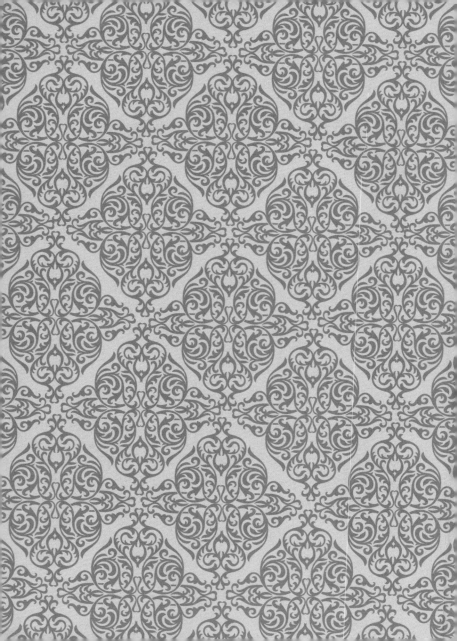

DONNA K. MALTESE

365 Devotions
ON THE

Daily Inspiration from Classic Prayers

BARBOUR BOOKS
An Imprint of Barbour Publishing, Inc.

Published by Barbour Books, an imprint of Barbour Publishing, Inc., 1810 Barbour Drive, Uhrichsville, Ohio 44683, www.barbourbooks.com

Our mission is to inspire the world with the life-changing message of the Bible.

Member of the
Evangelical Christian
Publishers Association

Printed in China.

INTRODUCTION

For thousands of years, men and women of faith have penned powerful prayers, for themselves and the masses. Here, for the first time ever, 365 classic prayers are available under one cover for readers who want to tap into the power of the ages. Each daily reading begins with a short devotional reading and a supporting Bible verse, followed by a classic prayer that can reach across the oceans of time to touch the heart, lift the spirit, embolden the soul, brighten the mind, and strengthen the faith. Included in the back of the book are brief biographies of the authors of the classic prayers. There you will also find an index of topics—such as adversity, aging, blessings, contentment, discouragement, faith, fear, guidance, hope, joy, plans, relationships, purpose, thoughts, truth, and more—so you can access specific help any day of the year!

May this book be a blessing in your life, helping your prayers pick up power, fueled by the belief that:

All things, whatsoever ye shall ask in
prayer, believing, ye shall receive.
MATTHEW 21:22

DAY 1

Each morning we choose which path we are going to follow: our own or God's. If we choose our own, we may find ourselves drifting off course in turbulent waters. But if we align our will with God's at the outset and listen for His voice throughout the day, we know we'll be cruising in the right direction, with God at the helm. Which course will you choose as you launch yourself into this day?

---

*And therefore will the LORD wait, that he may be gracious
unto you, and therefore will he be exalted, that he may have mercy
upon you. . .blessed are all they that wait for him. . . . Thine ears shall
hear a word behind thee, saying, This is the way, walk ye in it,
when ye turn to the right hand, and when ye turn to the left. . . .
And the LORD shall cause his glorious voice to be heard.*
ISAIAH 30:18, 21, 30

Afresh I seek thee. Lead me—once more I pray—
Even should it be against my will, thy way.
Let me not feel thee foreign any hour,
Or shrink from thee as an estranged power.
Through doubt, through faith,
through bliss, through stark dismay,
Through sunshine, wind, or snow, or fog, or shower,
Draw me to thee who art my only day.
GEORGE MACDONALD, *DIARY OF AN OLD SOUL*, MAY 15 READING

DAY 2

Each day we take pains to make sure we look good on the outside. But we all know beauty is only skin deep. What lies in our heart is the true teller of who we are. Spend some moments today becoming heart healthy by seeking to follow Jesus' example. It will change your life.

Keep thy heart with all diligence; for out of it are the issues of life.
PROVERBS 4:23

Dear Lord,
May I be no man's enemy, and may I be
the friend of that which is eternal and abides.
May I never quarrel with those nearest me;
and if I do, may I be reconciled quickly.
May I never devise evil against any person.
If any devise evil against me, may I escape
uninjured and without the need of hurting them.
May I love, seek and attain only that which is good.
May I wish for all humanity's happiness and envy none.
May I, to the extent of my power, give all needful
help to my friends and to all who are in want.
May I respect myself.
May I always keep tame that which rages in me.
May I accustom myself to be gentle, and never be
angry with people because of circumstances.
May I never discuss who is wicked and what wicked things he has
done, but know good people and follow in their footsteps.
EUSEBIUS OF CAESAREA

DAY 3

God requires our obedience. Not because He wants to make life difficult for us, but because He alone knows what's good for us. For when we are walking in His will and way, we're able to avoid the pitfalls and predicaments that distract and discourage us. In fact, when we live in obedience, we find ourselves enjoying all God has planned for us. Whether or not we think, from our limited knowledge, what He's telling us makes sense, and whether or not we understand, with our limited perspective, where He's leading us, we can trust that the Father truly does know best and sees all.

By faith Abraham, when he was called to go out into a place which he should after receive for an inheritance, obeyed; and he went out, not knowing whither he went. By faith he sojourned in the land of promise, as in a strange country. . . . For he looked for a city which hath foundations, whose builder and maker is God.
HEBREWS 11:8–10

Almighty and everlasting God, only speak to us that we may hear thee. Then speak to us again and yet again so that when in our hearts we answer thee by saying No, we may at least know well to whom we say it, and what it costs us to say it, and what it costs our brothers, and what it costs thee.
FREDERICK BUECHNER

DAY 4

God wants our hearts totally devoted and dedicated to Him. Yet sometimes His gifts to us get in the way. When we're feeling well, have a full stomach, and are successful in our work and relationships, we may begin making God a secondary priority. But when those gifts are removed, when we're ill, in want of food, or facing failure, we may find ourselves suddenly on our knees, crying out to God, making Him our *first* priority. Remember that all you have—health, food, success, and more—is not yours but God's. And none of those gifts are to stand between you and Him. God is giving you all of Himself. And that's what He wants back—all of you. For then His strength becomes fully active.

For the eyes of the LORD run to and fro throughout the
whole earth, to shew himself strong in the behalf of
them whose heart is perfect toward him.
2 CHRONICLES 16:9

Lord, you gave me health and I forgot you. You take it away and I come back to you. What infinite compassion that God, in order to give himself to me, takes away his gifts which I allowed to come between me and him. All is yours. You are the Lord. Dispose everything, comforts, success, health. Take all the things that possess me instead of you that I may be wholly yours.
FRANÇOIS FÉNELON

DAY 5

Nothing will happen today that God hasn't already seen coming. So rest assured that God's got you. That His constant thoughts toward you are filled with peace as He works out His plans for your life. Secure in that knowledge, you can have patience and be at peace no matter what your day brings. You and your life are in God's hands.

For I know the thoughts that I think toward you, saith the LORD, thoughts of peace, and not of evil, to give you an expected end. Then shall ye call upon me, and ye shall go and pray unto me, and I will hearken unto you. And ye shall seek me, and find me, when ye shall search for me with all your heart.
JEREMIAH 29:11–13

I do not know, O God, what will happen to me today,
I only know that nothing will happen to me but what has been foreseen by you from all eternity, and that is sufficient, O my God, to keep me in peace. I adore your eternal designs. I submit to them with all my heart. I desire them all and accept them all. I make a sacrifice of everything. I unite this sacrifice to that of your dear Son, my Saviour, begging you by His infinite merits, for the patience in troubles, and the perfect submission which is due to you in all that you will and design for me.
ÉLISABETH OF FRANCE

DAY 6

Why not make your whole being—mind, body, soul, and spirit—a united expression of gratitude to God! Give Him a standing ovation for all the blessings He's poured down upon you—within and without, seen and unseen. Thank Him for all the intangible and tangible blessings you've received. Thank Him for all the blessings in His storehouse waiting to pour down upon you. You'll be blessed when you do. For thanking God not only gladdens you but Him as well!

Come before his presence with singing. Know ye that the LORD he is God: it is he that hath made us, and not we ourselves; we are his people, and the sheep of his pasture. Enter into his gates with thanksgiving, and into his courts with praise: be thankful unto him, and bless his name.

PSALM 100:2–4

May my whole being, O God, be one thanksgiving unto Thee; may all within me praise Thee and love Thee; for all which Thou hast forgiven, and for all which Thou hast given; for Thine unknown hidden blessings, and for those which, in my negligence or thoughtlessness, I passed over; for any and every gift of nature or of grace; for my power of loving; for all blessings within and without; and for all which Thou hast yet in store for me; for everything whereby Thou hast drawn me to Thyself, whether joy or sorrow; for all whereby Thou willest to make Thine own forever. Amen.

EDWARD B. PUSEY

DAY 7

Silence. It can be hard to come by these days. But it's in the silence and stillness where you can find your way to God, to His presence, to a place where you can hear His still, small voice and feel His touch. Jeanne Guyon, the French mystic and author of *Experiencing the Depths of Jesus Christ*, advised people to "practice silent prayer for a long, uninterrupted period of time." For a person new to this idea, she suggested combining "spoken prayer with silent prayer." Below today's Bible verse are three different expressions Guyon said could be offered to the Lord—but they must be offered from the heart. See if one speaks to your inner spirit. Then take it with you as you enter the silence of heaven and come before your loving Lord.

And when he had opened the seventh seal, there was silence in heaven about the space of half an hour. . . . And another angel came and stood at the altar, having a golden censer; and there was given unto him much incense, that he should offer it with the prayers of all saints.
REVELATION 8:1, 3

"Oh my God, let me be wholly Yours."
"Let me love You purely for Yourself, for You are infinitely lovely."
"Oh my God, be my all! Let everything else be as nothing to me."
JEANNE GUYON

DAY 8

Where do you go when trouble comes knocking at your door? To whom or what do you turn for courage to face whatever's coming against you? In the prayer below, Oswald Chambers reminds you to go to God. To look to Him for all the help you need. To take courage from God's promise that He is your helper. He will never leave nor forsake you. God says so. So you know it's the truth. You know it's a solid promise. Because God will never leave you, you can boldly say, "I will not fear." Make it your outlook this second, this moment, this day, this life! When you do, God will not fail you! Because His help is not on its way—it's right there within you!

He hath said, I will never leave thee, nor forsake thee.
So that we may boldly say, The Lord is my helper,
and I will not fear what man shall do unto me.
HEBREWS 13:5–6

The Lord is my helper, I will not fear—I will not be haunted by apprehension. . . . I will remember God's say-so. I will be full of courage. . . . "The Lord is my Helper, this second, in my present outlook. . . . I will not fear." It does not matter what evil or wrong may be in the way, He has said—"I will never leave thee. . . . I will in no wise fail you." The Lord is my helper.

OSWALD CHAMBERS, *MY UTMOST FOR HIS HIGHEST*, JUNE 5 READING

DAY 9

Troubles, abounding for believers and nonbelievers alike, can become downright depressing, making us feel we're in the belly of Jonah's whale. Deep waters engulf us. Seaweed wraps around our heads. Just as we're about to sink to the bottom, we remember God, His love for us and ours for Him. And we pray. We become quiet, awaiting God's deliverance, knowing it will come. It's then we're spit out on the shores and find our footing on the Rock of our faith.

The waters compassed me about, even to the soul:
the depth closed me round about, the weeds were wrapped
about my head. . . . When my soul fainted within me I
remembered the LORD: and my prayer came in unto thee.
JONAH 2:5, 7

O Lord, my God! The amazing horrors of darkness were gathered about me, and covered all over, and I saw no way to go forth; I felt the depth and extent of the misery of my fellow-creatures separate from the Divine harmony, and it was heavier than I could bear, and I was crushed down under it; I lifted up my hand, I stretched out my arm but there was none to help me; I looked round about, and was amazed. In the depths of misery, O Lord, I remembered that Thou art omnipotent; that I had called Thee Father; and I felt that I loved Thee, and I was made quiet in my will, and I waited for deliverance from Thee.

JOHN WOOLMAN

DAY 10

God instructs you to "work with your own hands" so you'll "have lack of nothing" (1 Thessalonians 4:11–12). Sounds like a good plan, for you know that if you do your work for God's pleasure, He will praise you, saying, "Well done, good and faithful servant" (Matthew 25:23). Yet problems may arise when you look to the results of your work instead of just doing your work. God wants you neither diverted by what prospers you nor worrying about the outcome of your efforts. He doesn't want you comparing your work to that of others either. Instead, endeavor to leave all the results of your work in God's hands, to keep your attention on Him alone, and to improve upon the talents He's given you.

In the morning sow thy seed, and in the evening withhold not thine hand: for thou knowest not whether shall prosper, either this or that, or whether they both shall be alike good.
ECCLESIASTES 11:6

O God, who has commanded that no man should be idle, but that we should all work with our hands the thing that is good; grant that I may diligently do my duty in that station of life to which thou hast been pleased to call me. Give me grace, that I may honestly improve the talents thou hast committed to my trust, and that no worldly pleasures may ever divert me from the thoughts of the life to come, through Jesus Christ our Lord.
SABINE BARING-GOULD

DAY 11

God is exactly what you need when and where you need it. He's the pillar of fire going before you, leading you through the darkness of the wilderness path. He's the star above you, the bright light guiding you to the child-King. He's the smooth path that lies below you, keeping you on your feet. He's the good and gentle shepherd behind you, steering you to still waters, a place where He can restore your soul. God is all those things before, above, below, and behind you every moment of your life. And He will never take away His guidance, His provision, or His promises, nor remove Himself from you. Allow this all-encompassing God to meet your needs in this moment, to be what and where you need Him today, tonight, and forever.

And the LORD went before them by day in a pillar of a cloud, to lead them the way; and by night in a pillar of fire, to give them light; to go by day and night: He took not away the pillar of the cloud by day, nor the pillar of fire by night, from before the people.
EXODUS 13:21–22

Be thou a bright flame before me,
Be thou a guiding star above me,
Be thou a smooth path below me,
Be thou a kindly shepherd behind me,
Today—tonight—and forever.
SAINT COLUMBA OF IONA

DAY 12

A society can begin to fracture when children no longer respect or obey their parents. That's why God made it one of the ten commandments—and the only one with a promise! When kids respect their elders, things go a lot better—for you, them, and society as a whole. At the same time, parents are not to provoke kids, not to aggravate them.

If you have an argument with your parents or children, be humble enough to consider that you may have been wrong. Consider apologizing, if needed. And forgive them, just as God forgives you. Respecting and loving each other is a two-way street. Bless all children and parents. Love them. Respect them. Pray for them. When you do, things will be well with you, them, and God.

Children, obey your parents in the Lord: for this is right. Honour thy father and mother; which is the first commandment with promise; that it may be well with thee, and thou mayest live long on the earth. And, ye fathers, provoke not your children to wrath: but bring them up in the nurture and admonition of the Lord.

EPHESIANS 6:1–4

Give, I pray Thee, to all children grace reverently to love their parents, and lovingly to obey them. Teach us all that filial duty never ends or lessens; and bless all parents in their children, and all children in their parents.

CHRISTINA ROSSETTI

DAY 13

Discouragement can bring you down, so low that you feel as if God's at a distance, too far to reach. But it's not He who's moved; it's you. Remember, God's constantly pouring out His love upon you, yearning for you to just look up at Him. When you do, you'll find yourself uplifted. For He's there, ready to satiate your hunger, quench your thirst for Him. Look up.

As the hart panteth after the water brooks, so panteth my soul after thee, O God. My soul thirsteth for God, for the living God: when shall I come and appear before God? My tears have been my meat day and night, while they continually say unto me, Where is thy God?
PSALM 42:1–3

O Lord, our God, we desire to feel Thee near us in spirit and in body at this time. We know that in Thee we live and move and have our being, but we are cast down and easily disquieted, and we wander in many a sad wilderness where we lose the conscious experience of Thy presence. Yet the deepest yearning of our hearts is unto Thee. As the hart panteth after the waterbrooks, so pant our souls after Thee, O God. Nothing less than Thyself can still the hunger or quench the thirst with which Thou hast inspired us. Power of our souls! enter Thou into them and fit them for Thyself, making them pure with Christ's purity, loving and lovable with His love.
SAMUEL MCCOMB

DAY 14

How awesome that nothing can overcome the light of Jesus (John 1:5). And that Jesus has charged you to spread His light among others (Matthew 5:16). Even more amazing—because you're a believer who's given up yourself for Christ, you, like Him, are a sweet fragrant sacrifice to God. Today, pray for Christ to totally possess you so that you become more and more like Him, more of a shining and fragrant conduit of His light and aroma. When you do, others will look at you but see and smell only Christ.

Now thanks be unto God, which always causeth us to triumph in Christ, and maketh manifest the savour of his knowledge by us in every place. For we are unto God a sweet savour of Christ, in them that are saved.
2 CORINTHIANS 2:14–15

Dear Jesus, help me to spread Thy fragrance everywhere I go. Flood my soul with Thy spirit and love. Penetrate and possess my whole being so utterly that all my life may only be a radiance of Thine. Shine through me and be so in me that every soul I come in contact with may feel Thy presence in my soul. Let them look up and see no longer me but only Jesus. Stay with me and then I shall begin to shine as you shine, so to shine as to be a light to others.
MOTHER TERESA, FROM THE VIDEO *EVERYONE, EVERYWHERE*

DAY 15

Do you pray with a sense of expectancy? Do you believe that God has heard your prayers and that He will, if your desire is in line with His, answer those prayers with a resounding "Yes!"? Know this: God *requires* you to live in a state of expectancy. For Christ has promised "if we ask any thing according to his will, he heareth us: and if we know that he hear us, whatsoever we ask, we know that we have the petitions that we desired of him" (1 John 5:14–15). That means God *will* answer your prayers. And you put more power behind them when you expect God to answer in the affirmative—and go beyond what you'd imagined. Andrew Murray writes, "Beware in your prayers, above everything else, of limiting God, not only by unbelief, but by fancying that you know what He can do." That's powerful stuff.

So don't delay. Pray. Expect. And believe God will do more than you could ever ask.

I will look unto the LORD; I will wait for the God of my salvation: my God will hear me.
MICAH 7:7

Teach us, O gracious Lord, to begin our daily tasks with fear, to go on with obedience, and to finish them in love, and then to wait patiently in hope, and with cheerful confidence to look up to thee, whose promises are faithful and rewards infinite; through Jesus Christ our Lord.
GEORGE HICKES

DAY 16

God knows exactly what you need before you even ask Him. It's true! Jesus says so (Matthew 6:8)! Yet He still wants you to come to Him, to put what you desire into words so that you're clear on what you're asking. And God Himself will separate the good desires from the ones that are not so good for you, making sure you get all the best. What God *doesn't* want you to do is worry about the when, what, where, or through whom of how He's going to provide for you. Be content to leave all those details to Him. Just continue seeking, praising, and worshipping your provider. Trust Him for all. He's got you covered!

O taste and see that the LORD is good: blessed is the man that trusteth in him. O fear the LORD, ye his saints: for there is no want to them that fear him. The young lions do lack, and suffer hunger: but they that seek the LORD shall not want any good thing.
PSALM 34:8–10

Almighty God, who knowest our necessities before we ask, and our ignorance in asking: Set free thy servants from all anxious thoughts for the morrow; give us contentment with thy good gifts; and confirm our faith that according as we seek thy kingdom, thou wilt not suffer us to lack any good thing; through Jesus Christ our Lord.
SAINT AUGUSTINE

DAY 17

God has been with you since the day you were created in your mother's womb. He's still with you today, in this moment, as you read these words. He'll be with you tomorrow and the next day, until you are old and gray—and He'll be with you in the heavenly beyond. So keep on trusting God no matter what the days bring.

O Lord GOD: thou art my trust from my youth. . . . Cast me not off in the time of old age; forsake me not when my strength faileth. . . . Now also when I am old and greyheaded, O God, forsake me not; until I have shewed thy strength unto this generation, and thy power to every one that is to come.
PSALM 71:5, 9, 18

Almighty God, by whose mercy my life has continued for another year, I pray that, as my years increase, my sins may not increase. As age advances, let me become more open, more faithful and more trusting in you. Let me not be distracted by lesser things from what is truly important. And if I become infirm as I grow old, may I not be overwhelmed by self-pity or bitterness. Continue and increase your loving kindness towards me so that, when you finally call me to yourself, I may enter into eternal happiness with you, through Christ my Lord. Amen.
SAMUEL JOHNSON

DAY 18

What do you do when faced with the seemingly unconquerable? Pray, right? That's what King Jehoshaphat did when armies threatened to invade his kingdom. On his knees, he sought God's face and prayed for deliverance. He proclaimed his own helplessness, as well as his faith in God, saying, "We have no might against this great company that cometh against us; neither know we what to do: but our eyes are upon thee" (2 Chronicles 20:12). God responded by saying, "No problem. I've got this." The next day, the king told his people to just believe. Then he had his singers (praise) go out ahead of his army (strength), and "when they began to sing and to praise" (2 Chronicles 20:22), God went to work, defeating the enemy and leaving the spoils for Jehoshaphat's people. The point? It's great to pray. But end in praise. When you do, God brings the victory!

Believe in the LORD your God, so shall ye be established; believe his prophets, so shall ye prosper. . . . He appointed singers unto the LORD, and that should praise the beauty of holiness, as they went out before the army, and to say, Praise the LORD; for his mercy endureth for ever.

2 CHRONICLES 20:20–21

Open wide the window of our spirits and fill us full of light;
open wide the door of our hearts, that we receive and
entertain Thee with all our powers of adoration and love.

CHRISTINA ROSSETTI

DAY 19

Waiting *continually* on God (Hosea 12:6) with calm endurance seems almost impossible. And it is—without God. But with God, all is possible. Psalm 37 gives some tips on how to get there from here: Trust in God and do good where you are. Feed on your faith while you're waiting. Rest in God without worry, knowing He's working things out according to His plan, has everything under control. Just keep calmly walking in the way He's already laid out for you. The next thing you know, you'll have let go of your worry and gained His peace.

Trust in the LORD, and do good; so shalt thou dwell in the land, and verily thou shalt be fed. . . . Rest in the LORD, and wait patiently for him: fret not thyself. . . . Wait on the LORD, and keep his way, and he shall exalt thee to inherit the land.
PSALM 37:3, 7, 34

God, teach me to be patient, teach me to go slow,
Teach me how to wait on You when my way I do not know.
Teach me sweet forbearance when things do not go right
So I remain unruffled when others grow uptight.
Teach me how to quiet my racing, rising heart
So I might hear the answer You are trying to impart.
Teach me to let go, dear God, and pray undisturbed until
My heart is filled with inner peace and I learn to know Your will.
HELEN STEINER RICE

DAY 20

It's great to read the Bible, memorize verses, study different passages, and hear sermons. But if you don't put the message into action, if you don't put God's Word to work, both you and the world suffer. So don't just love the Word, live it. Be God's hands and feet. Put His plans, will, and ideas above your own. Let His light shine through you and thus onto the people around you. Follow as Jesus follows. Speak as He speaks. Love as He loves. Shine as He shines. Glow as He glows. When you put the Word into action, everyone prospers.

But be ye doers of the word, and not hearers only, deceiving your own selves. For if any be a hearer of the word, and not a doer, he is like unto a man beholding his natural face in a glass: For he beholdeth himself, and goeth his way, and straightway forgetteth what manner of man he was.
JAMES 1:22–24

We most humbly beg you to give us grace not only to be hearers of the Word, but doers also of the same; not only to love, but also to live your gospel; not only to favor, but also to follow your godly doctrine; not only to profess, but also to practice your blessed commandments, to the honor of your Holy Name, and the health of our souls.
THOMAS BECON

DAY 21

Thank God for the Spirit who leads you into truth, interpreting your groans, relaying your true needs to the Lord of all. Pray the prayer below with all your heart.

We know not what we should pray for as we ought: but the Spirit itself maketh intercession for us with groanings which cannot be uttered.
ROMANS 8:26

O God, forgive the poverty, the pettiness, Lord, the childish folly of our prayers. Listen not to our words, but to the groanings that cannot be uttered; hearken, not to our petitions, but to the crying of our need. So often we pray for that which is already ours, neglected and unappropriated; so often for that which never can be ours; so often for that which we must win ourselves; and then labour endlessly for that which can only come to us in prayer. How often we have prayed for the coming of Thy kingdom, yet when it has sought to come through us we have sometimes barred the way; we have wanted it without in others, but not in our own hearts. We feel it is we who stand between man's need and Thee; between ourselves and what we might be; and we have no trust in our own strength, or loyalty, or courage. O give us to love Thy will, and seek Thy kingdom first of all. Sweep away our fears, our compromise, our weakness, lest at last we be found fighting against Thee. Amen.
WILLIAM EDWIN ORCHARD

DAY 22

Often preoccupied with our own little fiefdoms, we forget we're to be working as servants in *God's* kingdom—not lording over ours! Instead of making things go our way, we're to ensure they go *God's* way. When Jesus taught us how to pray, He began by having us acknowledge who God is. And the very next sentence is about God's kingdom come, His will being done on earth, just as in heaven. Letting God have full reign is His primary purpose for us. Make it your purpose today—and every day—till His kingdom comes.

Pray ye: Our Father which art in heaven, Hallowed be thy name.
Thy kingdom come, Thy will be done in earth, as it is in heaven.
MATTHEW 6:9–10

O God, our leader and our Master and our Friend, forgive our imperfections and our little motives, take us and make us one with Thy great purpose, use us and do not reject us, make us all servants of Thy kingdom, weave our lives into Thy struggle to conquer and to bring peace and union to the world. We are small and feeble creatures, we are feeble in speech, feebler still in action, nevertheless let but Thy light shine upon us, and there is not one of us who cannot be lit by Thy fire and who cannot lose himself in Thy salvation. Take us into Thy purposes, O God. Let Thy kingdom come into our hearts and into this world.

H. G. WELLS

DAY 23

When the storms of life rise up, hunker down into your refuge, the rock of God. Cry out, and He'll bring you out. Even better, He'll still the waves, calm the wind. Jesus did it for His disciples when their boat was rocked. He'll do it for you too. So flee to the one who has power over all creation. Allow Him to calm you. When you do, you'll reach just what you've been striving for, that desired haven—peace in God within, no matter what befalls you without.

Then they cry unto the Lord in their trouble, and he bringeth them out of their distresses. He maketh the storm a calm, so that the waves thereof are still. Then are they glad because they be quiet; so he bringeth them unto their desired haven.

PSALM 107:28–30

Almighty God, the Refuge of all that are distressed, grant unto us that, in all trouble of this our mortal life, we may flee to the knowledge of Thy lovingkindness and tender mercy; that so, sheltering ourselves therein, the storms of life may pass over us, and not shake the peace of God that is within us. Whatsoever this life may bring us, grant that it may never take from us the full faith that Thou art our Father. Grant us Thy light, that we may have life, through Jesus Christ our Lord. Amen.

GEORGE DAWSON

DAY 24

Lady Jane Grey wrote the prayer below while held in the Tower of London, shortly before her execution in 1554. What a testament of faith amid adversity! Although you may not have your head on a chopping block, when trouble comes, there's a way out: looking to God to give you the strength and peace to endure, come what may.

I will love thee, O LORD, my strength. The LORD is my rock, and my fortress, and my deliverer; my God, my strength, in whom I will trust; my buckler, and the horn of my salvation, and my high tower.

PSALM 18:1–2

O Merciful God, be Thou now unto me a strong tower of defence, I humbly entreat Thee. Give me grace to await Thy leisure, and patiently to bear what Thou doest unto me; nothing doubting or mistrusting Thy goodness towards me; for Thou knowest what is good for me better than I do. Therefore do with me in all things what Thou wilt; only arm me, I beseech Thee, with Thine armour, that I may stand fast; above all things, taking to me the shield of faith; praying always that I may refer myself wholly to Thy will, abiding Thy pleasure, and comforting myself in those troubles which it shall please Thee to send me, seeing such troubles as are profitable for me; and I am assuredly persuaded that all Thou doest cannot but be well; and unto Thee be all honour and glory. Amen.

LADY JANE GREY

DAY 25

Anxious thoughts can so easily lead one astray, creating fear and turmoil within. The solution is to run to God, your defense, your rock of refuge—the one place you can go when your foot begins slipping, when you begin losing your spiritual balance. As you flee to His side, the God of all creation will help you pass through your anxious thoughts. In His might He will break up the fears amassed around your soul. Call and wait upon the Lord from deep within your heart. For He is not only your hope but your ultimate comforter. He will give you the power to stay calm amid your days of trouble (Psalm 94:13).

When I said, My foot slippeth; thy mercy, O Lord, held me up. In the multitude of my thoughts within me thy comforts delight my soul. . . . The Lord is my defence; and my God is the rock of my refuge.

PSALM 94:18–19, 22

O Lord, my God, be not Thou far from me; my God, have regard to help me, for there have risen up against me sundry thoughts, and great fears, afflicting my soul. How shall I pass through unhurt? How shall I break them to pieces? This is my hope, my one only consolation, to flee unto Thee in every tribulation, to trust in Thee, to call upon Thee from my inmost heart, and to wait patiently for Thy consolation. Amen.

THOMAS À KEMPIS

DAY 26

How wonderful to live with a heart open to the Spirit, His moving, His breath, His knock. When you possess this open awareness and an acceptance that whatever happens is for your good, you'll find joy. For then you're living for God, not for what He may provide. So open the door of your heart. Let the light and love in!

I stand at the door, and knock: if any man hear my voice,
and open the door, I will come in to him.
REVELATION 3:20

O Thou Divine Spirit that, in all events in life, art knocking
at the door of my heart, help me to respond to Thee. I would
not be driven blindly as the stars over their courses. I would
not be made to work out Thy will unwillingly, to fulfil Thy law
unintelligently, to obey Thy mandates unsympathetically. I would
take the events of my life as good and perfect gifts from Thee;
I would receive even the sorrows of life as disguised gifts from
Thee. I would have my heart open at all times to receive Thee—
at morning, noon and night; in spring, and summer, and winter.
Whether Thou comest to me in sunshine or in rain, I would
take Thee into my heart joyfully. Thou art Thyself more than the
sunshine; Thou art Thyself compensation for the rain; it is Thee
and not Thy gifts I crave; knock, and I shall open unto Thee.
GEORGE MATHESON

DAY 27

God has a task just for you, one He has uniquely qualified you to perform. It's one you have been created for. Are you in a posture to hear God's message? Have you gone and lain down in your place? When you do, when you're silent and still before Him, the Lord will come and stand before you. He'll call out your name. That's when you answer Him with the words, "Speak, Lord, I'm listening." God will then give you *His* words, tell you what He's up to, what He wants you to do. And, as His servant, you'll perform the task He speaks of.

Try it today. Go to God. Sit down in your secret place. Lay yourself before Him. When your heart, mind, soul, and spirit are in tune with God's, when you hear Him call your name, respond by saying, "Speak, Lord, I'm listening." Then willingly do as He instructs.

Samuel went and lay down in his place. And the LORD came, and stood, and called as at other times, Samuel, Samuel. Then Samuel answered, Speak; for thy servant heareth.
1 SAMUEL 3:9–10

Speak, gracious Lord, oh speak; thy servant hears;
For I'm thy servant and I'll still be so;
Speak words of comfort in my willing ears;
And since my tongue is in thy praises slow,
And since that thine all rhetoric exceeds;
Speak thou in words, but let me speak in deeds!
ALEXANDER POPE

DAY 28

There are days when you feel empty. When your faith feels weak at best. When your heart is cold toward others, perhaps even toward yourself and God. When your doubts seem stronger than your trust in the invisible God.

Amazingly enough, the former priest, monk, and leader of the Protestant Reformation—Martin Luther—felt all those things. So did the disciples. At times, Jesus referred to them as "O ye of little faith" (Matthew 8:26). So don't be ashamed if you find yourself feeling spiritually bereft. Instead, take all that you're experiencing to God. Be humble before Him. Tell Him where you're lacking and ask Him to fill the need. When you do, Christ will meet you where you are—and replenish you until your cup runneth over once again.

And he said unto me, My grace is sufficient for thee: for my strength is made perfect in weakness. Most gladly therefore will I rather glory in my infirmities, that the power of Christ may rest upon me.
2 CORINTHIANS 12:9

Behold, Lord, an empty vessel that needs to be filled. My Lord, fill it. I am weak in the faith; strengthen me. I am cold in love; warm me and make me fervent, that my love may go out to my neighbor. I do not have a strong and firm faith; at times I doubt and am unable to trust you altogether. O Lord, help me. Strengthen my faith and trust in you.

MARTIN LUTHER

DAY 29

Today's prayer is similar to Psalm 139:23–24—"Search me, O God, and know my heart: try me, and know my thoughts: And see if there be any wicked way in me, and lead me in the way everlasting"—but with one big, clarifying difference. The person praying is asking God to not just search him and know his heart, but help himself know it! He's asking God to not just test him and know all his innermost and lowest thoughts, purposes, and ambitions; he's actually asking God to help *him* know and understand them. He's not just asking God to reveal to him a harmful path, but to lead him away from it and onto God's! He is, in effect, asking God to search him well and then reveal himself to himself! Pray to know thyself today.

O LORD, thou hast searched me, and known me. Thou knowest
my downsitting and mine uprising, thou understandest my
thought afar off. Thou compassest my path and my lying
down, and art acquainted with all my ways.
PSALM 139:1–3

Search me, oh God, and know my heart and help me know it; try me and know my innermost, undermost thoughts and purposes and ambitions, and help me know them; and see what way there be in me that is a grief to Thee; and then lead me out of that way unto Thy way, the way everlasting. For Jesus' sake; aye for men's sake, too.
S. D. GORDON

DAY 30

Oh, to be free of temptation. To not be enticed to eat that chocolate cake, lie to improve one's standing, buy that unaffordable item, smoke that cigarette, or get involved in ungodly media. Temptation itself isn't bad, but giving in to it is. Because when temptation is satisfied, God is not. Because when one is drawn away by temptation, the urge can become an automatic habit, leading to a besetting sin that begins to control your life instead of God. So, ask God to cool your desire. Pray for Him to be with you in the storm of temptation. He'll lead you away!

And lead us not into temptation, but deliver us from evil: For thine is the kingdom, and the power, and the glory, for ever. Amen.
MATTHEW 6:13

Blessed are all Thy saints, O God and King, who have travelled over the tempestuous sea of this life and have made the harbour of peace and felicity. Watch over us who are still on our dangerous voyage; and remember such as lie exposed to the rough storms of trouble and temptations. Frail is our vessel, and the ocean is wide; but as in Thy mercy Thou hast set our course, so steer the vessel of our life towards the everlasting shore of peace, and bring us at length to the quiet haven of our heart's desire, where Thou, O God, art blessed and livest and reignest for ever. Amen.

SAINT AUGUSTINE

DAY 31

British writer Caryll Houselander wrote, "The one thing she [Mary] did and does is the one thing that we all have to do, namely, to bear Christ into the world." And her prayer below helps you get there from here. It's about presenting yourself to God so you can become like Jesus and bear Christ into your world. That means giving Him your body, eyes, mind, feet, hands, and heart in exchange for His humanity, vision, thoughts, path, prayer, and will to love. The more you give of yourself to enter that state of Christ, the more you will actually become like Him. He will increase and you will decrease. And although to lessen yourself sounds scary, it's actually more miraculous. For in that process, you will become *more* yourself, more the person you were actually created to be! Praise God!

I beseech you therefore, brethren, by the mercies of God,
that ye present your bodies a living sacrifice, holy,
acceptable unto God, which is your reasonable service.
ROMANS 12:1

Be born in us Incarnate Love; take our flesh and
blood and give us Your humanity; take our eyes
and give us Your vision; take our minds and
give us Your pure thought; take our feet and
set them in Your path; take our hands and
fold them in Your prayer; take our hearts and
give them Your will to Love.
CARYLL HOUSELANDER

DAY 32

Today's prayer by Corrie ten Boom is a simple one. But to truly understand its power, one needs to look into its author. Corrie ten Boom lived with her sister Betsie and watchmaker father, Casper, in the Netherlands. It was there, in their own home, that they hid Jews in their closet, provided for them during a time of severe rationing, and helped them escape the Nazi Holocaust during World War II. The ten Booms' efforts to shield God's people from evil became known as the Dutch Resistance. When their subterfuge was discovered, the entire ten Boom family was arrested and sent to a German prison. Casper died ten days later. Corrie and Betsie landed in a German work camp where Betsie eventually died. Before leaving this world, she told her sister, "There is no pit so deep that He [God] is not deeper still." After her experiences, Corrie wrote the book *The Hiding Place*.

So that's the history behind this powerful prayer. Now you can make it part of your own. Know that God is the place where you can hide from any evil that comes against you. Know that He is your ultimate protector. Hope in Him and His Word with the assurance that there's no pit so deep that God is not deeper still.

Thou art my hiding place and my shield: I hope in thy word.
PSALM 119:114

Thank you, Lord Jesus, that you will be
our hiding place, whatever happens.
CORRIE TEN BOOM

DAY 33

God is not just interested in *who* you are. He's also interested in *where* you are. And not just sometimes—but *at all times*. Yet it seems easy to get so caught up in your own plans for who you want to be and where you want to be in the world that you find yourself forgetting God, forgetting that His plans should always come first, always override your own. So go to God in the morning. Seek out and hear His loving voice. Tell Him you trust Him to lead you in the right way, down the right path. Then ask Him to make His desires known to you, to tell you who and where He wants you to be—in both your inner and outer self. Lift up yourself to Him and He will tell you all you need to know.

Cause me to hear thy lovingkindness in the morning;
for in thee do I trust: cause me to know the way
wherein I should walk; for I lift up my soul unto thee.
PSALM 143:8

O God, grant that at all times you may find me as you desire me and where you would have me be, that you may lay hold on me fully, both by the Within and the Without of myself, grant that I may never break this double thread of my life.

TEILHARD DE CHARDIN

DAY 34

When you've made a misstep, you may find it difficult to go to God and ask for His forgiveness. Yet that's exactly what you should do. For when you ask Him to forgive you, God actually blots out of His mind whatever you've done. He does that because He *wants* you to turn to Him—for all things amid all circumstances! So, if you've intentionally or unintentionally stepped out of His Way by turning to the dark instead of staying in His light—if you've left a brother or sister wounded, if you've preferred your plans over His, if in your impatience you've outrun Him, if you've broken a commandment, if you've injured those you love, or if you've muttered something against His will for your life—go to God. Ask Him to forgive you. Next thing you know, you'll be back in His good graces.

I have blotted out, as a thick cloud, thy transgressions, and,
as a cloud, thy sins: return unto me; for I have redeemed thee.
ISAIAH 44:22

If my soul has turned perversely to the dark;
If I have left some brother wounded by the way;
If I have preferred my aims to Thine;
If I have been impatient and would not wait;
If I have marred the pattern drawn out for my life;
If I have cost tears to those I loved;
If my heart has murmured against Thy will,
O Lord, forgive.
F. B. MEYER

DAY 35

Imagine living your life with the awareness that God's strength was continually flowing into you. That that holy strength, that power from your Creator and the Source of all things, was enough to meet your every need.

It's a fact that God gives and is constantly exuding all power. That He's the one who's the source of all the strength you'd ever need to meet your challenges. *Your* job is to look for it, to hope for it, to expect it. That's what it means to wait upon God. And when you do, He'll power you up. You'll be stronger than you ever believed possible. You'll be able to rise up like an eagle. To run and never tire. To walk where He'd have you go and not stumble into exhaustion. Make today's prayer your constant belief, your mantra, every moment of every day. And finalize it with an *amen*, which means "so be it"! And it will be!

He giveth power to the faint; and to them that have no might he increaseth strength. . . . They that wait upon the LORD shall renew their strength; they shall mount up with wings as eagles; they shall run, and not be weary; and they shall walk, and not faint.

ISAIAH 40:29, 31

God's strength flows into me continually, and is sufficient for my every need. . . . So be it; amen!

AGNES SANFORD

DAY 36

Ending the day with a spirit of thanksgiving turned to God positively impacts you not only spiritually but emotionally, mentally, and physically! That's what today's science says—but the ancient writer of Psalm 4 knew it all along. Yet don't end at thanksgiving! Continue your prayer by asking God to bless those you love. Then put yourself in God's hands as you lie down in peace, knowing He'll watch over you tonight and prepare you for a good day tomorrow.

Thou hast put gladness in my heart. . . . I will both lay me down in peace, and sleep: for thou, Lord, only makest me dwell in safety.
PSALM 4:7–8

We come before Thee, O Lord, in the end of thy day with thanksgiving. Our beloved in the far parts of the earth, those who are now beginning the labours of the day what time we end them, and those with whom the sun now stands at the point of noon, bless, help, console, and prosper them. Our guard is relieved, the service of the day is over, and the hour come to rest. We resign into thy hands our sleeping bodies, our cold hearths, and open doors. Give us to awake with smiles, give us to labour smiling. As the sun returns in the east, so let our patience be renewed with dawn; as the sun lightens the world, so let our loving-kindness make bright this house of our habitation.

ROBERT LOUIS STEVENSON

DAY 37

C. S. Lewis, along with fellow Christians and authors Charles Williams and Hugo Dyson, belonged to a literary group known as the Inklings. When Williams died, Lewis recorded Dyson as saying, "It is not blasphemous to believe that what was true of Our Lord is, in its less degree, true of all who are with Him. They go away in order to be with us in a new way, even closer than before."

Let today's prayer and the idea that the one you've lost is still with you in some way hearten you as you mourn the physical death of your loved one. Just as Jesus is still with you, so is the dear one who resides with Him now.

Lo, I am with you always, even unto the end of the world. Amen.
MATTHEW 28:20

Lord, my loved ones are near me. I know that they live in the spirit.
My eyes can't see them because they have left their bodies for a
moment, as one steps out of one's clothing. Their souls, deprived
of their bodily vesture, no longer communicate with me.

But in you, Lord, I hear them calling me.
I see them beckoning to me.
I hear them giving me advice.
For they are now more vividly present.
Before, our bodies touched but not our souls.
Now I meet them when I meet you.
I receive them when I receive you.
I love them when I love you.
MICHEL QUOIST

DAY 38

This is a noisy world. It's easy to get caught up in the din of media and the voices and gossip of others. It's even hard to find a decent role model, whether on TV, in the movies, or in "real life." Fortunately, the author of Colossians, the apostle Paul, gives you some good advice in this area. He urges you to seek things above, not here below. To set your heart, desires, and eyes on the things of heaven. To shut out all the worldly distractions by thinking, talking, and focusing on the higher things. Because, after all, you've been called to a higher life in Christ. When you change your thoughts and mind-set to Him, you lift the world.

If ye then be risen with Christ, seek those things which are above, where Christ sitteth on the right hand of God. Set your affection on things above, not on things on the earth. For ye are dead, and your life is hid with Christ in God.
COLOSSIANS 3:1–3

We pray shut us out from the world's clamour and the wagging tongues and the noisy booming voices, and the example that would lead us not toward Thee, but toward the world. Save us from it and shut us in with Thee, and may we think and talk and meditate on holy things today. This message now with Thy blessing may grace and mercy and peace be with us through Jesus Christ our Lord.
A. W. TOZER

DAY 39

You've had an idea in mind. And it seems like a good one. So you figured out a plan, the steps you would take to get there. But for some reason, things aren't working out. Even plan B seems to miss the mark. You keep hitting a wall. You begin to wonder what's happening, what to do.

The same thing happened to Paul and Timothy. They thought they should go one way, but the Holy Spirit forbade them to do so. Then they determined to go another. But the Spirit prevented that step too. Finally, Paul had a vision and they concluded that God was leading them in a different direction. (See Acts 16:6–10.)

If you find doors of opportunity being shut in your face, if you've come to a place where you don't know where to go next, turn to God. He'll let you in on His plans. . .if not today, then tomorrow. Just when the timing is absolutely right in His eyes, He'll let you know what He's trying to teach you, to tell you. He'll direct your steps down the right path.

A man's heart deviseth his way: but the LORD directeth his steps.
PROVERBS 16:9

Lord, we've tried everything we can think of.
Every road has seemed a dead end. Doors have
been so consistently shut in our faces that You must
be trying to teach us something. Tell us what it is.
CATHERINE MARSHALL

DAY 40

Worry can eat up your life. In fact, the word *fret*, a synonym for *worry*, comes from the Old English *fretan*, which means to "devour, feed upon, consume"!

The remedy for worry is to go to the God who resides within your heart. Spend time in His calming presence. Reawaken your awareness of how much bigger He is than your troubles. In Him you'll find all the hope and power you need to ward off worry—and more.

For God is not the author of confusion, but of peace.
1 Corinthians 14:33

God of our secret life, weary of ourselves, we come to Your shelter. Our span of troubled days we bring within Your calm eternity. Over our path of pilgrimage, we feel the spaces of Your immensity. In the strife of life and the sadness of mortality, we find a spirit of power and of hope in Your providence. Infinite Ruler of creation, whose spirit dwells in every world: we look not to the heavens for You, though You are there; we search not in the oceans for Your presence, though it murmurs with Your voice; we wait not for the wings of the wind to bring You near, though they are Your messengers; for You are in our hearts, O God. You make Your abode in the deep places of our thought and love. In each gentle affection, each contrite sorrow, each noble aspiration, we would worship You.

James Martineau

DAY 41

Jesus stopped at Martha's house. And while "Martha was cumbered about much serving" (Luke 10:40), Mary "sat at Jesus' feet, and heard his word" (Luke 10:39). When Martha asked Jesus to tell Mary to help her, He said, "Martha, Martha, thou art careful and troubled about many things: *But* one thing is needful: and Mary hath chosen that good part, which shall not be taken away from her" (Luke 10:41–42, emphasis added).

Whenever God and Jesus begin speaking with a "but," they're calling your attention to something important. "*But* seek ye first the kingdom of God." That's the number-one priority God wants you to have. When you put sitting at His feet and listening above all things, everything else falls into place.

But seek ye first the kingdom of God, and his righteousness;
and all these things shall be added unto you.
MATTHEW 6:33

O Father, calm the turbulence of our passions; quiet the
throbbings of our hopes; repress the waywardness of our wills;
direct the motions of our affections; and sanctify the varieties of
our lot. Be Thou all in all to us; and may all things earthly, while
we bend them to our growth in grace, dwell lightly in our hearts,
so that we may readily, or even joyfully, give up whatever Thou
dost ask for. May we seek first Thy kingdom and righteousness;
resting assured that then all things needful shall be added unto us.
MARY CARPENTER

DAY 42

God's Word is your doorway to knowledge. It's what gives you direction as it enfolds you, enlightening your spirit, informing your mind, touching your heart, guiding your spirit. When you stay within the light of God's Word, you are kept from going astray, from walking out of the path He's set before you, the one you alone can and were designed to walk.

When you bring God's Word before Him, He delights in your quest for knowledge, your thirst for hearing what He has to say. So, seek God's wisdom and knowledge every day. Allow His Word to unfold before you. Ask Him to reveal the pattern you are to abide by. Meditate on the precepts, the ideas He is laying upon your heart. And then as you rise up from the pages He's written just for you, follow that Light, the one that leads you to life everlasting.

Thy word is a lamp unto my feet, and a light unto
my path. . . . The entrance of thy words giveth light;
it giveth understanding unto the simple.
PSALM 119:105, 130

Lord, thou hast given us thy Word for a light to shine upon our path; grant us so to meditate on that Word, and to follow its teaching, that we may find in it the light that shines more and more until the perfect day; through Jesus Christ our Lord.

SAINT JEROME

DAY 43

In Jeremiah 23:23–24, you'll find these words: "Am I a God at hand, saith the LORD, and not a God afar off? Can any hide himself in secret places that I shall not see him? saith the LORD. Do not I fill heaven and earth? saith the LORD." Three times here the words "saith the LORD" appear. Sounds as if God is making sure you get the point.

There is nowhere you can go that God is not near. And very near at that. He's within you, around you, above you, below you. He's at your right hand and your left. Beneath your feet and above. He's nearer than your very own breath.

God is nearer than you can ever imagine. For it's in Him that you live and move and have your being (Acts 17:28). Live your life with that knowledge embedded deep in your heart and mind.

Whither shall I go from thy spirit? or whither shall I flee
from thy presence? If I ascend up into heaven, thou art there:
if I make my bed in hell, behold, thou art there. If I take the
wings of the morning, and dwell in the uttermost parts of the sea;
Even there shall thy hand lead me, and thy right hand shall hold me.
PSALM 139:7–10

Lord, you are closer to me
than my own breathing,
nearer than my hands and feet.
SAINT TERESA OF ÁVILA

DAY 44

When you lose your God-focus, you may become distracted and perhaps stumble along the way. To regain your sight, ask God to show you the one thing *He* wants you to do.

After Saul was blinded on the road to Damascus, God said to the believer Ananias, "Arise, and go. . .and enquire" (Acts 9:11). Following God's specific instructions and directions, Ananias found Saul and laid his hands upon him—and the scales fell from Saul's eyes!

God wants you to follow Ananias's behavior. To open your eyes to the visions He imparts. To then do what He calls you to do, eagerly and determinedly. Who knows whose sight will be restored when you open your *own* eyes and obey?

To him said the Lord in a vision, Ananias. And he said, Behold, I am here, Lord. And the Lord said unto him, Arise, and go. . . and enquire. . .for one called Saul, of Tarsus: for, behold, he prayeth, and hath seen in a vision a man named Ananias coming in, and putting his hand on him, that he might receive his sight.
ACTS 9:10–12

Grant me, O Lord, the single eye, that I may see the one thing needful, the thing that you want done. Don't let my vision be blurred by looking at too many things, or longing to please anyone but you. Give me simplicity of heart, quiet confidence in you, and eagerness to know and do your will.
GEORGE APPLETON

DAY 45

Author E. M. Bounds said, "Prayers are deathless. They outlive the lives of those who uttered them." It's true! Your prayers go up to heaven. There, angels hold golden bowls full of incense "which are the prayers of saints" (Revelation 5:8)! The prayers are then hurled back to earth, sprayed among God's people (Revelation 8:3–5). All cries to God go full circle *eternally and continually!*

Today's prayer of blessings for you, written by Saint Thérèse, is still alive! It's there for you to read, to take strength from, especially when you doubt where you are, where you're heading. Allow the saint's prayer to give you the peace you need. To trust you're *exactly* where God wants you. Take in her encouragement to hope, use your talents, pass on God's love, and live in contentment. Then bring yourself and your own prayers before God, settling into the reality of His presence and the foreverness of prayer.

And the smoke of the incense, which came with the prayers of the saints, ascended up before God out of the angel's hand.
REVELATION 8:4

May today there be peace within. May you trust God that you are exactly where you are meant to be. May you not forget the infinite possibilities that are born of faith. May you use those gifts that you have received, and pass on the love that has been given to you. May you be content knowing you are a child of God.
SAINT THÉRÈSE OF LISIEUX

DAY 46

Ah, to be totally yielded up to God, to allow Him to use you as He would, to do what He'd have you do. To leave all the plans, ideas, steps up to Him, knowing He's wiser than you. Have you so wholly given yourself, your life—all that you are—up to God?

Pray for that today. For God has chosen you for a specific purpose, one you alone can fulfill when you let Him work through you, no holds barred. When you willingly give Him all of you—mind, spirit, body, soul, and heart—you'll be amazed at the freedom in which you'll abide, the answers to prayer you'll receive, and the blessings that will be worked through you and into the world!

Ye have not chosen me, but I have chosen you, and ordained you, that ye should go and bring forth fruit, and that your fruit should remain: that whatsoever ye shall ask of the Father in my name, he may give it you.

JOHN 15:16

O Lord, I give myself to thee, I trust thee wholly. Thou art wiser than I, more loving to me than I myself. Deign to fulfil thy high purposes in me whatever they be; work in me and through me. I am born to serve thee, to be thine, to be thy instrument. Let me be thy blind instrument. I ask not to see, I ask not to know, I ask simply to be used. Amen.

JOHN HENRY NEWMAN

DAY 47

Few things are more precious than those friends that God has put into your life. Today, think about your friends. Thank God for connecting your paths. Then, in love, offer up your prayer for them to the greatest friend you'll ever have—Jesus.

---

*This is my commandment, That ye love
one another, as I have loved you.*
JOHN 15:12

O blessed Lord and Saviour, who hast commanded us to love one another, grant us grace that, having received Thine undeserved bounty, we may love every man in Thee and for Thee. We implore Thy clemency for all; but especially for the friends whom Thy love has given to us. Love Thou them, O Thou fountain of love, and make them to love Thee with all their heart, with all their mind, and with all their soul, that those things only which are pleasing to Thee they may will, and speak, and do. And though our prayer is cold, because our charity is so little fervent, yet Thou art rich in mercy. Measure not to them Thy goodness by the dulness of our devotion; but as Thy kindness surpasseth all human affection, so let Thy hearing transcend our prayer. Do Thou that they, being always and everywhere ruled and protected by Thee, may attain in the end to everlasting life; and to Thee, with the Father and the Holy Spirit, be all honour and praise for ever and ever. Amen.

SAINT ANSELM

DAY 48

Some days your mind may be too crowded with thoughts of what you should do. Unfortunately, such thoughts are often followed by worry over where you'll ever get the strength to do what needs to be done. Here's where God needs to enter the equation.

Open your mind to God's presence. Ask Him to shine His light on your thoughts. To fill your mind with the light of His wisdom. To revise your plans for this day so they're more in line with His plans for your life. Then know He'll give you the power to do what He's called you to do—for the glory of God, His Son, and His Spirit.

[I pray] that the God of our Lord Jesus Christ, the Father of glory, may give unto you the spirit of wisdom and revelation in the knowledge of him: The eyes of your understanding being enlightened; that ye may know what is the hope of his calling, and what the riches of the glory of his inheritance in the saints, and what is the exceeding greatness of his power to us-ward.
Ephesians 1:17–19

We beseech thee, O Lord, to enlighten our minds and to strengthen our wills, that we may know what we ought to do, and be enabled to do it, through the grace of thy most Holy Spirit, and for the merits of thy Son, Jesus Christ our Lord.
William Bright

DAY 49

Not only does worry rob you of energy, it robs you of your life. And it blinds you from seeing what the Son is doing, within and without. So turn your thoughts of worry to thanks of wonder! By doing so, you won't miss the Light and where it's leading you.

Therefore I say unto you, Take no thought for your life. . . .
Which of you by taking thought can add one cubit unto his stature?
MATTHEW 6:25, 27

O God, we thank Thee for this universe, our great home; for its vastness and its riches, and for the manifoldness of the life which teems upon it and of which we are a part. We praise Thee for the arching sky and the blessed winds, for the driving clouds and the constellations on high. We praise Thee for the salt sea and the running water, for the everlasting hills, for the trees, and for the grass under our feet. We thank Thee for our senses by which we can see the splendor of the morning, and hear the jubilant songs of love, and smell the breath of the springtime. Grant us, we pray Thee, a heart wide open to all this joy and beauty, and save our souls from being so steeped in care or so darkened by passion that we pass heedless and unseeing when even the thornbush by the wayside is aflame with the glory of God.

WALTER RAUSCHENBUSCH

DAY 50

When you feel weak, when you're tired of your work, your pleasures, your postponed hopes, and your very own self, go to the one who sees you, knows you, and longs to bring you out of yourself and into Him. Go to Jesus. He'll be your hiding place. The one who shelters you from the wind and the storms of life. Your Lord, your King looks upon you with compassion and tenderness. He wants to be the rock you look to, the one you stand on. The rock that will provide you with shade when the sun is at its hottest. Allow Him to be all that—and more. When you do, He'll gently draw you to Himself. And give you the true rest you need in this wearying land.

Behold, a king shall reign in righteousness, and princes shall rule in judgment. And a man shall be as an hiding place from the wind, and a covert from the tempest; as rivers of water in a dry place, as the shadow of a great rock in a weary land.
ISAIAH 32:1–2

O Lord, who art the shadow of a great rock in a weary land, who beholdest thy weak creatures, weary of labour, weary of pleasures, weary of heart from hope deferred, and weary of self. In thine abundant compassion and unutterable tenderness bring us we pray thee, unto thy rest, through Jesus Christ, thy Son, our Saviour.
CHRISTINA ROSSETTI

DAY 51

Sometimes you may find your eyes glazing over at the name *God*. Perhaps, because it's used so often in your prayers, it's lost its power for you. If so, consider using a name the Hebrews used for Him, one that reflects His many aspects, one that sparks your heart and fits your current need.

When the slave Hagar was running away from her mistress, Sarah, God found her in the desert, then spoke to, encouraged, and instructed her. There she referred to Him as the God Who Watches Over Me.

You too can address God by His many aspects by referring to Him as the Lord Is There, the Lord Is My Shepherd, the Lord Will Provide, Strong Tower, God Most High, Refuge, Shield, Fortress, the Lord Is Peace, the Lord My Rock, or Dwelling Place. Call God by the name your heart needs to bring more power to your prayer and life!

We will walk in the name of the LORD our God for ever and ever.
MICAH 4:5

God, this word we call you by is almost dead and meaningless,
transient and empty like all the words men use.
We ask you to renew its force and meaning, to make
it once again a name that brings your promise to us.
Make it a living word which tells us that you will be for us
as you have always been—trustworthy and hidden
and very close to us, Our God, now and for ever.
HUUB OOSTERHUIS

DAY 52

Some days you may find yourself so wrapped up in your daily doings, so driven by the stress of your day, so involved in running around to and from appointments or from deadline to deadline that you have drifted away from Jesus—not so much physically but mentally, emotionally, and spiritually. That's when you need to pray for Jesus to draw you to Himself. For when your awareness, your consciousness, of Him fills every thought and every space of your spirit and heart, you will become more His, more open to His voice, direction, love, peace, and light.

When under stress, look up to the one who can take you out of yourself and into Him. Allow Jesus to gather you into His arms, carry you close to His chest, and gently lead you into His peace of heart and mind (Isaiah 40:11).

No man can come to me, except the Father which hath sent
me draw him: and I will raise him up at the last day. . . .
And I, if I be lifted up from the earth, will draw all men unto me.
JOHN 6:44; 12:32

Yea, Lord Jesus Christ, whether we be far off or near, far away
from Thee in the human swarm, in business, in earthly cares,
in temporal joys, in merely human highness, or far from all this,
forsaken, unappreciated, in lowliness, and with this the nearer
to Thee, do Thou draw us, draw us entirely to Thyself.

SØREN KIERKEGAARD

DAY 53

In Matthew 25:31–40, Jesus told a parable about a King who, upon His return, will say to the ones right with God, "You are blessed because when I was hungry, you fed me; when I was thirsty, you gave me a drink. When I was a stranger to you, you welcomed me. When I was naked, you dressed me. When I was sick or in prison, you came to see me." And the people asked, "When did we see you hungry, thirsty, a stranger, naked, and sick or imprisoned, then feed, quench, welcome, clothe, and visit you?" And the King replied, "When you did those things for the lowest of the low, you did them for me."

In other words, Jesus says whatever you do for someone else, you do for Him. So when you look at that person—whether it be a friend or foe, a stranger or a relative—you're to see Jesus standing before you. You're to love all whom you encounter. To see them as God Himself. When you do so, that's love not only personified but love perfected!

Ask God to give you the power to see His face in everyone's.

No man hath seen God at any time. If we love one another,
God dwelleth in us, and his love is perfected in us.
1 JOHN 4:12

Grant me to recognize in other men,
Lord God, the radiance of your own face.
TEILHARD DE CHARDIN

DAY 54

The Holy Three—God, Jesus, and the Spirit—are an unfathomable mystery but are there for you, deep within. Spend time exploring the truth of their presence today.

And I will pray the Father, and he shall give you another Comforter,
that he may abide with you for ever; even the Spirit of truth; whom
the world cannot receive, because it seeth him not, neither knoweth
him: but ye know him; for he dwelleth with you, and shall be in you.
JOHN 14:16–17

You, O eternal Trinity, are a deep sea, into which the more I enter the more I find, and the more I find the more I seek. The soul cannot be satisfied in your abyss, for she continually hungers after you, the eternal Trinity, desiring to see you with the light of your light. As the hart desires the springs of living water, so my soul desires to leave the prison of this dark body and see you in truth. O abyss, O eternal Godhead, O sea profound, what more could you give me than yourself? You are the fire that ever burns without being consumed; you consumed in your heat all the soul's self-love; you are the fire which takes away cold; with your light you illuminate me so that I may know all your truth. Clothe me, clothe me with yourself, eternal truth, so that I may run this mortal life with true obedience, and with the light of your most holy faith.

CATHERINE OF SIENA

DAY 55

You rise from prayer to begin your duties. You feel set to meet the challenges before you, with God at the forefront of your eyes, ears, and thoughts. But then you actually *begin* your work, get caught up in the busyness of your day, and your consciousness of God has taken flight!

Today's prayer meets that contingency. It admits to God that a busy day lies ahead. But it asks, before the worker enters it, for God to keep her duties in line with God's. To keep her spiritual life on God's course whether or not her being is aware of God's presence. You may want to pray today's prayer *every* day to keep your duties on God's track!

Commit thy works unto the LORD,
and thy thoughts shall be established.
PROVERBS 16:3

O Lord, I have a busy world around me; eye, ear, and thought will be needed for all my work to be done in that busy world. Now, before I enter upon it, I would commit eye, ear, and thought, to thee! Do thou bless them and keep their work thine, such as, through thy natural laws, my heart beats and my blood flows without any thought of mine for them, so may my spiritual life hold on its course at those times when my mind cannot consciously turn to thee to commit each particular thought to thy service. Hear my prayer for my dear Redeemer's sake. Amen.

THOMAS ARNOLD

DAY 56

When you feel weak in your own power, when you're confused as to who you truly are, when you feel hopeless, that's the time to go to the one who never changes. Seek God, without whom you're powerless. Ask Him to take away all that's not of Him and to fill you with the fruits of His Spirit. Flee to the refuge that holds all promise for your life, trusting He'll bring you through. He'll renew you. As you wait on God, expect that He'll power you up. He'll be your arm of strength, your defense every morning, and help you meet whatever your day brings.

O LORD, be gracious unto us; we have waited for thee: be thou their arm every morning, our salvation also in the time of trouble.
ISAIAH 33:2

O Lord, reassure me with Your quickening Spirit;
without You I can do nothing.

Mortify in me all ambition, vanity, vainglory,
worldliness, pride, selfishness, and resistance from God,
and fill me with love, peace, and all the fruits of the Spirit.

O Lord, I know not what I am, but to You I flee for refuge.

I would surrender myself to You, trusting Your
precious promises and against hope believing in hope.

You are the same yesterday, today, and forever;
and therefore, waiting on Thee, Lord,
I trust that I shall at length renew my strength.

WILLIAM WILBERFORCE

DAY 57

It's God who searches us, who sees beyond our disguises. His love bears all our missteps, overlooks all our mistakes, and helps us see ourselves as we truly are. And only then, when our vision is totally clear, can *we* see things as they truly are. For then we're seeing with the eyes of God.

Allow today's prayer to draw you near to God. Let Him search you from top to bottom. He'll give you the strength to bear the truth of what you see and to rise fearless in Him.

But God hath revealed them unto us by his Spirit: for the Spirit searcheth all things, yea, the deep things of God.
1 Corinthians 2:10

O God, whose spirit searcheth all things, and whose love beareth all things, encourage us to draw near to Thee in sincerity and in truth. Save us from a worship of the lips while our hearts are far away. Save us from the useless labour of attempting to conceal ourselves from Thee who searchest the heart. Enable us to lay aside all those cloaks and disguises which we wear in the light of day and here to bare ourselves, with all our weakness, disease and sin, naked to Thy sight. Make us strong enough to bear the vision of the truth, and to have done with all falsehood, pretence, and hypocrisy, so that we may see things as they are, and fear no more.

William Edwin Orchard

DAY 58

Your character is determined by what you allow to reign over you. Is Christ on the throne of your life, thoughts, and spirit, or has something else taken possession of you, leading you down the wrong path? Although you may have no power to resist the thoughts that war against the law of your mind, Christ does. So call Him in! Invite the King of Peace to take over the throne of your mind once again. He *will* deliver you!

But I see another law in my members, warring against the law of my mind, and bringing me into captivity to the law of sin which is in my members. . . . Who shall deliver me from the body of this death? I thank God through Jesus Christ our Lord. So then with the mind I myself serve the law of God; but with the flesh the law of sin.
ROMANS 7:23–25

O Lord, come quickly and reign on Thy throne, for now ofttimes something rises up within me, and tries to take possession of Thy throne: pride, covetousness, uncleanness, and sloth want to be my kings; and then evil-speaking, anger, hatred, and the whole train of vices join with me in warring against myself, and try to reign over me. I resist them, I cry out against them, and say, "I have no other king than Christ." O King of Peace, come and reign in me, for I will have no king but Thee! Amen.
SAINT BERNARD

DAY 59

When worry causes a storm of unease to rise within, your sole recourse is to turn to God. He's the only one powerful enough to calm the troubled sea of your heart. And when His peace overrides your storm, you can focus your all on Him, your Refuge.

———————————————

O Lord, thou art my God; I will exalt thee, I will praise thy name; for thou hast done wonderful things. . . . For thou hast been a strength to the poor, a strength to the needy in his distress, a refuge from the storm, a shadow from the heat.
ISAIAH 25:1, 4

———————————————

Oh, Lord, unto whom all hearts are open, Thou canst govern the vessel of my soul far better than I can. Arise, O Lord, and command the stormy wind and the troubled sea of my heart to be still, and at peace in Thee, that I may look up to Thee undisturbed, and abide in union with Thee, my Lord. Let me not be carried hither and thither by wandering thoughts; but forgetting all else, let me see and hear Thee. Renew my spirit; kindle me in Thy light, that it may shine within me, and my heart may burn in love and adoration towards Thee. Let Thy Holy Spirit dwell in me continually, and make me Thy temple and sanctuary, and fill me with divine love and light and life, with devout and heavenly thoughts, with comfort and strength, with joy and peace. Amen.
JOHANN ARNDT

DAY 60

Oh, how often our thoughts go wild, leading us astray from God's reality. Based on what we see before us, we consider an idea. Usually a mistaken idea that plays on our fears. Then we find ourselves driven to add on to that first mistaken premise with even more wild imaginings, notions we consider and choose to treat as facts! Before we know it, our false notions have built up an entirely false scenario, a fabrication, a dark castle of resentment, despair, and doubt.

To keep yourself thinking right, pray that God would help you live in *His* reality—not yours! Ask Him for more faith, for Him to exchange your thoughts for His. Know that it is His reality, His words that will lead you to the truth and will restore you to your faith in Him.

I have spread out my hands all the day unto a rebellious people,
which walketh in a way that was not good, after their own thoughts.
ISAIAH 65:2

Oh, let me live in thy realities,
Nor substitute my notions for thy facts,
Notion with notion making leagues and pacts;
They are to truth but as dream-deeds to acts,
And questioned, make me doubt of everything.
"O Lord, my God," my heart gets up and cries,
"Come thy own self, and with thee my faith bring."
GEORGE MACDONALD, *DIARY OF AN OLD SOUL*, JULY 28 READING

DAY 61

Your heart is an important part of you. It's your very center. Out of it flow your feelings, thoughts, and will. As such, you're to guard it above all other things (Proverbs 4:23).

And you're to use your *entire* heart when it comes to seeking out God, to inquiring for Him and requiring Him as a vital and necessary part of your life.

Because your heart is so important, pray that God would give you one that's true to Him alone. Ask Him to give you a heart that cannot be conquered by trouble or be waylaid by something unworthy of His will, His plan for your life.

With such a pure heart that beats only for and seeks only God, you'll find a faithfulness that envelops God with more love and passion than you could ever imagine.

But if from thence thou shalt seek the LORD thy God, thou shalt find him, if thou seek him with all thy heart and with all thy soul.
DEUTERONOMY 4:29

Give me, O Lord, a steadfast heart, which no unworthy affection may drag downwards; give me an unconquered heart, which no tribulation can wear out; give me an upright heart, which no unworthy purpose may tempt aside. Bestow upon me also, O Lord my God, understanding to know Thee, diligence to seek Thee, wisdom to find Thee, and a faithfulness that may finally embrace Thee. Amen.

SAINT THOMAS AQUINAS

When you're not sure where you're going or where God's leading you, trust God, as did Abraham. God called him to go to a place he'd never seen before. And Abraham went, he obeyed, he followed—because he had complete trust in God. He believed in God's promises. He walked, keeping his eyes on his Source. And God credited it to him as righteousness (Genesis 15:6)! Determine in your heart and soul to do the same.

By faith Abraham, when he was called to go out into a place which he should after receive for an inheritance, obeyed; and he went out, not knowing whither he went. By faith he sojourned in the land of promise, as in a strange country. . . . For he looked for a city which hath foundations, whose builder and maker is God.
HEBREWS 11:8–10

O Thou Eternal, in Whose appointment our life standeth! Thou hast committed our work to us, and we could commit our cares to Thee. May we feel that we are not our own, and that Thou wilt heed our wants, while we are intent upon Thy will. May we never dwell carelessly or say in our hearts, "I am here, and there is none over me"; nor anxiously, as though our path were hid; but with a mind simply fixed upon our trust, and choosing nothing but the dispositions of Thy Providence.
JAMES MARTINEAU

DAY 63

How wonderful that you have someone who not only loves you throughout your life but will continue to love you when the storms of life have passed! His name is God. And it's because of His Son, Jesus, that there's a place waiting for you in heaven.

Even now, because of Jesus, you've already entered into this heavenly existence. In Him, nothing can touch your very spirit. So fly to the arms of the Shepherd waiting to guide, protect, and carry you if need be. He'll still the seas, calm the waves of worry. He'll hide you when you need a refuge and then renew and strengthen you, as you wait out the storm. And at the very end, He will bring you to your haven, a place where there's no more pain or sorrow. Only light and love.

Blessed be the God and Father of our Lord Jesus Christ,
which according to his abundant mercy hath begotten us
again unto a lively hope by the resurrection of Jesus Christ
from the dead, to an inheritance incorruptible, and undefiled,
and that fadeth not away, reserved in heaven for you.
1 PETER 1:3–4

Jesus, Lover of my soul, Let me to Thy bosom fly,
While the nearer waters roll, While the tempest still is high:
Hide me, O my Saviour, hide, Till the storm of life is past;
Safe into the haven guide, O receive my soul at last.
CHARLES WESLEY

DAY 64

The Holy Spirit takes on many forms. As the wind or breath, the Holy Spirit invisibly but powerfully enters your world (Acts 2:2). As the dove, the Holy Spirit takes on the characteristics of the gentleness and peace He provides you with (Luke 3:22). As water, the Holy Spirit cleanses and washes you (John 7:37–39). As a cloud, the Holy Spirit leads you down the right road (Exodus 16:10). As dew, the Holy Spirit refreshes you (Genesis 2:4–6). As the fire, the Holy Spirit refines you, bringing out the best in you (Isaiah 4:4). As the anointing oil, the Holy Spirit soothes and heals you (Acts 10:38). As the still, small voice, the Holy Spirit whispers to your innermost self (1 Kings 19:11–13).

Pray to the Holy Spirit today, in all His facets. Allow Him to be your power, peace, cleanser, guide, refresher, refiner, soother, and intimate adviser.

I tell you the truth; It is expedient for you that I go away:
for if I go not away, the Comforter will not come unto
you; but if I depart, I will send him unto you.
JOHN 16:7

As the wind is thy symbol so forward our goings.
As the dove so launch us heavenwards.
As water so purify our spirits.
As a cloud so abate our temptation.
As dew so revive our languor.
As fire so purge out our dross.
CHRISTINA ROSSETTI

DAY 65

The word *praise* appears 259 times in the King James Bible! In the book of Psalms, it shows up 150 times! But what are the who, what, where, when, how, and why of praise? Psalm 150 gives you guidance in this area. Who is to give the Lord praise, thanks for all He's done? "Every thing that hath breath" (Psalm 150:6). How and with what? With the sound of a musical instrument, which could include your voice, and with dancing (Psalm 150:3–5). Where? "In his sanctuary" (Psalm 150:1) and where He now resides—within you (1 Corinthians 3:16)! For what? Praise God "for his mighty acts. . . according to his excellent greatness" (Psalm 150:2).

This is just the beginning of the list. Your job is to praise God continually—and be even more blessed as you do so. Consider exploring what more the Bible says about praise. For the sake of you and your Lord Jesus Christ.

For here have we no continuing city, but we seek one to come. By [Jesus] therefore let us offer the sacrifice of praise to God continually, that is, the fruit of our lips giving thanks to his name.
HEBREWS 13:14–15

O God our Father, we would thank thee for all the bright things of life. Help us to see them, and to count them, and to remember them, that our lives may flow in ceaseless praise; for the sake of Jesus Christ our Lord.
JOHN HENRY JOWETT

DAY 66

There are some things you just can't do on your own. And one of those things is managing yourself. That's when you need to admit that you are the clay and *God* is the potter. You are the work of His hand. So give yourself up to Him. Let God take you over completely. When you do, then He will mold you into what He wants you to be, something that is more than good in His eyes. Then you will be equipped, enabled, and empowered to do His good work.

If a man therefore purge himself from these [things that are
dishonorable], he shall be a vessel unto honour, sanctified,
and meet for the master's use, and prepared unto every good work.
2 TIMOTHY 2:21

Here, Lord, I abandon myself to Thee. I have tried in every way
I could think of to manage myself, and to make myself what I
know I ought to be but have always failed. Now I give it up to
Thee. Do Thou take entire possession of me. Work in me all
the good pleasure of Thy will. Mold and fashion me into such
a vessel as seemeth good to Thee. I leave myself in Thy hands,
and I believe Thou wilt, according to Thy promise, make me
into a vessel unto Thy own honor, "sanctified, and meet for
the Master's use, and prepared unto every good work."
HANNAH WHITALL SMITH

DAY 67

At times, you may feel as if the vision you had for your life is fading. You don't understand why things have turned out the way they have. You're uncertain of the way forward.

Pray for God to help you continue to trust Him. Allow Him to take you by the hand, as a loving father would a small child. He'll give you confident hope to quiet your heart and mind.

Behold, what manner of love the Father hath bestowed
upon us, that we should be called the sons of God.
1 JOHN 3:1

Grant unto us, Almighty God, that when our vision fails, and our understanding is darkened; when the ways of life seem hard, and the brightness of life is gone—to us grant the wisdom that deepens faith when the sight is dim, and enlarges trust when the understanding is not clear. And whensoever Thy ways in nature or in the soul are hard to be understood, then may our quiet confidence, our patient trust, our loving faith in Thee, be great, and as children knowing that they are loved, cared for, guarded, kept, may we with a quiet mind at all times put our trust in the unseen God. So may we face life without fear, and death without fainting; and, whatsoever may be in the life to come, give us confident hope that whatsoever is best for us both here and hereafter is Thy good pleasure and will be Thy law. Amen.

GEORGE DAWSON

DAY 68

God has enlightened your mind so that you can see Him and desire Him. Because of your love for Him, a supernatural joy has blossomed in your heart. And because you serve Him, He's powered up your will, enabling you to become a coworker in His plans for this world. But this is only the beginning!

Pray that God will allow you to know Him even *more*, to consistently see His hand working in your life, and so *increase* your sincere love for Him. And because of that love, serve Him *more* fully. For in that greater knowledge, in that increased love, in that fuller service, you'll find your eternal and perfect freedom in Jesus!

And we know that we are of God. . . . And we know that the Son of God is come, and hath given us an understanding, that we may know him that is true, and we are in him that is true, even in his Son Jesus Christ. This is the true God, and eternal life.
1 John 5:19–20

Eternal God, who are the light of the minds that know you, the joy of the hearts that love you, and the strength of the wills that serve you; grant us so to know you, that we may truly love you, and so to love you that we may fully serve you, whom to serve is perfect freedom, in Jesus Christ our Lord.
Saint Augustine

DAY 69

So you're on your Christian walk, working at what will give God the most pleasure; that is becoming more like Christ. But you'll need a few things for this journey—namely, how to understand, discern, seek, find, know, meditate upon, hear, see, and proclaim God.

To get there from here, go to God with today's prayer. Ask Him for all you need—intellect, reason, diligence, wisdom, a spirit, a heart, ears, eyes, a tongue, a way of life, patience, and perseverance—and more. He'll grant all your requests to continue His—and your—good work.

I thank my God. . .always in every prayer of mine for you all making request with joy, for your fellowship in the gospel from the first day until now; being confident of this very thing, that he which hath begun a good work in you will perform it until the day of Jesus Christ.
PHILIPPIANS 1:3–6

Gracious and Holy Father,
Please give me: intellect to understand you,
reason to discern you, diligence to seek you,
wisdom to find you, a spirit to know you,
a heart to meditate upon you, ears to hear you,
eyes to see you, a tongue to proclaim you,
a way of life pleasing to you, patience to wait for you
and perseverance to look for you. Grant me a perfect end,
your holy presence, a blessed resurrection and life everlasting.
SAINT BENEDICT OF NURSIA

DAY 70

Jesus was all about love. He showed God's love by dying for you before you even knew Him. He loved you then and loves you now. His great plea was for you to love God with all your being. And to love others as you love yourself. Jesus knew that's what this world needs—more love, first and foremost for Him. For all other love flows from that Source. So pray for more love of Jesus. When you do, you'll be so full of the King of love that fear will have no room to reside.

God is love; and he that dwelleth in love dwelleth in God, and God in him. . . . There is no fear in love; but perfect love casteth out fear.
1 JOHN 4:16, 18

Lord Jesus Christ, that we may be able rightly to pray Thee for all things, we pray first for one: help us to love Thee much, increase love and inflame it. Oh, this is a prayer Thou wilt surely hear, Thou who indeed art not love of such a sort—so cruel a sort—that Thou art only the object, indifferent to whether any one loves Thee or not; Thou indeed art not love of such a sort—in wrath—that Thou art only judgment, jealous of who loves Thee and who does not. Oh, no, such Thou art not; Thou wouldst thus only inspire fear and dread, it would then be terrible "to come to Thee," frightful "to abide with Thee," and Thou wouldst not be the perfect love which castest out fear. No, compassionate, or loving, or in love, Thou art love of such a sort that Thou Thyself dost woo forth the love which loves Thee, dost foster it to love Thee much.

SØREN KIERKEGAARD

DAY 71

When things get desperate, all you need is a short prayer: "Lord, hold me up! Hold me, Lord, by my right hand!" That's today's prayer, and it's a good one.

And today's verses reveal how well God backs up this eleven-word plea. He promises you *twice* that you need not fear. Because He's with you. He's God. He'll give you all the strength you need. *Twice* He says He'll help. *Twice* He says He'll hold your right hand. And *three* times God tells you all those people, things, and situations against you will be as nothing!

So take the verses below to heart. Then memorize this eleven-word prayer. It's packed with all the power you need—and more!

Fear thou not; for I am with thee: be not dismayed; for I am thy God: I will strengthen thee; yea, I will help thee; yea, I will uphold thee with the right hand of my righteousness. Behold, all they that were incensed against thee shall be ashamed and confounded: they shall be as nothing; and they that strive with thee shall perish. Thou shalt seek them, and shalt not find them, even them that contended with thee: they that war against thee shall be as nothing, and as a thing of nought. For I the LORD thy God will hold thy right hand, saying unto thee, Fear not; I will help thee.

ISAIAH 41:10–13

Lord, hold me up! Hold me, Lord, by my right hand!

CHARLES SPURGEON

DAY 72

God has such power. He made the earth, sea, and land. He brought life and light to all creatures. He can do anything! So, need help? Ask God. Pray He would save those in trouble, have mercy on the fallen, reveal Himself to those in need, heal believers and nonbelievers alike, bring in sheep that have wandered, lift those with no strength, give ease to the broken in mind and heart. When you pray, God will do all that. Why? Because *all* are His sheep, in His fold, under the care, protection, and guidance of Christ the Shepherd. They're in His good hands—as are you.

The sea is his, and he made it: and his hands formed the dry land. O come, let us worship and bow down: let us kneel before the LORD our maker. For he is our God; and we are the people of his pasture, and the sheep of his hand.
PSALM 95:5–7

We beseech Thee, Lord and Master, to be our help and succor. Save those who are in tribulation; have mercy on the lonely; lift up the fallen; show Thyself unto the needy; heal the ungodly; convert the wanderers of Thy people; feed the hungry; raise up the weak; comfort the faint-hearted. Let all the peoples know that Thou art God alone, and Jesus Christ is Thy Son, and we are Thy people and the sheep of Thy pasture; for the sake of Christ Jesus. Amen.
SAINT CLEMENT OF ROME

DAY 73

Lies. Some are casual, some half truths, some "little white lies." But they're basically the same. One little lie, one deception, leads to another, then another, then another.

It began in the garden of Eden when Eve, in response to the serpent's question "Did God actually say. . . ?" adds her own "edited" version of God's instructions. And then the serpent responds with "Ye shall not surely die" (Genesis 3:4), a half truth at best—because lie-believing Eve not only dies but opens the door to death for all.

The point is, lies are not what God wants His people to hear or utter. That's why He sent the Holy Spirit, to speak and lead you into truth—within and without.

Lie not one to another, seeing that ye have put off the old man with his deeds; and have put on the new man, which is renewed in knowledge after the image of him that created him.
COLOSSIANS 3:9–10

Almighty God, who hast sent the Spirit of truth unto us to guide us into all truth, so rule our lives by thy power, that we may be truthful in word, deed, and thought. O keep us, most merciful Saviour, with thy gracious protection, that no fear or hope may ever make us false in act or speech. Cast out from us whatsoever loveth or maketh a lie, and bring us all to the perfect freedom of thy truth; through Jesus Christ thy Son our Lord.
BROOKE FOSS WESTCOTT

DAY 74

Your vision of the world affects your environs—both inner and outer. Pray for yourself and others to have a God perspective. It will change the world.

Fear not. . .thou art mine.
Isaiah 43:1

O Thou, who art the ever-blessed God, the underlying Peace of the world, and who wouldst draw all men into the companionship of Thy joy; speak, we beseech Thee, to this Thy servant, for whom we pray. Take him by the hand and say unto him, "Fear not; for I am with thee. I have called thee by my name; thou art mine." Put such a spirit of trust within him that all fear and foreboding shall be cast out, and that right reason and calm assurance may rule his thoughts and impulses. Let quietness and confidence be his strength. Reveal to him the vision of a universe guided and governed by Thy wise and loving care; and show him that around and about him are Thy unseen and beneficent powers. Lift up his whole being into communion with Thy life and thought. Let him ever remember that Thou dost not give to any the spirit of fearfulness, but a spirit of power and love and self-mastery. In this faith, grant, O Lord, that he may summon the energies of his soul against the miseries that cast him down. Give him courage, confidence, an untroubled heart, and a love that loves all creatures, great and small, for Thy love's sake. Amen.
Samuel McComb

DAY 75

God sees you. Your entire being. You are in His spotlight. You are His loved one, His chosen one, His special lamb. He's made you for His pleasure. And although He knows about and sees your past and future, right now, in this present moment, He wants you to take your eyes off yourself and out of the world around you—and turn to Him. For it's when you return to and rest in God that you're saved—from worries, fears, agitations, misgivings, misperceptions, and so much more.

Return to God. Rest in Him. Entrust yourself to His care, protection, and guidance. Put your confidence not in the world and what it might provide you, but in God alone. When you do, you'll find your entire being quieted and all the strength and calm you need to truly rest in Him.

For thus saith the Lord GOD, the Holy One of Israel;
In returning and rest shall ye be saved; in quietness
and in confidence shall be your strength.
ISAIAH 30:15

O Omnipotent God, who cares for each of us as if no one else existed and for all of us as if we were all but one! Blessed is the person who loves You. To You I entrust my whole being and all I have received from You. You made me for Yourself, and my heart is restless until it rests in You.
SAINT AUGUSTINE

DAY 76

It's easy to hang on to past grievances, but it's not very profitable to either your well-being or that of others. Why? Because the burning bitterness of unforgiveness keeps you from moving forward *and* from loving others. So, do as Jesus would have you do and what He does for you. Forgive, in His love. And move on—in His love.

Let all bitterness, and wrath, and anger, and clamour,
and evil speaking, be put away from you, with all malice:
And be ye kind one to another, tenderhearted, forgiving one
another, even as God for Christ's sake hath forgiven you.
EPHESIANS 4:31–32

I offer to Thee prayers for the pardon of those especially, who have in any way injured, grieved or reproached me; or have caused me any harm or annoyance. And I offer also for all those whom I have in any way grieved, vexed, oppressed, and scandalized, by word or deed, knowingly or unknowingly; that Thou mayest equally forgive us all our sins, and all our offences against each other. Take away, O Lord, from our hearts all suspiciousness, indignation, anger, and contention, and whatever is calculated to wound charity, and to lessen brotherly love. Have mercy, O Lord, have mercy on those who seek Thy mercy; give grace to the needy; make us so to live that we may be found worthy to enjoy the fruition of Thy grace, and that we may attain to eternal life. Amen.
THOMAS À KEMPIS

DAY 77

Worry is like a dark, heavy cloud of distorted thoughts that comes between you and the Prince of Peace. It follows you around, keeping you from seeing the light Christ would shine upon your mind. It's formed when you're in a place of uncertainty, when you panic, thinking you have to come up with your own solutions. But your God is a God of certainty and wisdom. So put all your what-ifs in His hands. And thank Him for all the what-ares in your life. When you do, He'll remove from you all the faithless fears that weigh you down and may never come to pass. Pray for Christ to beam His light upon you. Then rise up in peace and victory.

Humble yourselves therefore under the mighty
hand of God, that he may exalt you in due time:
Casting all your care upon him; for he careth for you.
1 PETER 5:6–7

O most loving Father, you who will us to give thanks for all things, to dread nothing but the loss of yourself, and to cast all our care on you, who care for us; preserve us from faithless fears and worldly anxieties, and grant that no clouds of this mortal life may hide from us the light of that love which is immortal, and which you have manifested unto us in your Son, Jesus Christ our Lord.

WILLIAM BRIGHT

DAY 78

How pliable are you when it comes to God shaping and reshaping you? How yielded are you to the ministrations of the Master Craftsman who created and knew you before you were even born? How much do you moan, groan, complain about, or, even worse, resist God's work? Envision how blessed your life becomes when you totally put yourself in the Master's hand!

Begin a yielded life today. Allow yourself to be remade in God's image. Pray for Him to recreate you as you lie compliant in His hands, being what He would have you be, doing what He would have you do.

But now, O LORD, thou art our father; we are the clay,
and thou our potter; and we all are the work of thy hand.
ISAIAH 64:8

I leave myself, Father, in thy hands; make and re-make this clay, shape it or grind it to atoms; it is thine own, it has nought to say; only let it always be subservient to thine ever-blessed designs, and let nothing in me oppose thy good pleasure for which I was created. Require, command, forbid; what wouldst Thou have me do? what not do? Exalted or abased, rejoicing or suffering, doing thy work or laid aside, I will always praise Thee alike, ever yielding up all my own will to Thine! Nothing remains for me but to adopt the language of Mary: "Be it unto me according to thy word" (Luke 1:38).

FRANÇOIS FÉNELON

DAY 79

Imagine someone who thinks he knows it all, is perfect, and has all the talent in the world. He believes he's better than good and the humblest of the humble. He's got so much "religion" and strength that he needs no help from God—at all. How insufferable that person would be! Yet it won't be long before he falls. Hard. For he's self-reliant, not God-reliant.

God doesn't want you puffing yourself up in your own mind. He wants you humbly coming to Him, seeking more teaching, correction, grace, goodness, atonement, light, and strength. For when you are God-reliant, you're continuing to grow, to progress in a life with Christ, helping to build God's kingdom up—not tear it down.

Pray for God to guide you closer to Him today. To help you never become so proud that you think you can handle life without His help. To make you humble before Him, sticking to His path and walking forward in the way He's laid out—just for you.

Pride goeth before destruction, and an haughty spirit before a fall.
PROVERBS 16:18

Suffer me never to think that I have knowledge enough to
need no teaching, wisdom enough to need no correction,
talents enough to need no grace, goodness enough to need no
progress, humility enough to need no repentance, devotion
enough to need no quickening, strength enough without
thy Spirit; lest, standing still, I fall back for evermore.
ERIC MILNER-WHITE

DAY 80

When you see the word *work*, your mind might automatically define it as what one does to make a living, to earn money. But work comes in other forms, such as needlework, housework, even homework. And God will bless all that work, whatever you put your hand to—sacred or secular—when you offer Him your efforts, talents, skills, and experience and leave their results to Him.

Pray today for God not only to use you and your work but to ensure that He and His love shine through it all. For His sake.

------

*Let thy work appear unto thy servants, and thy glory unto their children. And let the beauty of the L*ORD *our God be upon us: and establish thou the work of our hands upon us; yea, the work of our hands establish thou it.*
PSALM 90:16–17

I want to begin this day with thankfulness, and continue it with eagerness. I shall be busy; let me set about things in the spirit of service to you and to my fellows, that Jesus knew in the carpenter's shop in Nazareth. I am glad that he drew no line between work sacred and secular. Take the skill that resides in my hands, and use it today; take the experience that life has given me, and use it; keep my eyes open, and my imagination alert, that I may see how things look to others, especially the unwell, the worried, the overlooked. For your love's sake. Amen.
RITA SNOWDEN

DAY 81

You might shake your head at the Israelites, how their lack of trust and faith in God, their murmuring and complaining, led them to wandering forty years in the wilderness. And how they did so in spite of the miracles they'd seen God work to rescue, defend, and provide for them! Yet do you not sometimes do the same? Complaining to God about what's happened in your life? Wondering what He might've been thinking to land you where you are?

Time to turn that thinking into thankfulness. To get in line with God's will for you and not reason against it. Pray that you would be content in your life, whatever God brings into it. Consider God's working of His will in your life the best thing that could've happened!

For it is God which worketh in you both to will and to do of his good pleasure. Do all things without murmurings and disputings: That ye may be blameless and harmless, the sons of God, without rebuke. . .among whom ye shine as lights in the world.
PHILIPPIANS 2:13–15

Grant, gracious Father, that I may never dispute the reasonableness of thy will, but ever close with it, as the best that can happen. Prepare me always for what thy providence shall bring forth. Let me never murmur, be dejected, or impatient, under any of the troubles of this life, but ever find rest and comfort in this, this is the will of my Father, and of my God; grant this for Jesus Christ's sake. Amen.
THOMAS WILSON

DAY 82

The king of Syria sent his horses and chariots to attack Dothan, where the prophet Elisha was staying. The king's army surrounded the city at night. When Elisha's servant woke and saw all the horses and chariots, he panicked. But Elisha said, "Fear not: for they that be with us are more than they that be with them" (2 Kings 6:16), then prayed for God to open the servant's eyes. That's when the servant saw God's army!

When you view your troubles as steamrollers about to flatten you, pray that God would open your eyes to His heavenly help. He'll then reveal a chariot in which you can ride above your troubles!

And Elisha prayed, and said, LORD, I pray thee, open his eyes,
that he may see. And the LORD opened the eyes of the young
man; and he saw: and, behold, the mountain was full
of horses and chariots of fire round about Elisha.
2 KINGS 6:17

Lord, open our eyes that we may see, for the world all around us, as well as around the prophet, is full of [Your] horses and chariots, waiting to carry us to places of glorious victory. And when our eyes are thus opened, we shall see in all the events of life, whether great or small, whether joyful or sad, a "chariot" for our souls.

HANNAH WHITALL SMITH,
ADAPTED FROM *THE CHRISTIAN'S SECRET OF A HAPPY LIFE*

DAY 83

External events can be powerful enough to scatter your thoughts, which then disturbs your internal peace, keeping you from hearing what God is speaking into your life. At those times, when worry blocks you from God's voice, make Isaiah 26:3 your mantra. For there God promises that if you keep your mind focused on Him *and* trust Him, He'll keep you in a place of perfect peace.

Thou wilt keep him in perfect peace, whose mind
is stayed on thee: because he trusteth in thee.
Isaiah 26:3

O Lord, this is all my desire—to walk along the path of life
that Thou hast appointed me, even as Jesus my Lord would
walk along it, in steadfastness of faith, in meekness of spirit,
in lowliness of heart, in gentleness of love. And because
outward events have so much power in scattering my thoughts
and disturbing the inward peace in which alone the voice of
Thy Spirit is heard, do Thou, gracious Lord, calm and settle my
soul by that subduing power which alone can bring all thoughts
and desires of the heart into captivity to Thyself. All I have is
Thine; do Thou with all as seems best to Thy divine will; for I
know not what is best. Let not the cares or duties of this life
press on me too heavily; but lighten my burden, that I may
follow Thy way in quietness, filled with thankfulness for Thy
mercy, and rendering acceptable service unto Thee. Amen.

Maria Hare

DAY 84

When some people think of God, they see Him as an angry, laying-down-the-law father. Feeling unable to satisfy Him, their heart lurches. It reacts like a panicked bird flapping its wings, unable to settle down, to find a way out. Others may see God as a mother figure. Loving and comforting, she nurses them at her breast, carries them on her hips, bounces them up and down on her knees. With this perception of God, their heart soars, longing to be with Him.

Pray today that when the thought of God stirs in your heart, it doesn't awaken like a panicked bird but stirs like a child just waking from a good night's sleep, joy upon its face, ready to run to its mother's arms and be brought up into her lap where comfort, love, and provision are found.

For thus saith the LORD, Behold, I will extend peace to her like a river. . .then shall ye suck, ye shall be borne upon her sides, and be dandled upon her knees. As one whom his mother comforteth, so will I comfort you. . . And when ye see this, your heart shall rejoice, and your bones shall flourish.
ISAIAH 66:12–14

Father in heaven! When the thought of Thee wakes in our hearts let it not awaken like a frightened bird that flies about in dismay, but like a child waking from its sleep with a heavenly smile.
SØREN KIERKEGAARD

DAY 85

Sleep can at times be elusive. We find ourselves tossing and turning; the regrets and mistakes of yesterday, the worrisome events of the day just past, and the fears of an unknown tomorrow are ricocheting around in our minds, keeping sleep at bay.

When this happens, remind yourself who God is. That He has chosen you, loves you, and listens to you when you call upon Him. Look into your heart. Gather up your regrets, missteps, worries, fears, and uncertainties and put them in His hands. Find a comfortable position and then relax your body from the tip of your head to your toes. Trust that He who never sleeps is watching over you and will continue to do so throughout the night and in the coming day. He will defend and protect you. You're safe in His strong and loving arms.

But know that the LORD hath set apart him that is godly for himself: the LORD will hear when I call unto him. . . . Commune with your own heart upon your bed, and be still. . . . Put your trust in the LORD. . . . I will both lay me down in peace, and sleep: for thou, LORD, only makest me dwell in safety.
PSALM 4:3–5, 8

O Thou, whose captain I account myself,
To Thee I do commend my watchful soul,
Ere I let fall the windows of mine eyes:
Sleeping and waking, O! defend me still.
WILLIAM SHAKESPEARE

DAY 86

You're Jesus' servant, His hands, feet, mouth, mind, and heart here on earth. Your purpose is to do whatever He desires in whatever way He moves you. Yet you cannot live out His will in your own power. Instead, you're to come to God as an empty vessel for Him to fill. So bring your heart, soul, mind, and mouth to Him. Ask God to fill them.

We preach not ourselves, but Christ Jesus the Lord; and ourselves your servants for Jesus' sake. For God, who commanded the light to shine out of darkness, hath shined in our hearts, to give the light of the knowledge of the glory of God in the face of Jesus Christ. But we have this treasure in earthen vessels, that the excellency of the power may be of God, and not of us.
2 Corinthians 4:5–7

Use me then, my Saviour, for whatever purpose, and in whatever way, Thou mayest require. Here is my poor heart, an empty vessel; fill it with Thy grace. Here is my sinful and troubled soul; quicken it and refresh it with Thy love. Take my heart for Thine abode; my mouth to spread abroad the glory of Thy name; my love and all my powers, for the advancement of believing people; and never suffer the steadfastness and confidence of my faith to abate—that so at all times I may be enabled from the heart to say, "Jesus needs me, and I Him."

D. L. Moody

DAY 87

Whether or not you have children of your own, you have an influencing effect on their lives. The apostle Timothy, born of a pagan Greek father and a pious Jewish mother, was raised Jewish. Both his mother and grandmother laid his spiritual groundwork. Then, after hearing Paul preach, Timothy became a Christian—and Paul his spiritual father!

Pray that God would bless His children. That their overseers—parents, grandparents, etc.—would care for and raise them in Christ's love and wisdom. That their households would reflect God's kingdom. And while you're at it, ask God to open your heart to how you might present God in a child's life and so become a spiritual father or mother yourself!

To Timothy, my dearly beloved son. . .I thank God. . .When I call to remembrance the unfeigned faith that is in thee, which dwelt first in thy grandmother Lois, and thy mother Eunice; and I am persuaded that in thee also.
2 TIMOTHY 1:2–3, 5

Heavenly Father, from whom all fatherhood in heaven and earth is named, bless, we beg you, all children, and give to their parents and to all in whose charge they may be, your Spirit of wisdom and love; so that the home in which they grow up may be to them an image of your kingdom, and the care of their parents a likeness of your love; through Jesus Christ our Lord.
LESLIE HUNTER

DAY 88

Imagine being alive when the disciples discovered Jesus' empty tomb. Then imagine being one of the two disciples who, on that same day, journeyed to Emmaus. While you're talking about the day's events, Jesus draws near. But you don't recognize Him. You tell Him the story of Jesus. And then He opens the Word to you, explaining why things had to happen this way. Suddenly you see Him for who He truly is!

Pray that Jesus would open your eyes to His message as you walk in the way. That He would make your heart burn within you as you listen to His words. That you would then journey on in the strength of His presence and His amazing truth, all the way to the end of your road where you'll see Him again in all His glory!

And their eyes were opened, and they knew him; and [Jesus]
vanished out of their sight. And they said one to another,
Did not our heart burn within us, while he talked with us
by the way, and while he opened to us the scriptures?
LUKE 24:31–32

Make our hearts to burn within us, O Christ, as we walk
with Thee in the way and listen to Thy words; that we may
go in the strength of Thy presence and Thy truth all our
journey through, and at its end behold Thee, in the glory
of the Eternal Trinity, God for ever and ever.
ERIC MILNER-WHITE

DAY 89

When you're distraught, need forgiveness, in the dark, sick, sorrowful of heart and soul, burdened, or weary of everything, stretch out your hands toward God. When you do, you'll find the hope you so desperately need—the eternal hope of God that pours upon you courage, mercy, strength, and love.

If thou prepare thine heart, and stretch out thine hands toward him. . .thou shalt be secure, because there is hope; yea, thou shalt dig about thee, and thou shalt take thy rest in safety.
JOB 11:13, 18

Grant unto us, Almighty God, in all time of sore distress, the comfort of the forgiveness of our sins. In time of darkness give us blessed hope, in time of sickness of body give us quiet courage; and when the heart is bowed down, and the soul is very heavy, and life is a burden, and pleasure a weariness, and the sun is too bright, and life too mirthful, then may that Spirit, the Spirit of the Comforter, come upon us, and after our darkness may there be the clear shining of the heavenly light; that so, being uplifted again by Thy mercy, we may pass on through this our mortal life with quiet courage, patient hope, and unshaken trust, hoping through Thy loving-kindness and tender mercy to be delivered from death into the large life of the eternal years. Hear us of Thy mercy, through Jesus Christ our Lord. Amen.

GEORGE DAWSON

DAY 90

It's tempting to look to ourselves or others to help us. Yet humans are not only fallible but have limited power, strength, and resources. So if we're trusting in people—or material things—to save us, disappointment and heartache are bound to follow. But when we look to and trust Jesus to deliver us, we find a myriad of blessings. For He has all the power in the world. As the King of creation, Jesus can provide unlimited relief, renewal, strength, and resources.

So be wise. Determine to put your wholehearted trust in Jesus. He, your arm of strength, is here, right beside you, waiting for you to turn to Him. When you do, your life will bloom!

Thus saith the LORD; Cursed be the man that trusteth in man, and maketh flesh his arm, and whose heart departeth from the LORD. For he shall be like the heath in the desert, and shall not see when good cometh. . . . Blessed is the man that trusteth in the LORD, and whose hope the LORD is. For he shall be as a tree planted by the waters, and that spreadeth out her roots by the river, and shall not see when heat cometh, but her leaf shall be green; and shall not be careful in the year of drought, neither shall cease from yielding fruit.
JEREMIAH 17:5–8

Dear Jesus. . .how foolish of me to have
called for human help when You are here.
CORRIE TEN BOOM

DAY 91

When Jesus walked this earth, the same earth you now walk, He experienced grief, rejection, sorrow, hatred, weakness, and trouble. He did so to save you. To ensure you would know that everything you have gone through or are currently going through can be more than endured. For although Jesus had more than His fair share of trouble, He had something else: a close and abiding relationship with God. This connection to Abba God gave Jesus all He needed: joy, acceptance, happiness, love, power, and peace. And because you know Jesus, you too have access to those same blessings.

So ask God for His strength. Pray He would bestow upon you all the love and joy your relationship with Jesus provides. Ask Him to help you over the troubles of this life. Know that you can get through anything with God Almighty in your corner, Jesus the invincible at your side, and the Holy Spirit of comfort within.

He is despised and rejected of men; a man of sorrows,
and acquainted with grief: and we hid as it were our
faces from him; he was despised, and we esteemed him not.
Surely he hath borne our griefs, and carried our sorrows.
ISAIAH 53:3–4

Almighty God, grant unto us Thy love, that we may greatly rejoice; that we, knowing trouble, and acquainted with grief, may, through the goodly deliverance of faith and hope, come to the large joy of the peace that passeth all understanding. Amen.
GEORGE DAWSON

DAY 92

You may not know what today will bring. And that's okay. No one does. Except for God of course. He's got it all planned out. So instead of giving in to uncertainties and fear, trust in God. Be confident that He—who's promised to be with and support you—will give you all the strength and courage you need to move into today. When you do, you'll find yourself automatically walking His way.

Be strong and of a good courage, fear not, nor be afraid of them: for the LORD thy God, he it is that doth go with thee; he will not fail thee, nor forsake thee.
DEUTERONOMY 31:6

Eternal God, who commits to us the swift and solemn trust of life: since we know not what a day may bring forth, but only that the hour for serving You is always present, may we wake to Your instant claims, not waiting for tomorrow, but yielding today. Lay to rest the resistance of our passion, indolence, or fear. Consecrate the way our feet may go, and the humblest work will shine, and the roughest places be made plain. Lift us above unrighteous anger and mistrust into faith and hope and charity, through steady reliance on You. So may we be modest in our time of wealth, patient under disappointment, ready for danger, serene in death. In all things, draw us to Yourself that Your lost image may be traced again, and we may be at one with You.

JAMES MARTINEAU

DAY 93

Need some wisdom? Seek God and His Word and you'll get it! That's what King Asa did. He sought God, found Him, got wisdom, and then did things to please Him—like tear down idols.

Then one day Zerah, the Ethiopian, came with an army of a million men to war against Asa's army of only 580,000. So Asa prayed to God. As a result, not only did Asa and his people gain the strength to defeat the million-man army, but they also "carried away very much spoil" (2 Chronicles 14:13).

Need wisdom? Seek God and you'll get it—and more!

---

*And Asa cried unto the LORD his God, and said, LORD,
it is nothing with thee to help, whether with many, or with
them that have no power: help us, O LORD our God; for we
rest on thee, and in thy name we go against this multitude.
O LORD, thou art our God; let no man prevail against thee.*
2 CHRONICLES 14:11

Strengthen me, O God, by the grace of Thy Holy Spirit;
grant me to be strengthened with might in the inner
man, and to empty my heart of all useless care and anguish.
O Lord, grant me heavenly wisdom, that I may learn above
all things to seek and to find Thee, above all things to relish
and to love Thee, and to think of all other things as being,
what indeed they are, at the disposal of Thy wisdom. Amen.
THOMAS À KEMPIS

DAY 94

When we find ourselves ensconced in our own little world, our vision can become somewhat skewed and God's presence a little blurry. That's when it's time for an eye/I exam. Take a look at the Creator's creation. Look at God's people and animals. Raise your eyes to His skies, stars, trees—all the nature that surrounds you. Ask Jesus to fill you with the Spirit so you can see God in everything. When you do, your actions will become more aligned to God and His will for all His creation.

But ask now the beasts, and they shall teach thee; and the fowls of the air, and they shall tell thee: Or speak to the earth, and it shall teach thee: and the fishes of the sea shall declare unto thee. Who knoweth not in all these that the hand of the LORD hath wrought this? In whose hand is the soul of every living thing, and the breath of all mankind.
JOB 12:7–10

Fulfil us, Lord Jesus, with the grace of thy Holy Spirit, that everything we see may represent to us the presence, the excellency, and the power of God, and our conversation with the creatures lead us unto the Creator; that so our actions may be done more frequently with an eye to God's presence, by our often seeing him in the glass of creation; who with thee and the Holy Spirit liveth and reigneth, ever one God, world without end. Amen.

JEREMY TAYLOR

DAY 95

It's one thing to rise—to roll out of bed and into your day. It's another thing to actually rise and *shine*—to be aware of God's presence, be stirred by the Holy Spirit, and feel Christ's light within. For when you awaken to the awareness of the Holy Three, you can have that heart-to-heart talk you need with God before you speak to anyone else. Then you gain the strength you need to not only face your day but truly enjoy it—no matter what. Then you're actually rising and shining—and the Son of righteousness with you, with healing in His wings, causing you to leap into your day and to dance to an inner song only you can hear! So awaken, sleepyhead, with full awareness of the Trinity, and Christ will give you all the light you need for today's path.

But all things that are reproved are made manifest by the light: for whatsoever doth make manifest is light. Wherefore he saith, Awake thou that sleepest, and arise from the dead, and Christ shall give thee light.
Ephesians 5:13–14

O Lord, when I awake and day begins,
waken me to Thy Presence;
waken me to Thine indwelling;
waken me to inward sight of Thee,
and speech with Thee,
and strength from Thee;
that all my earthly walk may waken into song
and my spirit leap up to Thee all day, all ways.
Eric Milner-White

DAY 96

It's amazing how God created you, fashioning you into something He desires. How He breathed the breath of life into you and gave you the power to rise out of the darkness and into His light. How He made you for a specific reason, purpose, function, to live in this moment of time. Imagine how God sacrificed His Son for you, thousands of years ago, so that you could commune with Him in this moment. And how when you became a believer, He sent the Holy Spirit to live within you, guiding you, translating your prayers for you. All this is hard to grasp. For God is so much higher than you. Yet still, He resides within.

It's good to remind yourself of the wonder of God every day and the role you play in His plan for this world. Pray and praise Him. Thank Him for giving you life, reason, knowledge, good desires, and all else. For without Him, you'd be nothing!

For my thoughts are not your thoughts, neither are your ways my ways, saith the LORD. For as the heavens are higher than the earth, so are my ways higher than your ways, and my thoughts than your thoughts.
ISAIAH 55:8–9

God is what thought cannot better; God is whom thought cannot reach; God no thinking can even conceive. Without God, men can have no being, no reason, no knowledge, no good desire, naught. Thou, O God, art what thou art, transcending all.
ERIC MILNER-WHITE

DAY 97

All your strength lies in God's Spirit within you. Jesus says you have all the power you need to live this life. That nothing can hurt you. Pray for that strength and power. Believe it's yours. And it will be.

Behold, I give unto you power to tread on serpents and scorpions, and over all the power of the enemy: and nothing shall by any means hurt you. Notwithstanding in this rejoice not, that the spirits are subject unto you; but rather rejoice, because your names are written in heaven.
Luke 10:19–20

O Thou divine Spirit, let me find my strength in Thee. I need Thee, that I may be strong everywhere. I long to be independent of all circumstances, alike of the cloud and of the sunshine. I want a power to save me from sinking in despondency, and to rescue me from soaring in pride. I want both a pillar of fire and a pillar of cloud; a refuge from the night of adversity, and a shield from the day of prosperity. I can find them in Thee. Thou hast proved Thy power over the night and over the day. Come into my heart, and Thy power shall be my power. I shall be victorious over all circumstances, at home in all scenes, restful in all fortunes. I shall have power to tread on scorpions, and they shall do me no hurt; the world shall be mine when Thy Spirit is in me. Amen.
George Matheson

DAY 98

When Jesus heard Lazarus was dying, "he abode two days still in the same place where he was" (John 11:6). *Then* He walked to Bethany and found that Lazarus had already been dead for four days (John 11:17)! Of course, Jesus had known He'd raise Lazarus from the dead. It was all so people would see God's glory.

Throughout the New Testament, we witness Jesus' unwavering trust in God. He knew and had faith in God's plan. That's why He never rushed.

You trust in God. You believe everything will work out for your and God's good. And when reading His Word, you glean knowledge of God's plan. Like Jesus, you too don't need to stress. So stop. Ask God to slow you down so you won't trip up. Realize you're already living in eternity, so there's no real need to hurry. Instead of stressing, take the time to know God, enjoy His gifts, and get better acquainted with others along your way.

Also, that the soul be without knowledge, it is not good;
and he that hasteth with his feet sinneth.
PROVERBS 19:2

In the name of Jesus Christ who was never in a hurry, we pray,
O God, that You will slow us down, for we know that we live
too fast. With all eternity before us, make us take time to live—
time to get acquainted with You, time to enjoy Your blessing,
and time to know each other.

PETER MARSHALL

DAY 99

It's through God's love for you that you have gained Jesus Christ. It's through Him you gained the Holy Spirit. Within you, you have the divine strength that nothing can overcome, that leads you down the path of godliness. You have the promise-filled Word that helps you escape the darkness of this world and see the God-reality in your life. You are able to take on the divine nature, to become more and more like Jesus, who is over and above all things in this world. In Him alone, you have all you need to be content—and so much more!

Pray today and every day that God would give you what you require—*Himself*. So doing, you will never be in need.

According as his divine power hath given unto us all things that pertain unto life and godliness, through the knowledge of him that hath called us to glory and virtue: Whereby are given unto us exceeding great and precious promises: that by these ye might be partakers of the divine nature, having escaped the corruption that is in the world through lust.

2 Peter 1:3–4

God, of your goodness, give me yourself; for you are sufficient for me. I cannot properly ask anything less, to be worthy of you. If I were to ask less, I should always be in want. In you alone do I have all.

Julian of Norwich

DAY 100

Today's evening prayer gives you a starting point for thanking God for the myriad of people in your life. As you pray, consider naming names!

[I] cease not to give thanks for you,
making mention of you in my prayers.
<small>EPHESIANS 1:16</small>

Eternal and ever-blessed God, we give thee thanks, as the day comes to an end, for those who mean so much to us, and without whom life could never be the same. We thank thee for those to whom we can go at any time and never feel a nuisance. We thank thee for those to whom we can go when we are tired, knowing that they have, for the weary feet, the gift of rest. We thank thee for those with whom we can talk, and keep nothing back, knowing that they will not laugh at our dreams or mock at our failures. We thank thee for those in whose presence it is easier to be good. We thank thee for those in whose company joys are double dear, and sorrow's bitterness is soothed. We thank thee for those who by their warning counsel and their rebuke have kept us from mistakes we might have made, and sins we might have committed. And above all we thank thee for Jesus, the pattern of our lives, the Lord of our hearts, and the Saviour of our souls. Accept this our thanksgiving, and grant us tonight a good night's rest; through Jesus Christ our Lord.

<small>WILLIAM BARCLAY</small>

DAY 101

When you need a little pick-me-up, take a deep breath, close your eyes, and go to Jesus. Imagine His face smiling upon you. Feel His Spirit giving you the energy you desire. Then be as the lame man who, after being healed in Jesus' name, found his feet strengthened and "leaping up stood, and walked" (Acts 3:8). Dance as David did in the joy he felt at bringing home the ark, the presence of God. Sing and be glad, knowing the joy of the Lord is your strength! Pray for that joy to be yours today!

When the Lord turned again the captivity of Zion, we were like them that dream. Then was our mouth filled with laughter, and our tongue with singing: then said they among the heathen, The Lord hath done great things for them. The Lord hath done great things for us; whereof we are glad.
Psalm 126:1–3

Come and help us, Lord Jesus. A vision of your face will brighten us; but to feel your Spirit touching us will make us vigorous. Oh! for the leaping and walking of the man born lame. May we today dance with holy joy, like David before the ark of God. May a holy exhilaration take possession of every part of us; may we be glad in the Lord; may our mouth be filled with laughter, and our tongue with singing, "for the Lord hath done great things for us whereof we are glad."
Charles Spurgeon

DAY 102

We naturally tend to be self-focused. We've got our own ideas, plans, possessions, and goals. So when we're presented with having to fulfill the needs of others, we feel put out—even when it's just for a few minutes. But God would have us willingly and eagerly be the opposite. He wants us less self-focused and more others-focused. He wants us to be like Jesus!

So, when putting yourself aside to help others, pray for Jesus to give you not only patience and fortitude but grace. To give others first priority—even if it means putting your plans on hold, making an effort to go out of your way. For when you put others before yourself, you are in reality putting Jesus first. For whatever you do for them, you are actually doing for Him—the one who sacrificed all for you!

Let nothing be done through strife or vainglory; but in lowliness of mind let each esteem other better than themselves. Look not every man on his own things, but every man also on the things of others.
PHILIPPIANS 2:3–4

Give us patience and fortitude to put self aside for you in the most unlikely people: to know that every man's and any man's suffering is our own first business, for which we must be willing to go out of our way and to leave our own interests.
CARYLL HOUSELANDER

DAY 103

You're a work in progress. So eschew discouragement when things don't seem to be going your way. Perhaps God's putting challenges in your path, ones to test and teach you, to exercise your faith. Consider such times as your opportunity to change your perspective, to take another tack, to get yourself aligned with God's efforts instead of resisting them.

In George MacDonald's book *Warlock o' Glenwarlock*, a student asks his teacher how to make the best of this life. The teacher says, "Simply by falling in with God's design in the making of you. That design must be worked out—cannot be worked out without you. You must walk in the front of things with the will of God—not be dragged . . .behind him!" Then he advises the student to pray today's prayer.

Why not do the same? Trade discouragement for design! Run to God, as a child runs to her Abba. Willingly fall in with His making the best you. Ask what you can do to help!

[I] will be a Father unto you, and ye shall be
my sons and daughters, saith the Lord Almighty.
2 Corinthians 6:18

O Maker of me, go on making me, and let me help Thee.
Come, oh Father, here I am: let us go on. I know my words
are those of a child, but it is Thy child that prays to Thee.
It is Thy dark I walk in, it is Thy hand I hold.
George MacDonald

DAY 104

King David was the apple of God's eye because he obeyed, trusted, and had faith in God. When God delivered him from his enemies, David called God a buckler, which was a small round shield, a personal item held by a handle at arm's length or worn on the left arm. In other words, David held his Protector close.

Pray for a close, personal trust in God to lead you out of darkness.

———————————

For thou art my lamp, O LORD: and the LORD will lighten my darkness. For by thee I have run through a troop: by my God have I leaped over a wall. As for God, his way is perfect; the word of the LORD is tried: he is a buckler to all them that trust in him.
2 SAMUEL 22:29–31 (SEE ALSO PSALM 18:28–30)

———————————

It has pleased Thee to hide from us a perfect knowledge, yet Thou callest for a perfect trust in Thee. We cannot see to-morrow, we know not the way that we take, darkness hangs about our path and mystery meets us at every turn. Yet Thou hast shut us up to a final faith in goodness, justice, truth; that loving these for themselves alone, we may find the love that passeth knowledge, and look upon Thy face. O suffer us not for any terror of darkness or from any torment of mind to sin against our souls, or to fail at last of Thee. Amen.
WILLIAM EDWIN ORCHARD

DAY 105

Jesus is your Good Shepherd (John 10:11–18). He knows you—and you know Him. He calls you—and you discern His voice. Thus, you never lack for direction and support, guidance and wisdom. No matter where you are, you simply need to listen, and Jesus will lead you, every step of the way.

Put yourself in Jesus' hands. He'll breathe into you what He desires of you, the path He wants you to choose. And as you follow each nudge of His inspiration, you'll find yourself becoming more and more like your Good Shepherd.

———

The LORD is my shepherd; I shall not want. He maketh me to lie down in green pastures: he leadeth me beside the still waters. He restoreth my soul: he leadeth me in the paths of righteousness for his name's sake. Yea, though I walk through the valley of the shadow of death, I will fear no evil: for thou art with me; thy rod and thy staff they comfort me.

PSALM 23:1–4

———

My God, I want Thy guidance and direction in all I do. Let Thy wisdom counsel me, Thy hand lead me, and Thine arm support me. I put myself into Thy hands. Breathe into my soul holy and heavenly desires. Conform me to Thine own image. Make me like my Saviour. Enable me in some measure to live here on earth as He lived, and to act in all things as He would have acted.

ASHTON OXENDEN

DAY 106

God has placed your soul within a body and sent you on a journey. Yet He doesn't want you to set your anchor in earthly things but to steer straight for His kingdom. To help you stay afloat, God's Spirit speaks to yours, inspiring you, giving you guidance—until you reach your heavenly haven.

Pray that God would open your awareness to the provisions He's supplied—within and without—as you journey ever closer to Him.

———————————————

But ye are not in the flesh, but in the Spirit, if so be that the Spirit of God dwell in you. . . . And if Christ be in you, the body is dead because of sin; but the Spirit is life because of righteousness. But if the Spirit of him that raised up Jesus from the dead dwell in you, he that raised up Christ from the dead shall also quicken your mortal bodies by his Spirit that dwelleth in you.
ROMANS 8:9–11

———————————————

O God, whose eternal providence has embarked our souls
in our bodies, not to expect any port of anchorage on the
sea of this world, to steer directly through it to your glorious
kingdom, preserve us from the dangers that on all sides assault
us, and keep our affections still fitly disposed to receive your
holy inspirations, that being carried strongly forward by your
Holy Spirit we may happily arrive at last in the haven of
eternal salvation, through our Lord Jesus Christ.
JOHN WESLEY

DAY 107

Some days we may be mired in confusion, doubt, and uncertainty. We cannot seem to see the forest for the trees, and thus find ourselves unable to move forward. But not to worry! God guides the meek. Light rises up in the darkness for all God followers—of which you are one!

So simply ask God for His wisdom—and He'll give it (James 1:5). He'll tell you what to do, nudge you in the right direction. He'll save you from making a mistake. He'll give you all the light you need for your path when you trust in the shadow of His wings!

How excellent is thy lovingkindness, O God! therefore the children of men put their trust under the shadow of thy wings. They shall be abundantly satisfied. . .and thou shalt make them drink of the river of thy pleasures. For with thee is the fountain of life: in thy light shall we see light.
PSALM 36:7–9

O God, by whom the meek are guided in judgment, and light riseth up in darkness for the godly; grant us, in all our doubts and uncertainties, the grace to ask what Thou wouldst have us to do; that the spirit of wisdom may save us from all false choices, and that in Thy light we may see light, and in Thy straight path may not stumble, through Jesus Christ our Lord.
WILLIAM BRIGHT

DAY 108

God loves you. And because He loves you, He sent His Son, Jesus, to save you. And you've "seen" Jesus—the personification of Love! Because of that love, God wants you to love others. When you do, it's obvious God is in you—and you in Him.

Do you see how love comes full circle? How your love of others shows the perfection, the completeness, of God's love?

If you need more love from God so you can love others, pray for it, every moment of your day. For when God overwhelms you with His love, only then will you have the power to love as fully as your Shepherd of love, Jesus Christ.

Herein is love, not that we loved God, but that he loved us, and sent his Son to be the propitiation for our sins. Beloved, if God so loved us, we ought also to love one another. No man hath seen God at any time. If we love one another, God dwelleth in us, and his love is perfected in us.

1 John 4:10–12

O God, Fountain of love, pour Thy love into our souls, that we may love those whom Thou lovest, with the love Thou givest us, and think and speak of them tenderly, meekly, lovingly; and so loving our brethren and sisters for Thy sake, may grow in Thy love, and dwelling in love may dwell in Thee; for Jesus Christ's sake. Amen.

Edward B. Pusey

DAY 109

Others may scoff at your beliefs, perhaps even mock you. But you know that no matter what the world says, you're living the right way, in the truth of God's Word. So content yourself with hearing God speak through His Word. Rest easy knowing He has the final say-so; He will love you and lead you down the right path to Himself. Care only for God's approval. Do things His way—even if it means going against the world's ways. For God is your true treasure. He's the Light of your world, the Love of your life, the Master of your heart and soul, from here to eternity! He'll give you the strength and passion to turn from the world and to Him.

We were bold in our God to speak unto you the gospel of God with much contention. . . . But as we were allowed of God to be put in trust with the gospel, even so we speak; not as pleasing men, but God. . . . So being affectionately desirous of you, we were willing to have imparted unto you, not the gospel of God only, but also our own souls, because ye were dear unto us.
1 THESSALONIANS 2:2, 4, 8

O Lord God, grant us always, whatever the world may say, to content ourselves with what thou wilt say, and to care only for thine approval, which will outweigh all words.
CHARLES GEORGE GORDON

DAY 110

Thank God for God. When you don't have the strength to do what He's telling you to do, He'll give you that strength! With His unlimited resources, He'll equip you with whatever you need to carry out the plan for your life. He'll give you the energy to keep trying, to persevere. For God not only works *on* you; He works *in* you, empowering you with the same power He used to raise Jesus from the dead! Even more amazing is that He'll give you all the peace you need as you go through this process of hearing, obeying, and doing. Oh what a God you have! There is no greater help available to you than that of the Holy Three working within and without.

Now the God of peace, that brought again from the dead our Lord Jesus, that great shepherd of the sheep, through the blood of the everlasting covenant, make you perfect in every good work to do his will, working in you that which is wellpleasing in his sight, through Jesus Christ; to whom be glory for ever and ever. Amen.
HEBREWS 13:20–21

From this moment on I promise that I'll try to do whatever You tell me for the rest of my life, insofar as You'll make it clear to me what Your wishes are. I'm weak and many times I'll probably want to renege on this. But Lord, You'll have to help me with that too.
CATHERINE MARSHALL, *BEYOND OUR SELVES*, PAGE 43

DAY 111

Boldly is the only form of the word *bold* that appears in the Gospels in the King James Version. And it does so only twice. One refers to how Jesus spoke (John 7:26). The other is in Mark 15:43—"Joseph of Arimathaea. . .went in boldly unto Pilate, and craved the body of Jesus." All the other New Testament forms of *bold* appear *after* Christ followers received the Holy Spirit.

Like other Christ followers, you too have been given the Holy Spirit, your comforter and interpreter. And because Jesus is your high priest, you can boldly go to God in prayer so you'll have what you need to perform both the little daily duties and the greater acts that come your way.

Let us therefore come boldly unto the throne of grace, that we
may obtain mercy, and find grace to help in time of need.
HEBREWS 4:16

Our Lord, our Guide even unto death, grant us, we pray
Thee, grace to follow Thee whithersoever Thou goest. In little
daily duties to which Thou callest us, bow down our wills to
simple obedience, patience under pain or provocation, strict
truthfulness of word and manner, humility, kindness: in great
acts of duty or perfection if Thou shouldest call us to them,
uplift us to self-sacrifice, heroic courage, laying down
of life for Thy Truth's sake or for a brother. Amen.
CHRISTINA ROSSETTI

DAY 112

Jesus gave you two rules: love God with all your heart, soul, and mind, and love others as yourself. To fulfill that second rule, you need to be clothed in mercy, kindness, humility, gentleness, patience, forbearance, and forgiveness! And above all those things, you're to put on love. All because of what Christ did for you.

That "wardrobe" is what you should be praying for every day. For the more you clothe yourself with those qualities, the more friends you'll make, the more like Christ you'll become, and the better the world will be! Make it your prayer today.

Put on therefore, as the elect of God, holy and beloved, bowels of mercies, kindness, humbleness of mind, meekness, longsuffering; forbearing one another, and forgiving one another, if any man have a quarrel against any: even as Christ forgave you, so also do ye. And above all these things put on charity, which is the bond of perfectness.
Colossians 3:12–14

Almighty and most merciful Father, who has given us a new commandment that we should love one another, give us also grace that we may fulfil it. Make us gentle, courteous, and forbearing. Direct our lives so that we may look each to the good of others in word and deed. And hallow all our friendships by the blessing of thy spirit, for his sake, who loveth us and gave himself for us, Jesus Christ our Lord. Amen.
Brooke Foss Westcott

DAY 113

Let's face it. At times, you are tempted. But you don't have to give in to those things that threaten to come between you and God. Besides, God promises He won't let you be tempted more than you're able to handle. And with the temptation, God will give you an escape route so you can bear up under it.

Pray that God would enable you to follow Him, and to love, trust, and delight in Him, so that if any temptation *does* come your way, it won't drive you away but will draw you closer to Him!

There hath no temptation taken you but such as is common to man: but God is faithful, who will not suffer you to be tempted above that ye are able; but will with the temptation also make a way to escape, that ye may be able to bear it.
1 CORINTHIANS 10:13

Oh, teach us to know you, our God, and enable us to do your will as we ought to do. Give us hearts to love you, to trust and delight in you. That no temptations may draw us, nor any tribulations drive us from you; but that all your dispensations to us, and all your dealings with us, may be the messengers of your love to our souls, to bring us still nearer to your blessed self, and to make us still fitter for your heavenly kingdom.

BENJAMIN JENKS

DAY 114

Because you trust God, He lives in your heart. That's the first amazing benefit. The next is that you get to run to God, to the "secret place of the most High" (Psalm 91:1), and dwell there with Him. You get to hang out in God's presence. You can be in that place where God reigns, "abide under the shadow of the Almighty" (v. 1), away from the heat of the day. When you claim God as your refuge and your fortress, when you declare to yourself, to God, and to the world that it is *He* you rely on, lean on, and trust—that He has all your confidence—you gain everything: protection, provision, rest, healing, shielding, security, blessings, angelic assistance, power, long life, and God's ear. Pray that you learn how to abide in God 24-7—and you'll gain Him and so much more!

He that dwelleth in the secret place of the most High shall abide under the shadow of the Almighty. I will say of the LORD, He is my refuge and my fortress: my God; in him will I trust.
PSALM 91:1–2

Infinite One who fills the universe with Your unsearchable presence, and has a dwelling-place in every heart that trusts in You: I come now in a spirit of thanksgiving, and I would commune with You in prayer that I may learn to live in Your constant presence. Indeed, may I learn to pray as I ought in spirit and in truth.
JAMES MARTINEAU

DAY 115

God's Spirit hovered over the deep and dark waters. And then God spoke, and light was formed, bringing color. In its wake came forms of lands, seas, skies, and creatures.

God is the Master Craftsman. And all He's made is good. But do you *see* it?

Pray that today God would open your eyes to the beauty of His creation. That you would notice each leaf, snowflake, or creature that dwells in your midst. That you would take note of the sun and sky, the stars and moon that light up your little piece of heaven. That you would see every person you encounter as a reflection of God's light and love. That He would give you the mind and heart to take joy in all you see—and to celebrate His world.

In the beginning God created the heaven and the earth. And the earth was without form, and void; and darkness was upon the face of the deep. And the Spirit of God moved upon the face of the waters. And God said, Let there be light: and there was light. And God saw the light, that it was good: and God divided the light from the darkness.

GENESIS 1:1–4

Creator Spirit, who broodest everlastingly over the lands
and waters of the earth, enduing them with forms and
colours which no human skill can copy, give me today,
I beseech Thee, the mind and heart to rejoice in Thy creation.

JOHN BAILLIE

DAY 116

From the time you were hidden in your mother's womb to the moment you're reading these lines to the day you enter heaven, Christ is with you. Live and love Him from beginning to end.

My reward is with me, to give every man according as his work
shall be. I am Alpha and Omega, the beginning and the end,
the first and the last. . . . I Jesus have sent mine angel to
testify unto you these things in the churches.
REVELATION 22:12–13, 16

May Christ-Omega keep me always young "to the greater glory of God." For old age comes from him, old age leads on to him, and old age will touch me only in so far as he wills. To be "young" means to be hopeful, energetic, smiling—and clear-sighted. May I accept death in whatever guise it may come to me in Christ-Omega, that is within the process of the development of life. A smile (inward and outward) means facing with sweetness and gentleness whatever befalls me. Jesus-Omega, grant me to serve you, to proclaim you, to glorify you, to make you manifest, to the very end through all the time that remains to me of life, and above all through my death. Desperately, Lord Jesus, I commit to your care my last active years, and my death; do not let them impair or spoil my work I have so dreamed of achieving for you.

TEILHARD DE CHARDIN

DAY 117

Jesus has so much love for you, so much compassion for who and where you are. He demonstrated His love by showing you how God wants you to live, how God wants you to love Him, love yourself, and love others.

Nothing can separate you from the love personified by Jesus. Revel in that today. Allow His love to envelop you, to permeate your life. Let it so absorb your entire being that there's no room for anything else—fear, doubts, misgivings, worries, anger, or envy. Permit that love to lift you up and into His arms. Cuddle close, breathing slowly against His chest. You are in His love. And there's no better place to be.

Who shall separate us from the love of Christ? shall tribulation, or distress, or persecution, or famine, or nakedness, or peril, or sword?. . . Nay, in all these things we are more than conquerors through him that loved us. For I am persuaded, that neither death, nor life, nor angels, nor principalities, nor powers, nor things present, nor things to come, nor height, nor depth, nor any other creature, shall be able to separate us from the love of God, which is in Christ Jesus our Lord.
ROMANS 8:35, 37–39

Lord Jesus, may the sweet burning ardour of your love so absorb my soul entirely and make it a stranger to all that is not you or for you.
SAINT FRANCIS OF ASSISI

DAY 118

As believers in God, we're pilgrims upon this earth, strangers in this universe (1 Peter 2:11). Yet we're comforted by the fact that God not only becomes our sheltering home here but provides one for us in heaven. For when our bodies pass away, we'll have a room in the eternal heavenly house of God (2 Corinthians 5:1).

In the meantime, while we're walking the earth as Jesus did, we can find inspiration in those who've gone before, that great cloud of witnesses (Hebrews 12:1). As we read the stories of the Old and New Testaments, we gain fresh hope; we are renewed by the courage of fellow sojourners who overcame the things of this world.

Read about and consider the godly who've gone before. Feel the power of their stories. Allow it to refresh even your most tiresome tasks. Then praise God for our fellow pilgrims and for Him, our true home.

For whatsoever things were written aforetime were written for our learning, that we through patience and comfort of the scriptures might have hope.
ROMANS 15:4

Dear God, we are as strangers in Your wondrous universe, yet as children at home within Your shelter. You inspire joyful confidence in You. Enlightener of true seers and prophets, You are our Strength. May their faith and spirit rest upon all our life, refreshing the weariest task. In life and in death, You are the steadfast light of our hearts; You are our portion forever.

JAMES MARTINEAU

DAY 119

One of the first steps to becoming willing for God to have His way with you is to be willing to be made willing. And to tell *God* that you're willing to be made willing. Are you willing?

Perhaps you have misgivings or fears about God having His way with you. If so, get to know God better. He's already given you a heart to do so, knowing that when you know Him well, all mistrust and fears will fade away (Jeremiah 24:7). To grow your trust in God and your knowledge of Him, dig into His Word, seeking Him with your whole heart, hiding His wondrous, eye-opening Word there (Psalm 119:10–11, 18).

Today, let God know you're willing to be willing. Then *be* willing to be willing.

Come, and let us return unto the LORD: for he hath torn, and he will heal us; he hath smitten, and he will bind us up. After two days will he revive us: in the third day he will raise us up, and we shall live in his sight. Then shall we know, if we follow on to know the LORD. . . . For I desired mercy, and not sacrifice; and the knowledge of God more than burnt offerings.
HOSEA 6:1–3, 6

Lord, I am not yet willing for thee to have thy way with me, but I am willing to be made willing.
F. B. MEYER

DAY 120

When you need a vision for your life, go to God. He's the one who opens your eyes and ears and enters your heart. He's the life and strength of souls that love and seek Him. God enlightens and expands your mind; He lifts the vision of your heart so your thoughts and spirit can wing their way to His wisdom.

God's Spirit will lead you into all the knowledge you need to be a heavenly kingdom dweller on earth. As a believer with the mind of Christ, fly up into God today and raise the vision of your heart.

But as it is written, Eye hath not seen, nor ear heard, neither have entered into the heart of man, the things which God hath prepared for them that love him. But God hath revealed them unto us by his Spirit: for the Spirit searcheth all things, yea, the deep things of God. . . . For who hath known the mind of the Lord, that he may instruct him? but we have the mind of Christ.
1 Corinthians 2:9–10, 16

O God, light of the minds that see you, life of the souls that love you, and strength of the souls that seek you, enlarge our minds and raise the vision of our hearts, that, with swift wings of thought, our spirits may reach you, the eternal wisdom, you who live from everlasting to everlasting; through Jesus Christ our Lord. Amen.
Saint Augustine

DAY 121

Jesus is in everything. He "is the image of the invisible God" (Colossians 1:15). Through Him everything—visible and invisible, in heaven and on earth—was made. Jesus holds all things created together, including you!

Because Jesus is all in all, there is nothing for you to fear. Your heart can take courage in His words, "Be of good cheer; it is I; be not afraid" (Matthew 14:27).

So pray today that God would help you see and understand that Jesus is in everything that comes your way. That nothing will touch you that hasn't first gone through Him.

Jesus will reveal Himself to you in all things, all ways, all your days, if only you'll look to see His smiling face within all things.

[Jesus Christ] is the image of the invisible God, the firstborn of every creature: For by him were all things created, that are in heaven, and that are in earth, visible and invisible, whether they be thrones, or dominions, or principalities, or powers: all things were created by him, and for him: And he is before all things, and by him all things consist.

COLOSSIANS 1:15–17

Lord, purge our eyes to see
Within the seed a tree,
Within the glowing egg a bird,
Within the shroud a butterfly.
Till, taught by such we see
Beyond all creatures, Thee
And hearken to Thy tender word
And hear its "Fear not; it is I."

CHRISTINA ROSSETTI

DAY 122

Someone else's burden has been laid upon your heart. But you're not exactly sure what to pray for. You've heard the person's troubles and wishes—to be healed, find a job, be more joyful or less stressed, etc. But you're not sure what *God's* will is for this individual.

That's why today's prayer is so powerful. For it outlines the individual's issue but leaves the solution up to the Spirit. And it goes even further by asking the Spirit to "pray in me the prayer Thou art praying." All so that God's will would be done in Jesus' name. Use this prayer today and experience its power.

Likewise the Spirit also helpeth our infirmities: for we know not what we should pray for as we ought: but the Spirit itself maketh intercession for us with groanings which cannot be uttered. And he that searcheth the hearts knoweth what is the mind of the Spirit, because he maketh intercession for the saints according to the will of God.

ROMANS 8:26–27

Blessed Holy Spirit, Thou knowest this man, and what the lacking thing is in him. There is trouble there. Thou knowest this sick woman, and what the difficulty is there. This problem, and what the hindrance is in it. Blessed Spirit, pray in me the prayer Thou art praying for this man, and this thing, and this one. The prayer Thou art praying, I pray that, in Jesus' name. Thy will be done here under these circumstances.

S. D. GORDON

DAY 123

No matter where God has placed you or where He sends you, know He's always with you. In fact, you're in His hands. And Jesus says that once there, no one—no thing—will be able to snatch you away (John 10:28–29)! That eternal tie between you, God, Jesus, and the Spirit can never be severed.

At the same time, God will give you the strength to bear up under any burden laid upon you. That's a promise: "Cast thy burden upon the Lord, and he shall sustain thee" (Psalm 55:22).

Pray today for willingness to go where God sends you, knowing He'll stick with you. Pray that you're up for any burden as long as He sustains you—and He will. Allow Him to sever any ties, except that between Him and you. And you'll become a mighty servant of God.

I am continually with thee: thou hast holden me by my right hand. Thou shalt guide me with thy counsel, and afterward receive me to glory. Whom have I in heaven but thee? and there is none upon earth that I desire beside thee. My flesh and my heart faileth: but God is the strength of my heart, and my portion for ever.
Psalm 73:23–26

Lord, send me anywhere, only go with me. Lay any burden on me, only sustain me. Sever any ties, but the ties that bind me to your heart and to your service.
David Livingstone

DAY 124

Amid the darkness at the beginning of creation, God spoke the first words: "Let there be light" (Genesis 1:3). Pray for that light to shine within you. Doing so will lighten your heart, bringing you the joy of the Lord.

For God's light shining in your heart will drive away the darkness of sin and the mists of doubt, fear, and wrong thinking. It will guide your feet upon the way, keeping you from stumbling. Let there be light.

The sun shall be no more thy light by day; neither for brightness shall the moon give light unto thee: but the Lord shall be unto thee an everlasting light, and thy God thy glory. Thy sun shall no more go down; neither shall thy moon withdraw itself: for the Lord shall be thine everlasting light.
Isaiah 60:19–20

O Thou, who art the true Sun of the world, ever rising, and never going down; who, by Thy most wholesome appearing and sight dost nourish, and gladden all things in heaven and earth; we beseech Thee mercifully to shine into our hearts, that the night and darkness of sin, and the mists of error on every side, being driven away, by the brightness of Thy shining within our hearts, we may all our life walk without stumbling, as in the day-time, and, being pure and clean from the works of darkness, may abound in all good works which Thou hast prepared for us to walk in. Amen.

Erasmus

DAY 125

God is holy. And so is His Word. For when the scriptures speak, God speaks (Galatians 3:8). Thus, immerse yourself in the Word. Take it as God's voice speaking directly into your heart. And then live by it, allowing it to direct your feet, to light your pathway.

By staking your confidence in God's promises found in His pages, you'll find the courage, strength, and provisions to live the life God would have you live.

Pray for God's guidance before you read His Word. Ask Him to highlight the portions He's revealing to you, to interpret anything that seems unclear. And then slowly, thoughtfully delve into the scriptures, following the Spirit's direction. It will be the most important journey you embark upon today.

But continue thou in the things which thou hast learned and hast been assured of, knowing of whom thou hast learned them. . . . All scripture is given by inspiration of God, and is profitable for doctrine, for reproof, for correction, for instruction in righteousness: That the man of God may be perfect, thoroughly furnished unto all good works.
2 TIMOTHY 3:14, 16–17

O God, whose name is holy of itself, we pray that it may be hallowed also by us. To this end help us, O blessed Father in heaven, that thy word may be taught in truth and purity, and that we, as thy children, may lead holy lives in accordance with it; through Jesus Christ, thy Son, our Lord. Amen.
MARTIN LUTHER

DAY 126

Live with the hope that God, who orders the world, will also order your inner life so that you can understand the hidden wisdom He brings to light. Pray for that wisdom and hope today.

But we speak the wisdom of God in a mystery, even the hidden wisdom, which God ordained before the world unto our glory. . . . God hath revealed them unto us by his Spirit: for the Spirit searcheth all things, yea, the deep things of God.
1 Corinthians 2:7, 10

Almighty God, by Whose word all things work, by Whose guidance all things go, so order our inward life that we may be enabled to understand the things that we see; and by Thy guidance in the spiritual life and in charity, so order what there is disordered in our lives, so bring our minds to the truth, our consciences to the law, our eyes to the light, and our hearts to Thy true love, that amidst the seeming discords of life, we may hear the music of the heavenly will, and catch ofttimes the charms of the heavenly order. So give us hope that we may pass on through time, into the higher and better education of the eternal life to come, and that at last we may know those things that are hidden, and which now we cannot know, and learn the glorious beauty and the glorious loving of the eternal years.

George Dawson

DAY 127

Jesus has come to stand in your midst. His first words are "Peace be unto you." He shows you His hands and side, the wounds He suffered to save you, to bring you into the fold. Your heart rejoices, for you feel His light, power, joy, and love. He says, again, "Peace be unto you," and now you really feel it.

And then the Holy Three come into play. Jesus says, "As my Father hath sent me, even so send I you" (John 20:21). You feel His breath upon you as you hear His words, "Receive ye the Holy Ghost" (v. 22).

Breathe. Breathe in Jesus' presence, God's love, and the Holy Spirit's power.

Today, ask God to teach you how to breathe deeply in faith.

Then. . .when the doors were shut where the disciples were assembled for fear of the Jews, came Jesus and stood in the midst, and saith unto them, Peace be unto you. And when he had so said, he shewed unto them his hands and his side. Then were the disciples glad, when they saw the LORD. Then said Jesus to them again, Peace be unto you: as my Father hath sent me, even so send I you. And when he had said this, he breathed on them, and saith unto them, Receive ye the Holy Ghost.
JOHN 20:19–22

O God. . .teach me to breathe deeply in faith.
SØREN KIERKEGAARD

DAY 128

God is the one who loves, encourages, strengthens, and uplifts you so that you can meet all the challenges your day brings in His power. So ask for His blessings today. Know you have received them—and be sure to pass them on to those you meet along the way!

---

*And let us consider one another to
provoke unto love and to good works.*
HEBREWS 10:24

O God, our heavenly Father, we Thy children come to Thy feet with our supplications. We cannot live without Thy blessings. Life is too hard for us and duty is too large. We get discouraged, and our feeble hands hang down. We come to Thee with our weakness, asking Thee for strength. Help us always to be of good cheer. Let us not be disheartened by difficulties. Let us never doubt Thy love or any of Thy promises. Give us grace to be encouragers of others, never discouragers. Let us not go about with sadness or fear among men, but may we be a benediction to every one we meet, always making life easier, never harder, for those who come within our influence. Help us to be as Christ to others, that they may see something of His love in our lives and learn to love Him in us. We beseech Thee to hear us, to receive our prayer, and to forgive our sins, for Jesus Christ's sake. Amen.

J. R. MILLER

DAY 129

These words of Isaiah 29:13 are eye-openers: "This people draw near me with their mouth, and with their lips do honour me, but have removed their heart far from me." Do you feel their sting?

It's clear God doesn't want you to give Him lip service, to consent in your words while dissenting in your heart. He wants you to pray with your entire being—mind, soul, and strength—and from the heart.

So before you pray today, take a few moments to sit back and breathe. Think about your love for God and His love for you. Then pray the prayer below, changing up the wording if needed so that your words come deep from your heart, your very core. Add on whatever your heart is speaking to you, what it wants to say to your Daddy God. You'll find blessings galore as you do so, prompting you to be even more faithful in prayer day after day.

Blessed are they that keep his testimonies,
and that seek him with the whole heart.
PSALM 119:2

Assist me mercifully, O Lord, in all my supplications and prayers, that I may not draw near to thee with my lips while my heart is far from thee. Give me a hearty desire to pray, and grace to pray faithfully, that I may live under thy most mighty protection here, and praise thee hereafter; through Jesus Christ.
SABINE BARING-GOULD

DAY 130

Psalm 18 calls God your strength, rock, fortress, deliverer, shield, savior, and high tower. He's exactly who you need when you're caught in the riptide of affliction, being pulled under by grief. God rushes in at your cry, drawing you up out of the waters, then putting you down in a place where you can find your footing once again.

Pray. God will answer and lift you up.

In my distress I called upon the LORD, and cried unto my God: he heard my voice out of his temple, and my cry came before him, even into his ears. . . . He sent from above, he took me, he drew me out of many waters. . . . He brought me forth also into a large place; he delivered me, because he delighted in me.

PSALM 18:6, 16, 19

O holy and loving Father, Whose mercies are from everlasting to everlasting, we thank Thee that Thy children can flee for refuge in their afflictions to the blessed certainty of Thy love. From every grief that burdens our spirits, from the sense of solitude and loss, from the doubt and fainting of the soul in its trouble, we turn to Thee. Thou knowest our frame, Thou rememberest that we are dust. Be Thou our Strength and Deliverer; in our great need be Thou our Helper; pour Thy consolations into our hearts, and let the gospel of Thy beloved Son minister comfort and peace to our souls. Amen.

HENRY W. FOOTE

DAY 131

Today's prayer shows you the peace that can settle upon you when you leave all your expectations in God's hands—when you keep in mind that all that happens is according to His good plan, one that's so much better than anything you can imagine. Pray and experience the freedom gained when you leave all you have and are to the Master.

---

*My soul, wait thou only upon God; for my expectation
is from him. He only is my rock and my salvation:
he is my defence; I shall not be moved.*
PSALM 62:5–6

O Lord, Who hast breathed into me the breath of life, and endued me with an immortal spirit, which looks up unto Thee, and remembers it is made after Thine own image, behold with grace and favor the ardent desires which are in my heart, to recover a perfect likeness of Thee. Endue me with more contentedness in what is present, and less solicitude about what is future; with a patient mind to submit to any loss of what I have, or any disappointment of what I expect. Fill me, O Lord, with the knowledge of Thy will, in all wisdom and spiritual understanding. Fill me with goodness, and the fruits of righteousness. And fill me with all joy and peace in believing that Thou wilt never leave me nor forsake me, but make me perfect, stablish, strengthen, settle me, and be my God for ever and ever; my Guide unto death. Amen.

SIMON PATRICK

DAY 132

Love not only makes the world go round; it makes *God* go round. For when you love others, God is there. When you exhibit love in your thinking, speaking, and doing, God is there.

Before praying today, think about how much love God showed when He sent His one and only Son to save you, to show you how to live, how to love. Pray God would give you that same love to shine on, in, and through you.

Beloved, let us love one another: for love is of God; and every one that loveth is born of God, and knoweth God. He that loveth not knoweth not God; for God is love. In this was manifested the love of God toward us, because that God sent his only begotten Son.
1 JOHN 4:7–9

O God of love, we pray thee to give us love:
Love in our thinking, love in our speaking,
Love in our doing, and love in the hidden places of our souls;
Love of our neighbours near and far;
Love of our friends, old and new;
Love of those with whom we find it hard to bear,
And love of those who find it hard to bear with us;
Love of those with whom we work,
And love of those with whom we take our ease;
Love in joy, love in sorrow;
Love in life and love in death;
That so at length we may be worthy to dwell with thee,
Who art eternal love.

WILLIAM TEMPLE

DAY 133

God's Word molds you into the person God wants you to be. It teaches you about God's grace, the Gospel, and Jesus, God's gift of grace to you. When you instruct others about God and His Word, you need God's grace not only to teach but to learn as you teach and from those whom you teach.

Today's prayer asks God for grace to teach and learn. It asks for the Word of God to speak to you and give you the words to speak to others. It asks for the wisdom of God to educate you so that you and others can be taught by God.

The more you learn from God's Word, the more grace you gain, the more you live your life by God's promises, the more you find your needs fulfilled, and the more complete you become. Pray for the transforming power of God's Word of grace.

And now, brethren, I commend you to God, and to the word of his grace, which is able to build you up, and to give you an inheritance among all them which are sanctified.
ACTS 20:32

Lord Jesus, merciful and patient, grant us grace, I beg you, ever to teach in the teachable spirit; learning along with those we teach, and learning from them whenever you please. Word of God, speak to us, speak by us what you will. Wisdom of God, instruct us. . .that we and they may all be taught of God.
CHRISTINA ROSSETTI

DAY 134

God's light follows you everywhere you go, giving you rest whenever and wherever you need it. Secure in His presence, you know you need not fear at night. As you close your eyes, you know He is with you, guarding you as you sleep. If you awaken during the night, He will be there to soothe you, to give you ease of mind and heart. And when you awaken to a new day, you turn to His presence once again, to Jesus your sun, the Spirit your comforter.

With the Holy Three in your midst, you find the eagerness to face the tasks before you, the strength to meet whatever comes, and the guidance that leads you in the path of peace.

Pray today for the rest you find in God alone.

The dayspring from on high hath visited us, to give light to them that sit in darkness and in the shadow of death, to guide our feet into the way of peace.
LUKE 1:78–79

Go with each of us to rest; if any awake, temper them the dark hours of watching; and when the day returns, return to us, our sun and comforter, and call us up with morning faces and with morning hearts, eager to labour, eager to be happy, if happiness should be our portion, and if the day be marked for sorrow, strong to endure it. Amen.
ROBERT LOUIS STEVENSON

DAY 135

God doesn't just want your mind. Or your body. Or your soul. Or your spirit. He wants all of you. That means God wants your inner heart too. He wants you to give Him full possession of your very core, to open up and allow His Son to reign there so you'll follow His every nudge, be led down the right path.

God gave you life. So live for Him. God worked to make you. So work for His benefit. Jesus gave His life for you. So give yours to Him. Jesus promised to never leave you. So don't desert Him now.

Pray today's prayer, giving the Lord your whole heart. Live wholeheartedly and unashamedly for God's glory.

For this cause I bow my knees unto the Father of our Lord Jesus Christ, of whom the whole family in heaven and earth is named, that he would grant you, according to the riches of his glory, to be strengthened with might by his Spirit in the inner man; that Christ may dwell in your hearts by faith.
EPHESIANS 3:14–17

O Lord, take full possession of my heart, raise there your throne, and command there as you do in heaven.
Being created by you, let me live for you;
being created for you, let me always act for your glory;
being redeemed by you, let me give to you what is yours;
and let my spirit cling to you alone, for your name's sake.
JOHN WESLEY

DAY 136

One of the great things about being a God follower is that whether you're alive or dead, Christ is with you. Because He's "Lord both of the dead and living" (Romans 14:9)! So, while you're here, God the Father will support you, hold you up, strengthen you, imbue you with power—whatever needs to be given to keep you walking His way. And then, when your work here is done, Jesus will meet you at the gates of heaven where God the Father already has a place prepared for you, one that's safe, where you can rest in peace at last.

So no worries. Keep following God. Pray for His help while you're in the sun today and for His haven in heaven when your earthly days are done!

And I heard a voice from heaven saying unto me, Write, Blessed are the dead which die in the Lord from henceforth: Yea, saith the Spirit, that they may rest from their labours; and their works do follow them.
REVELATION 14:13

O Father, support me all the day long of this troublous life, until the shadows lengthen, and the evening comes, and the busy world is hushed, and the fever of life is over, and my work is done. Then, dear Father, in Thy mercy grant me a safe lodging, a holy rest, and a peace at the last; through Jesus Christ, Thy Son and my Lord. Amen.
JOHN HENRY NEWMAN

DAY 137

Today's prayer is like a love letter God has sent to your soul. Your soul reads God's letter then pens one of its own. And God's letter back to your soul brings it full circle. And that's what God's love is. A living, breathing thing that goes full circle. It begins with God loving you, yet He somehow lost you. So He's sent His beloved Son to bring you back. You accepted the Son. And now He lives within you. He in God and you in Him.

Today, let your soul speak its love to God.

I in them, and thou in me, that they may be made perfect in one; and that the world may know that thou hast sent me, and hast loved them, as thou hast loved me.

JOHN 17:23

AND GOD SAID TO THE SOUL:
I desired you before the world began. I desire you now
as you desire me. And where the desires of two
come together The love is perfected.

HOW THE SOUL SPEAKS TO GOD:
Lord, you are my lover, my longing, My flowing stream, my sun,
And I am your reflection.

HOW GOD ANSWERS THE SOUL:
It is my nature that makes me love you often,
For I am love itself.
It is my longing that makes me love you intensely,
For I yearn to be loved from the heart.
It is my eternity that makes me love you long,
For I have no end.

MECHTHILD OF MAGDEBURG

DAY 138

There's power in thanking God. When the ark of God was first brought into King Solomon's temple, the people lifted their voices in thanksgiving and praise to God, and the Lord's presence filled the meeting place!

Today's prayer begins with thanksgiving then follows with pleas where the petitioner admits people's imperfections. Yet you'll find it to be a power-filled and perfect prayer.

It came even to pass, as the trumpeters and singers were as one, to make one sound to be heard in praising and thanking the LORD; and when they lifted up their voice. . .and praised the LORD, saying, For he is good; for his mercy endureth for ever: that then the house was filled with a cloud, even the house of the LORD.

2 CHRONICLES 5:13

Lord, behold us here assembled. We thank Thee for this place in which we dwell; for the love that unites us; for the peace accorded us this day; for the hope with which we expect the morrow; for the health, the work, the food, and the bright skies, that make our lives delightful; for our friends in all parts of the earth. Let peace abound in our community. Purge out of every heart the lurking grudge. Give us grace and strength to forbear and to persevere.

Offenders, give us the grace to forgive offenders. Forgetful ourselves, help us to bear cheerfully the forgetfulness of others. Give us courage and gaiety and the quiet mind.

ROBERT LOUIS STEVENSON

DAY 139

God has formed you into the person you are now, the one reading these words. He has certain tasks He wants you to perform. He has a mission, duties, for you in this generation—to live as an example to others, shed your light, love and forgive all, be like Christ. But God needs some help.

God needs you to be willing. He needs you to be pliant, to bend to His will. That means not getting caught up in your own desires. Not letting fear rule over you. Not having a worldly mind-set. God wants you to give Him total control. To acknowledge that Christ rules your heart—and then let Him do it! To refer all things to the wisdom of the Holy Spirit within. To be humble and obedient.

And that's what today's four-word prayer is all about. Being humble and obedient, giving yourself up to God's will. To have that mind of Christ in you. And, in so doing, grasp the courage, peace, strength, and power that go with it!

Let this mind be in you, which was also in Christ Jesus: Who, being in the form of God, thought it not robbery to be equal with God: But made himself of no reputation, and took upon him the form of a servant, and was made in the likeness of men: And being found in fashion as a man, he humbled himself, and became obedient.
PHILIPPIANS 2:5–8

Oh, Lord, bend me!
EVAN ROBERTS

DAY 140

Consider how often God has been with you when the going got hard, how many things He's brought you through. He was with you amid the fire and flood. He dammed the tsunami of troubles in your life. When earthly burdens were weighing you down, He held you up. When you were as helpless as a little baby, unable to find your feet, God—your rock and foundation, refuge and strength, fortress and protector—was still with you. What a God! Praise Him!

When thou passest through the waters, I will be with thee; and through the rivers, they shall not overflow thee: when thou walkest through the fire, thou shalt not be burned; neither shall the flame kindle upon thee.
ISAIAH 43:2

It is in my heart to praise thee, O my God;
Let me never forget thee, what thou has been to me. . .
When the floods sought to sweep me away
Thou set a compass for them,
how far they should pass over;
When my way was through the sea,
and when I passed under the mountains
there was thou present with me;
When the weight of the hills was upon me
thou upheld me, else had I sunk under the earth;
When I was one altogether helpless,
when tribulation and anguish was upon me
day and night, and the earth was without foundation;
. . .Thou was with me and the Rock of thy Presence.
JAMES NAYLER

DAY 141

Be assured God has a plan. That He loves you and knows what's best. That's where you'll find the strength to wait on Him for guidance. Today, pray for patience, then believe you've received it. Experience the immediate calm that follows.

Walk worthy of the Lord unto all pleasing, being fruitful in every good work, and increasing in the knowledge of God; strengthened with all might, according to his glorious power, unto all patience and longsuffering with joyfulness; giving thanks unto the Father.
COLOSSIANS 1:10–12

O my God, Thou and Thou alone art all-wise and all-knowing! I believe that Thou knowest just what is best for me. I believe that Thou lovest me better than I love myself, that Thou art all-wise in Thy Providence and all-powerful in Thy protection. I thank Thee, with all my heart, that Thou hast taken me out of my own keeping, and hast bidden me to put myself in Thy hands. I can ask nothing better than this, to be Thy care, not my own. O my Lord, through Thy grace, I will follow Thee whithersoever Thou goest, and will not lead the way. I will wait on Thee for Thy guidance, and, on obtaining it, I will act in simplicity and without fear. And I promise that I will not be impatient, if at any time I am kept by Thee in darkness and perplexity; nor will I complain or fret if I come into any misfortune or anxiety. Amen.
JOHN HENRY NEWMAN

DAY 142

When those you care about are being tossed about by illness, weakness, or anxiety, lift them up to Jesus. If fear or sadness threatens to pull them down into the depths of the sea, pray for Him to rescue them. Ask that they would turn to Him who has power over the wind and waves. May your doing so loose their fears and strengthen their faith, leaving them awed by Jesus' love.

There arose a great tempest in the sea, insomuch that the ship was covered with the waves: but he was asleep. And his disciples came to him, and awoke him, saying, Lord, save us: we perish. And he saith unto them, Why are ye fearful, O ye of little faith? Then he arose, and rebuked the winds and the sea; and there was a great calm. But the men marvelled, saying, What manner of man is this, that even the winds and the sea obey him!
MATTHEW 8:24–27

Lord of great compassion, we pray to you for those who are
nervously ill, and too weak and anxious to lift themselves
above the fear and sadness that threaten to overwhelm them.
Do you yourself, O Lord, lift them up and deliver them,
as you delivered your disciples in the storm at sea, strengthening
their faith and banishing their fear. Turning to you, O Lord,
may they find you, and finding you may they find also all you
have laid up for them within the fortress of your love.

ELIZABETH GOUDGE

DAY 143

Running for his life, the prophet Elijah went into the wilderness. Stressed and strained, he was ready to give up and die. But God had other ideas. First, He allowed Elijah to get some much-needed rest and renewal. Then God told him to stand on the mountain before Him, where He would pass by. And after the wind, earthquake, and fire, God spoke to Elijah in a still, small voice.

When you find yourself on the run, stressing, straining, and striving, go to God. Turn your ear to His voice. When He speaks, allow His words to give you the peace you need.

And, behold, the Lord passed by, and a great and strong wind rent the mountains, and brake in pieces the rocks before the Lord; but the Lord was not in the wind: and after the wind an earthquake; but the Lord was not in the earthquake: and after the earthquake a fire; but the Lord was not in the fire: and after the fire a still small voice.

1 Kings 19:11–12

Drop Thy still dews of quietness,
Till all our strivings cease;
Take from our souls the strain and stress,
And let our ordered lives confess
The beauty of Thy peace.

Breathe through the heats of our desire
Thy coolness and Thy balm;
Let sense be dumb, let flesh retire;
Speak through the earthquake, wind and fire,
O still, small voice of calm!

John Greenleaf Whittier

DAY 144

According to *Strong's Bible Concordance*, the word *waiteth* in Psalm 62:1 comes from a Hebrew word implying "a state of silent stillness with quiet and trust." The word *wait* in verse 5 means "to hold peace, quiet yourself, rest, be still and silent." Most of us need to be taught how to wait before God in that way, to just *be* with Him so we can commune with Him in a way that silence promotes.

Make your primary goal today to wait quietly before God. Allow His Spirit to touch yours from the deepest place within. Begin by asking God to teach you how to find your silent refuge in Him. Then sit still quietly. . .and wait. Trust Him to lead you where He is.

Truly my soul waiteth upon God. . . . My soul, wait thou only upon God. . . . Trust in him at all times. . .God is a refuge for us.
PSALM 62:1, 5, 8

Teach us, O Spirit of God, that silent language which says all things. Teach our souls to remain silent in thy presence: that we may adore thee in the depths of our being and await all things from thee, whilst asking of thee nothing but the accomplishment of thy will. Teach us to remain quiet under thy action and produce in our soul that deep and simple prayer which says nothing and expresses everything, which specifies nothing and includes everything.

JEAN NICHOLAS GROU

DAY 145

In times of spiritual dryness, you may find yourself unwilling or unable to pray. Praying brings you neither comfort nor joy. Yet by *not* praying, you're stopping up the very source of power and renewal you so desperately need.

So, whether you want to or not, go to God. Ask Him to give you a heart longing for His presence, a spirit that finds solace in Him alone. Ask God to bring to your mind past blessings, present wonders, and future good. Pray for God to rekindle your soul.

Renew a right spirit within me.
PSALM 51:10

Gracious Father, who givest the hunger of desire, and satisfies our hunger with good things; quicken the heart of Thy servant who mourns because he cannot speak to Thee, nor hear Thee speak to him. Refresh, we beseech Thee, the dulness and dryness of his inner life. Grant him perseverance that he may never abandon the effort to pray, even though it brings for a time no comfort or joy. Enlarge his soul's desires that he may be drawn to Thee. Send forth Thy Spirit into his heart to help his infirmities; to give him freedom of utterance, and warmth of feeling. Let him muse upon Thy goodness; upon the blessings with which Thou hast strewn his path; upon the mystery of the world, and the shame of sin, and the sadness of death—until the fire kindles and the heart melts in prayer and praise and supplication.

SAMUEL McCOMB

DAY 146

Today's wonders of the sky and earth are but a poor reflection of the new heaven and earth that await you. A place where you will dwell in peace. Where the only light will be that of Christ. Where there will be no noise or silence but the music of angels. Where there will be no fear or hope but all things shared. Where there will be no beginning or end but a glorious eternity in a heavenly world without end.

As you pray today, ask God to bring you there in that glorious day. And to keep that vision in your mind, spirit, and heart as you face the hours before you.

And the city had no need of the sun, neither of the moon, to shine in it: for the glory of God did lighten it, and the Lamb is the light thereof. . . . And the gates of it shall not be shut at all by day: for there shall be no night there.

Revelation 21:23, 25

Bring us, O Lord God, at our last awakening into the house and gate of heaven to enter into that gate and dwell in that house, where there shall be no darkness nor dazzling, but one equal light; no noise nor silence, but one equal music; no fears nor hopes, but one equal possession; no ends nor beginnings, but one equal eternity; in the habitations of thy glory and dominion, world without end.

John Donne

DAY 147

God planted within your heart a desire to follow Him and His path for your life. But sometimes that path, what you thought it would look like, has fallen short of what you'd expected. When this happens, pray God would keep you on His path, regardless of where you think you should be by now. To keep your feet steady as you walk in His better way wherever that may lead. To give you the wisdom to follow Him and to do so cheerfully. To give you the strength to keep your hands strong in your labor for Him.

Now our Lord Jesus Christ himself, and God, even our Father, which hath loved us, and hath given us everlasting consolation and good hope through grace, comfort your hearts, and stablish you in every good word and work.
2 Thessalonians 2:16–17

O God, who hast in mercy taught us how good it is to follow the holy desires which Thou manifoldly puttest into our hearts, and how bitter is the grief of falling short of whatever beauty our minds behold, strengthen us, we beseech Thee, to walk steadfastly throughout life in the better path which our hearts once chose; and give us the wisdom to tread it prudently in Thy fear, as well as cheerfully in Thy love; so that, having been faithful to Thee all the days of our life here, we may be able hopefully to resign ourselves into Thy hands hereafter. Amen.
Rowland Williams

DAY 148

Parents aren't perfect. Yet even they won't give their son a stone when he asks for bread. So, if imperfect parents know how to give good gifts upon request, imagine how much more Father God will give good things to you—regardless of how imperfect you are. But you actually need to ask. Do so today and then expect God to give.

What man is there of you, whom if his son ask bread,
will he give him a stone? Or if he ask a fish, will he give
him a serpent? If ye then, being evil, know how to give good
gifts unto your children, how much more shall your Father
which is in heaven give good things to them that ask him?
MATTHEW 7:9–11

O my Lord! How can one ask you for favors who has served you so ill and has hardly been able to keep what you have already given? How can you have any confidence in one who has so often betrayed you? What, then, shall I do, comfort of the comfortless, and help of all who seek help from you? Can it be better to keep silence about my necessities, hoping that you will relieve them? No, indeed; for you, my Lord and my joy, knowing how many they must be and how it will alleviate them if we speak to you of them, do bid us pray to you and say that you will not fail to give.

SAINT TERESA OF ÁVILA

DAY 149

God wants to be with you when you plan your day. Then He wants to be consulted every step of the way. This may sound restricting, but when you practice asking Him, "What do You think, Lord?" at every turn, you find real freedom! For you know that when you're doing everything according to His desire, all your desires will be met and more!

So trust in God. Ask Him for advice for everything—from what to wear, to what to eat, to what to do, to whom to love! Rely on God's wisdom instead of your own intuition. See Him in everything you encounter and endeavor to do. Then you'll be on His path, walking His way. Then you'll neither stumble nor walk into a trap—because God's way is the right way.

Trust in the LORD with all thine heart; and lean not unto thine own understanding. In all thy ways acknowledge him, and he shall direct thy paths. . . . Then shalt thou walk in thy way safely, and thy foot shall not stumble. . . . For the LORD shall be thy confidence, and shall keep thy foot from being taken.
PROVERBS 3:5–6, 23, 26

Lord, enable me to regulate this day so as to please You!
Give me spiritual insight to discover what is Your will in
all the relations of my life. Guide me as to my pursuits,
my friendships, my reading, my dress, my Christian work.
HANNAH WHITALL SMITH

DAY 150

Today's prayer will put a smile on your face and joy in your heart. It was obviously written by someone who found happiness no matter what came around life's corner.

The key to such a merry heart and joy-filled spirit lies in knowing God. For with that knowledge grows trust in God, utter confidence that He will work all things out for your good.

A merry heart maketh a cheerful countenance: but by sorrow of the heart the spirit is broken. . . . A merry heart doeth good like a medicine: but a broken spirit drieth the bones.
PROVERBS 15:13; 17:22

Give us, Lord, a bit o' sun a bit o' work and a
bit o' fun; give us all, in the struggle and splutter,
our daily bread and a bit o' butter.

Give us health, our keep to make an' a bit to spare for poor
folks' sake; give us sense, for we're some of us duffers,
an' a heart to feel for all that suffers.

Give us, too, a bit o' song, an' a tale, an' a book
to help us along, an' give us our share o' sorrow's
lesson that we may see how grief's a blessing.

Give us, Lord, a chance to be our goodly best—brave,
wise and free; our goodly best for ourselves and others
'til all men learn to live as brothers.
OLD ENGLISH PRAYER

DAY 151

So often we go through life unconscious of our innermost feelings and thoughts. Yet for our spiritual health, God would have us examine ourselves, using the light of Christ to delve into the depths of our hearts and minds, to see if there's anything within that may tempt us to do something dishonorable without.

With God's help and power, give yourself a spiritual exam today. Ask the Christ within to clear out whatever might be standing in His way.

For though he was crucified through weakness, yet he liveth by the power of God. For we also are weak in him, but we shall live with him by the power of God. . . . Examine yourselves, whether ye be in the faith; prove your own selves. Know ye not your own selves, how that Jesus Christ is in you. . . ?

2 Corinthians 13:4–5

Almighty God, and most merciful Father, give us, we beseech Thee, that grace that we may duly examine the inmost of our hearts, and our most secret thoughts, how we stand before Thee; and that we may henceforward never be drawn to do anything that may dishonor Thy name: but may persevere in all good purposes, and in Thy Holy service, unto our life's end; and grant that we may now this present day, seeing it is as good as nothing that we have done hitherto, perfectly begin to walk before Thee, as becometh those that are called to an inheritance of light in Christ.

George Hickes

DAY 152

You're here to serve God in this generation. To not hide your talents in fear but to use them in the service of your Lord. Pray for God's grace to do what He calls you to do, so that at the end of the day, He will call you His good and faithful servant!

His lord said unto him, Well done, good and faithful servant; thou hast been faithful over a few things, I will make thee ruler over many things: enter thou into the joy of thy lord.
MATTHEW 25:23

O eternal God, Who has created me to do the work of God after the manner of men, and to serve Thee in this generation, and according to my capacities; give me Thy grace that I may be a prudent spender of my time, so as I may best prevent or resist all temptation, and be profitable to the Christian commonwealth; and, by discharging all my duty, may glorify Thy name. Take from me all slothfulness, and give me a diligent and an active spirit, and wisdom to choose my employment; that I may do works proportionable to my person, and to the dignity of a Christian, and may fill up all the spaces of my time with actions of religion and charity; improving my talent intrusted to me by Thee, my Lord, that I may enter into the joy of the Lord, to partake of Thy eternal felicities, even for Thy mercy's sake. Amen.

JEREMY TAYLOR

DAY 153

Each day, moment by moment, bit by bit, the Spirit of the Lord is remaking you, recreating you, transforming you into that perfect image of God that was marred through the fall. God knew you were coming. Way back when, He *chose* you to become like Christ: "For whom he did foreknow, he also did predestinate to be conformed to the image of his Son, that he might be the firstborn among many brethren" (Romans 8:29).

Yet to take on this image of Christ within you, you must be pliable, amenable to Christ's ministrations. That means replacing your desires with His. Letting the Lord of lords have full sway. Seeking Him first above all things. Getting to know Him better by reading and studying the Word and spending time in His presence. Allowing yourself to be less so He can be more.

Today, from the bottom of *your* heart, pray for Jesus to make you according to *His* heart. Believe He's doing so right now. And the next time you pass a mirror, you may be pleasantly surprised at what you see reflected back.

Now the Lord is that Spirit: and where the Spirit of the Lord is, there is liberty. But we all, with open face beholding as in a glass the glory of the Lord, are changed into the same image from glory to glory, even as by the Spirit of the Lord.
2 Corinthians 3:17–18

Lord, make me according to thy heart.
Brother Lawrence

DAY 154

God is always with you. You're never out of His sight. He's constantly looking out for you, giving you the power and strength to do what He's called you to do. From one task to the next, He's keeping your soul enlightened, your hands strong, and your mind alert. Take this knowledge with you throughout your day and night as you strive to do His work for Him and others. As God directs your course, commit yourself and your desires to Him while the moment is ripe.

For the eyes of the LORD run to and fro throughout the whole earth, to shew himself strong in the behalf of them whose heart is perfect toward him.
2 CHRONICLES 16:9

Eternal and infinite One, our hours of faithful duty follow us from the past and do not perish. Stir within us that we may redeem the time. Great Giver of the task, we live day and night beneath Your constant eyes. May we be steadfast through all faintness of soul and not rest by the roadside while Your errand waits. Daily may we drive out our selfishness and delight to bear one another's burden and uphold each other's faith and hope and love. May our minds be wholly turned to finish, without undue disquiet or contention, the work we strive to do for You. O Watcher of our days and nights, we would commit them all to You.

JAMES MARTINEAU

DAY 155

Amid trouble, turn to God. He'll answer you before you even call. While you're still praying, crying out to Him, He hears you. God's heart is breaking for you. He'll strengthen your faith, give you the hope, confidence, and patience to bear whatever's happening. Be resolved that in His time, He *will* deliver you safely. Meanwhile, know He's holding you close.

And it shall come to pass, that before they call, I will answer; and while they are yet speaking, I will hear.
ISAIAH 65:24

When I am afflicted, I think of God. O, where shall I turn, of whom else shall I think, in my cares and sufferings, but of thee, my God!...Thou hast said, Before they call, I will answer, and while they yet speak, I will answer, my heart is breaking for thee, and I must have mercy upon thee: therefore, I will not prescribe the time for thee to deliver me. Strengthen my faith by thy Holy Spirit; strengthen my faith, my hope, my confidence; give me patience and strength to bear my troubles. O my Father! thou hast never forsaken any one, forsake not me; thou hast always rejoiced the afflicted, rejoice me also; thou has assisted the wretched, assist me also; when, where, and as thou wilt, that all shall be according to thy wisdom, love, goodness and mercy. Be thou at peace, O my soul.
JOHANN FRIEDRICH STARCK

DAY 156

After leaving home, Jacob lay down and slept. In his dream, he saw a ladder between heaven and earth, and "angels of God ascending and descending on it" (Genesis 28:12). God, standing above the ladder, told Jacob, "I'm with you, and will watch over you. I'll never leave you until I've done all I said I would." When Jacob awoke, he said, "God's in this place—and I didn't even know it!"

As God is with you, you are with Him. No matter where you go, remember you are still together. Keep that glorious thought forever in mind as God keeps you forever in His!

I am with thee, and will keep thee in all places whither thou goest, and will bring thee again into this land; for I will not leave thee, until I have done that which I have spoken to thee of. And Jacob awaked out of his sleep, and he said, Surely the LORD is in this place; and I knew it not.
GENESIS 28:15–16

"Still, Still with Thee"

Still, still with Thee, when purple morning breaketh,
When the bird waketh, and the shadows flee;
Fairer than morning, lovelier than daylight,
Dawns the sweet consciousness, I am with Thee. . . .

So shall it be at last, in that bright morning,
When the soul waketh and life's shadows flee;
O in that hour, fairer than daylight dawning,
Shall rise the glorious thought, I am with Thee.
HARRIET BEECHER STOWE

DAY 157

Cry out to God if you're discouraged! The psalmists did, over and over again. But after crying out, reaffirm that God is your strength. That He will draw near and help you. As you hope in Him, He pulls you through.

———————————

Why art thou cast down, O my soul? and why art thou disquieted in me? hope thou in God: for I shall yet praise him for the help of his countenance. O my God, my soul is cast down within me. . . . Yet the LORD will command his lovingkindness in the day time, and in the night his song shall be with me, and my prayer unto the God of my life.
PSALM 42:5–6, 8

———————————

O God, my God, I am all weakness, but Thou art my Strength; I am ever anew bowed down by any trial, but Thou canst and willest to lift me up. Let me not fail, O God, my Strength; let me not be discouraged, O God, my Hope. Draw me each day, if it be but a little nearer to Thee; make me, each day, if it be but a little less unlike Thee; let me do or bear each day something for love of Thee, whereby I may be fitter for Thee. Let no day pass without my having done something pleasing unto Thee. Thus alone would I live, that I may live more unto Thee; thus would I die, longing to love Thee more. Amen.
EDWARD B. PUSEY

DAY 158

Today's prayer is a prayer for these days we live in. Although written over one hundred years ago, its pleas seem to meet every contingency, every emergency an individual may face. The prayer acknowledges God as the Helper of the helpless, asking Him to bring home the wanderer, heal the sick, free the captive, keep the old, comfort the weak, and liberate souls.

The world needs you to pray this prayer today.

Hear me when I call, O God of my righteousness: thou hast enlarged me when I was in distress; have mercy upon me, and hear my prayer.
PSALM 4:1

Grant us peace, and establish Thy truth in us; as Thou fillest all things living with plenteousness. Remember every faithful soul in trial; and comfort, if it be possible, every one in sorrow and distress.
O Helper of the helpless, bring the wanderer home, and give health to the sick, and deliverance to the captive. Sustain the aged, comfort the weak-hearted, set free those whose souls are bound in misery and iron; remember all those that are in affliction, necessity, and emergency everywhere. Let us dwell with Thee in peace, as children of light; and in Thy light, Lord, let us see the light. Direct, O Lord, in peace, the close of our life; trustfully, fearlessly, and, if it be Thy will, painlessly. Gather us when Thou wilt, into the abodes of Thy chosen; without shame, or stain, or sin. Amen.

ROWLAND WILLIAMS

DAY 159

God is clearly and consistently giving you clues that He's here, that He exists. Open your eyes and see the evidence of God's work in your life. Allow that proof to boost your faith. Let it enhance your belief that because of God, goodness does still exist. And you, as His follower, as His worker, are an extension of that goodness, a conduit of His light.

Pray, praise, and shine on.

Let your light so shine before men, that they may see your good works, and glorify your Father which is in heaven.
MATTHEW 5:16

How easy it is for me to live with you, Lord!
How easy it is for me to believe in You!
When my mind is distraught and my reason fails,
When the cleverest people do not see further
than this evening what must be done tomorrow
You grant me the clear confidence,
that You exist, and that You will take care
that not all the ways of goodness are stopped.
At the height of earthly fame I gaze with wonder
at that path through hopelessness—
to this point, from which even I have been able to convey
to men some reflection of the light which comes from You.
And you will enable me to go on doing
as much as needs to be done.
And in so far as I do not manage it—
that means that You have allotted the task to others.
ALEKSANDR SOLZHENITSYN

DAY 160

Jesus laid down His life for you—before you even knew Him. He was born for you—before you were conceived. He began watching out for you—before you ever saw Him. He loved you—before you loved Him. Jesus has done all this—and more—so you could get close to God. So you could be reunited with the Father of all creation. So you could be brought out of the darkness and led into the light. So your missteps and debts could be forgiven, wiped clean, once and for all. So you could have peace within regardless of what's happening without.

Today, thank Jesus for His sacrifice on your behalf. You're in the light of the Son's kingdom now. Thank God!

Thanks unto the Father, which hath made us meet to be partakers of the inheritance of the saints in light: Who hath delivered us from the power of darkness, and hath translated us into the kingdom of his dear Son: In whom we have redemption through his blood, even the forgiveness of sins. . . . Now hath he reconciled in the body of his flesh through death, to present you holy and unblameable and unreproveable in his sight: If ye continue in the faith grounded and settled, and be not moved away from the hope of the gospel.
COLOSSIANS 1:12–14, 21–23

I thank Thee, Savior, because Thou has died for me.
OLE HALLESBY

DAY 161

When you feel weakened by personal sorrow or brought down by the world's woes, go to God, your strength. Ask Him to send out His light so you can be led back into the peace of His presence. There you'll find the joy of God's hope, Jesus' love, and the Spirit's wisdom. There, music will stir your heart and a song of praise will form on your lips.

For thou art the God of my strength. . .why go I mourning because of the oppression of the enemy? O send out thy light and thy truth: let them lead me; let them bring me unto thy holy hill, and to thy tabernacles. Then will I go unto the altar of God, unto God my exceeding joy: yea, upon the harp will I praise thee, O God my God. Why art thou cast down, O my soul? and why art thou disquieted within me? hope in God: for I shall yet praise him, who is the health of my countenance, and my God.

PSALM 43:2–5

O Lord God, my soul is sorrowful, sometimes, even unto tears; sometimes also my spirit is disquieted, by reason of impending sufferings. I long after the joy of thy peace, the peace of thy children I earnestly crave. If thou give peace, if thou pour into me holy joy, the soul of thy servant shall be full of melody, and shall become devout in thy praise. Amen.

THOMAS À KEMPIS

DAY 162

How wonderful to become like Christ. To share all His attributes, to reflect Him to the point where people no longer see you but Him shining through. Yet such a feat cannot be done in your own power but must come through God's Spirit and voice.

Today, spend time in God's Word. Allow it to transform your mind, heart, soul, and spirit. After meditating upon the verses that have touched your inner being, commune with Jesus, taking on more and more of His persona deep within. Then pray that Christ would mold your soul to mirror Him alone so that those you meet would see and greet *His* grace and face.

And such trust have we through Christ to God-ward: Not that we are sufficient of ourselves to think any thing as of ourselves; but our sufficiency is of God; who also hath made us able ministers of the new testament; not of the letter, but of the spirit. . . . Now the Lord is that Spirit: and where the Spirit of the Lord is, there is liberty. But we all, with open face beholding as in a glass the glory of the Lord, are changed into the same image from glory to glory, even as by the Spirit of the Lord.
2 CORINTHIANS 3:4–6, 17–18

Lord, make my soul
To mirror Thee,
Thyself alone
To shine in me,
That men may see
Thy love, Thy grace,
Nor note the glass
That shows Thy face.
BLANCHE MARY KELLY

DAY 163

When you realize the abundant compassion God has for you, you can face anything as you trust that God, the highest power, favors you above all else. Pray and take courage as you lean into God's love and mercy surrounding you.

Be merciful unto me, O God. . . . O thou most High. What time I am afraid, I will trust in thee. In God I will praise his word, in God I have put my trust; I will not fear what flesh can do unto me.
PSALM 56:1–4

Father, we pray: Bless thou this truth. Oh God, thy mercies are abundant. Are not thy mercies full and free, and have they not, oh God, found out me? We thank thee for thy mercies, thy many, abundant, full mercies. Now we pray that thou will help us to lean back upon thy mercy and trust, and not be afraid; heed sin and love righteousness, flee from iniquity and follow after godliness, but always know that in all that we do mercy is around us like the air; underneath us as the earth; above us as the stars, and we live in a merciful world and serve a merciful God; live and swim and move and have our being in the abundant mercies of the triune God. Graciously grant us, we pray thee, properly to understand this and to apply it to our hearts, and we give thee praise through Jesus Christ our Lord. Amen.
A. W. TOZER

DAY 164

Do you trust God to make decisions for you? Do you believe He has your best interests at heart? Are you meek enough to accept God to do things His way and in His timing?

When you allow God to choose your path, when you believe in His love for you, when you submit to His way, timing, and reasonings, you'll find God's guidance in every decision you make—and the peace that comes with trusting Him for everything.

Today, lift up your soul to God. Bring Him your worries, issues, plans, and quandaries. Then pray today's nine-word prayer as you go through this day and every day, leaving all in His good hands.

Unto thee, O LORD, do I lift up my soul. O my God, I trust in thee . . . . Lead me in thy truth, and teach me: for thou art the God of my salvation; on thee do I wait all the day. . . . The meek will he guide in judgment: and the meek will he teach his way. . . . What man is he that feareth the LORD? him shall he teach in the way that he shall choose. His soul shall dwell at ease; and his seed shall inherit the earth.

PSALM 25:1–2, 5, 9, 12–13

Dear God, you choose. I choose what you choose.
S. D. GORDON

DAY 165

God knows the things of this world can never satisfy you. That's why He offers Himself to be your all in all. That's why He offers His grace to keep you from being snared by desires that pull you away from Him.

As you pray today's prayer, you'll find yourself drawn ever closer to the freedom of God and further away from the trappings of the world. You'll find God helping you to seek and desire Him above all. And as He raises your heart to Him, you'll find yourself overflowing with His supernatural love, peace, and power.

And the Word was made flesh, and dwelt among us, (and we beheld his glory, the glory as of the only begotten of the Father,) full of grace and truth. . . . And of his fulness have all we received, and grace for grace. For the law was given by Moses, but grace and truth came by Jesus Christ.
JOHN 1:14, 16–17

O my God, give me thy grace so that the things of this earth and things more naturally pleasing to me, may not be as close as thou art to me. Keep thou my eyes, my ears, my heart from clinging to the things of this world. Break my bonds, raise my heart. Keep my whole being fixed on thee. Let me never lose sight of thee; and while I gaze on thee, let my love of thee grow more and more every day.
JOHN HENRY NEWMAN

DAY 166

It's a credit to you and Jesus (and a benefit to others) when you follow His example. But to do so, you need help—lots of it—from Father God. You need His power to remain cheerful when things don't work out, to keep trying no matter what, to stay peaceful when stressed. And that's only the beginning of the list! Fortunately, God's on your side. With today's prayer and His divine aid, you'll get there from here.

But speaking the truth in love. . .grow up into
him in all things, which is the head, even Christ.
Ephesians 4:15

O God, our Father, help us all through this day so to live
that we may bring help to others, credit to ourselves and to
the name we bear, and joy to those that love us, and to you.
Cheerful when things go wrong;
Persevering when things are difficult;
Serene when things are irritating.
Enable us to be:
Helpful to those in difficulties;
Kind to those in need;
Sympathetic to those whose hearts are sore and sad.
Grant that:
Nothing may make us lose our tempers;
Nothing may take away our joy;
Nothing may ruffle our peace;
Nothing may make us bitter towards anyone.
So grant that through all this day all with whom we work,
and all those whom we meet, may see in us the reflection
of the master, whose we are, and whom we seek to serve.
This we ask for your love's sake.

William Barclay

DAY 167

God's Word is the doorway to understanding the one who holds the entire world in His hands. It gives you the opportunity to see into the highest of minds, His ways, His love, His plan for you. When you begin to delve into the Word, to believe in and claim God's promises to and for you, you cannot help but praise the Creator and Master Planner.

Today, pray for God to enlighten your mind by the power of the Holy Spirit. To give you the means and grace to understand and receive God's Word, accepting it as truth. Ask God to reveal what He would have you know in this time and place so you can walk Christ's way.

The entrance of thy words giveth light; it giveth understanding unto the simple. . . . Let my cry come near before thee, O LORD: give me understanding according to thy word. . . . My lips shall utter praise, when thou hast taught me thy statutes. My tongue shall speak of thy word: for all thy commandments are righteousness. Let thine hand help me; for I have chosen thy precepts.
PSALM 119:130, 169, 171–173

O Lord, heavenly Father, in whom is the fullness of light and wisdom, enlighten our minds by your Holy Spirit, and give us grace to receive your Word with reverence and humility, without which no one can understand your truth. For Christ's sake, amen.
JOHN CALVIN

DAY 168

When Jesus healed a deaf and mute man, the people "were beyond measure astonished, saying, He hath done all things well: he maketh both the deaf to hear, and the dumb to speak" (Mark 7:37). That may sound like ancient history—but be assured, it's your present reality. Jesus does do all things well!

To obtain the supernatural calmness of knowing all things are in Jesus' hands and the patient trust that He does all things well, pray today's prayer—and you'll get both!

For we are saved by hope. . . . We with patience wait for it. . . . The Spirit itself maketh intercession for us. . . . And he that searcheth the hearts knoweth what is the mind of the Spirit, because he maketh intercession for the saints according to the will of God. And we know that all things work together for good to them that love God.
ROMANS 8:24–28

O God, who makest cheerfulness the companion of strength, but apt to take wings in time of sorrow, we humbly beseech thee that if, in thy sovereign wisdom, thou sendest weakness, yet for thy mercy's sake deny us not the comfort of patience. Lay not more upon us to bear; and, since the fretfulness of our spirit is more hurtful than the heaviness of our burden, grant us that heavenly calmness which comes of owning thy hand in all things, and patience in the trust that thou doest all things well. Amen.

ROWLAND WILLIAMS

DAY 169

Never think you can stand alone, without needing God. Arrogance blocks the work God can do in your life, but your acknowledged need of Him makes it easy for Him to aid you in a powerful way.

Moses discovered how our need opens the door to God's power. The Egyptians had driven Moses and God's people to the edge. There was no escape. But Moses told the Israelites to calm down, to stand their ground at the edge of the Red Sea, that God would fight for them. And He did—using His power and Moses' upraised hand.

Without God's strong arm, you'll fall. With it, you'll not only stay standing but will rise up and win the day!

[Moses said to the people,] The Lord shall fight for you, and ye shall hold your peace. . . . And the angel of God, which went before the camp of Israel, removed and went behind them; and the pillar of the cloud went from before their face, and stood behind them. . . . And Moses stretched out his hand over the sea; and the Lord caused the sea to go back by a strong east wind all that night, and made the sea dry land, and the waters were divided. And the children of Israel went into the midst of the sea upon the dry ground.
Exodus 14:14, 19, 21–22

O Lord, never suffer us to think that we
can stand by ourselves, and not need thee.
John Donne

DAY 170

Don't just dive into a conversation. Listen. Then wait on God to lead you in what to say. Because if you don't listen, you may mishear, take offense, then speak out in anger. In the end, you'll find yourself having to extend *and* receive some forgiveness.

To help you become a better listener, one slow to anger, delve into the Word, anchoring it in your heart. It will save your soul!

Let every man be swift to hear, slow to speak, slow to wrath: For the wrath of man worketh not the righteousness of God. . . . Receive with meekness the engrafted word, which is able to save your souls.

JAMES 1:19–21

O Almighty God, give to Thy servant a meek and gentle spirit, that I may be slow to anger, and easy to mercy and forgiveness. Give me a wise and constant heart, that I may never be moved to an intemperate anger for any injury that is done or offered. Lord, let me ever be courteous, and easy to be entreated; let me never fall into a peevish or contentious spirit, but follow peace with all men; offering forgiveness, inviting them by courtesies, ready to confess my own errors, apt to make amends, and desirous to be reconciled. Let no sickness or cross accident, no employment or weariness, make me angry or ungentle and discontented, or unthankful, or uneasy to them that minister to me; but in all things make me like unto the holy Jesus. Amen.

JEREMY TAYLOR

DAY 171

The moment you received Christ, the Spirit began residing within you. He was with God in the beginning of creation, hovering upon the darkness of the water. And He's with you now.

Invite the Spirit into this moment. Pray today's prayer slowly, giving yourself the opportunity to commune with Him, spirit to Spirit.

And the spirit of the LORD shall rest upon him.
ISAIAH 11:2

"An Invocation to the Holy Spirit"

Come, true light. Come, life eternal. Come, hidden mystery.
Come, treasure without name. Come, reality beyond all words.
Come, person beyond all understanding.
Come, rejoicing without end. Come, light that knows
no evening. Come, unfailing expectation of the saved.
Come, raising of the fallen. Come, resurrection of the dead.
Come, all-powerful, for unceasingly you create, refashion and
change all things by your will alone.
Come, invisible whom none may touch and handle.
Come, for you continue always unmoved, yet at every
instant you are wholly in movement; you draw near to us
who lie in hell, yet you remain higher than the heavens.
Come, for your name fills our hearts with longing and is
ever on our lips; yet who you are and what your nature is,
we cannot say or know. Come, alone to the alone.
Come, for you are yourself the desire that is within me.
Come, my breath and my life. Come, the consolation of my
humble soul. Come, my joy, my glory, my endless delight.

SAINT SYMEON

DAY 172

God doesn't want you to consider your life a drudgery but a blessing, blooming where He has planted you to do His will—to His glory. For every day is a gift to you from God, as is your job, the tasks He puts into your hands, and the roles only you can fulfill. So enjoy your life. Take pleasure in what God's given you. Rejoice in your work. As God rewards you, reward Him right back by sharing your joy with Him.

And while you're living, don't waste time looking back at what might have been. Instead, be focused on the now, on today, knowing that no matter what happens, you'll be with God tomorrow.

Behold that which I have seen: it is good and comely for one to eat and to drink, and to enjoy the good of all his labour that he taketh under the sun all the days of his life, which God giveth him: for it is his portion. Every man also to whom God hath given riches and wealth, and hath given him power to eat thereof, and to take his portion, and to rejoice in his labour; this is the gift of God. For he shall not much remember the days of his life; because God answereth him in the joy of his heart.
ECCLESIASTES 5:18–20

Make us remember, O God, that every day is
your gift, to be used according to your command.
SAMUEL JOHNSON

DAY 173

What's the greatest thing God gives you? Love. What's the greatest thing He wants you to give Him? Love.

Ask God to free you from everything so you can love Him with everything.

And, behold, a certain lawyer stood up, and tempted him, saying, Master, what shall I do to inherit eternal life?... And he answering said, Thou shalt love the Lord thy God with all thy heart, and with all thy soul, and with all thy strength, and with all thy mind; and thy neighbour as thyself.

LUKE 10:25, 27

Let my heart be free from every unworthy thing that I may be free to love thee, my Lord God, with all my heart and soul and with all my strength. Free me from such narrow-mindedness as would make me set my affections upon anything apart from thee, O thou, who art the only true Lover and true Lord of all. When I love anything for the reason that it is from thee, then do I truly love thee, in that I love it for thy sake, for thou alone hast every claim over it for our good. Our service of thee, what else is it but a working out of thy loving salvation? Thou didst first show us love to win our love, not needing it, but solely because we cannot become what thou wouldst have us be unless we love thee.

WILLIAM OF SAINT-THIERRY

DAY 174

There's one path to God's presence, the place where you can find His light, goodness, deliverance, support, wisdom, and mercy. That gateway to Him lies in seeking and loving Him with all your heart and mind and soul and might. The word *might* refers to using all your energy and ability to love God. When you do so diligently, wholly, with your entire being, you'll find yourself wanting to obey Him and, in the process, discover that Promised Land in Him.

Today, pray to the God whom you seek and love. Do so often, with your entire being. And you'll find His land of promise and power.

Hear therefore, O Israel, and observe to do it; that it may be well with thee, and that ye may increase mightily, as the LORD God of thy fathers hath promised thee, in the land that floweth with milk and honey. Hear, O Israel: The LORD our God is one LORD: And thou shalt love the LORD thy God with all thine heart, and with all thy soul, and with all thy might.

DEUTERONOMY 6:3–5

O eternal Light, shine into our hearts; eternal Goodness, deliver us from evil; eternal Power, be thou our support; eternal Wisdom, scatter our ignorance; eternal Pit, have mercy upon us. Grant that with all our heart and mind and soul and strength we may seek thy face, and finally bring us, by thine infinite mercy, to thy holy presence, through Jesus Christ our Lord. Amen.

ALCUIN

DAY 175

Your best answer to prayer isn't the actual outcome of your pleas but the idea that God loves, cares for, and wants the best for you. Glory in God's presence as you pray. And you'll find all the answers you need.

O taste and see that the LORD is good:
blessed is the man that trusteth in him.
PSALM 34:8

We rejoice that in all time men have found a refuge in Thee, and that prayer is the voice of love, the voice of pleading, and the voice of thanksgiving. Our souls overflow toward Thee like a cup when full; nor can we forbear; nor shall we search to see if our prayers have been registered, or whether of the things asked we have received much, or more, or anything. That we have had permission to feel ourselves in Thy presence, to take upon ourselves something of the light of Thy countenance, to have a consciousness that Thy thoughts are upon us, to experience the inspiration of the Holy Spirit in any measure—this is an answer to prayer transcending all things that we can think of. We are glad that we can glorify Thee, that we can rejoice Thee, that it does make a difference to Thee what we do, and that Thou dost enfold us in a consciousness of Thy sympathy with us, of how much Thou art to us, and of what we are to Thee.

HENRY WARD BEECHER

DAY 176

When you're open to God, when you're willing to receive Him into every moment of your life, when you readily accept His kingdom, no matter what happens in this earthly world, you'll discover the peace found in Jesus alone. For He has *overcome* this world.

Knowing Jesus has gained victory here means you need not fear anything anywhere. That peace you find in Him gives you access to all the courage, resiliency, and joy you need to thrive. For you know no power in this world can harm you. Jesus is over all!

So on those days when you feel as if the bear has eaten you, go to Jesus. Open yourself up to His ministrations, power, love, light. Accept all He's willing to give you of His kingdom and Himself. Be as a child in your big Brother's hands, allowing His arms to protect you, His power to strengthen you, His love to bind you. Make Jesus your home, all the days of your life.

These things I have spoken unto you, that in me ye might have peace. In the world ye shall have tribulation: but be of good cheer; I have overcome the world.
JOHN 16:33

Make us receptive and open
and may we accept your kingdom
like children taking bread
from the hands of their father.
Let us live in your peace,
at home with you
all the days of our lives.
HUUB OOSTERHUIS

DAY 177

The first commandment Jesus gave you was to love God with your entire being. The second was to love others as you love yourself. That means putting others' needs and wants above your own at times. Doing so may require you to put your work aside so you can help someone with his work. To be vulnerable enough to depend on the courage, industry, or honesty of a fellow human being so she can shine. To trust in the wisdom of another instead of your own. In order to do this, remember that God is watching. He's taking care of you. And, at times, He'll be counting on you to count on others—to His glory and good end.

Be kindly affectioned one to another with brotherly love;
in honour preferring one another; not slothful in business;
fervent in spirit; serving the Lord. . .distributing to the
necessity of saints; given to hospitality. . . . Be of the same
mind one toward another. Mind not high things, but condescend
to men of low estate. Be not wise in your own conceits.
ROMANS 12:10–11, 13, 16

O God, you have bound us together in this bundle of life; give
us grace to understand how our lives depend on the courage, the
industry, the honesty and integrity of our fellow men; that we may
be mindful of their needs, grateful for their faithfulness, and faithful
in our responsibilities to them; through Jesus Christ our Lord.
REINHOLD NIEBUHR

DAY 178

Today, rise above life's turmoil and into the love of God with the power of prayer. Soar up to the Lord, letting your love for Him and His for you override all.

Let us lift up our heart with our hands unto God in the heavens. . . .
I called upon thy name, O LORD, out of the low dungeon. Thou hast
heard my voice. . . . Thou drewest near. . .thou saidst, Fear not.
LAMENTATIONS 3:41, 55–57

O God, my God, give me a heart to thank Thee; lift up my heart above myself, to Thee and Thine eternal throne; let it not linger here among the toils and turmoils of this lower world; let it not be oppressed by any earth-born clouds of care or anxiety or fear or suspicion; but bind it wholly to Thee and to Thy love; give me eyes to see Thy love in all things, and Thy grace in all around me; make me to thank Thee for Thy love and Thy grace to all and in all; give me wings of love, that I may soar up to Thee, and cling to Thee, and adore Thee, and praise Thee more and more, until I be fitted to enter into the joys of Thine everlasting love, everlasting to love Thee and Thy grace, whereby Thou didst make me such as Thou couldest love, such as could love Thee, O God, my God. Amen.
EDWARD B. PUSEY

DAY 179

Neither time nor space has dominion over God. He's all the time, everywhere. He's in, of, above, and over all things. He sees, knows, and understands all things. And all things are in His hands—including you. So hold nothing back.

Give God all of you—heart, mind, body, soul, and spirit. Give Him your pen, and the lines you write will dance upon the paper. Give Him your instrument, and the notes you play will shimmer upon the air. Give Him your brush, and the colors you paint will sing upon the canvas.

God brings out the truest meaning of all things. So pray, giving all you have and are to Him. And watch as He makes something amazing out of all.

O LORD my God, thou art very great. . . . Who coverest thyself with light as with a garment: who stretchest out the heavens like a curtain: Who layeth the beams of his chambers in the waters: who maketh the clouds his chariot: who walketh upon the wings of the wind: Who maketh his angels spirits. . .Who laid the foundations of the earth, that it should not be removed for ever.

PSALM 104:1–5

Thou takest the pen—and the lines dance.
Thou takest the flute—and the notes shimmer.
Thou takest the brush—and the colours sing.
So all things have meaning and beauty in that space beyond time where Thou art. How, then, can I hold back anything from Thee?

DAG HAMMARSKJÖLD

DAY 180

Today, use the power of prayer to reaffirm the trust you have in God to give you what you need when you need it.

God. . .is a shield unto them that put their trust in him. . . .
Give me neither poverty nor riches; feed me with food convenient
for me: Lest I be full, and deny thee, and say, Who is the LORD?
or lest I be poor, and steal, and take the name of my God in vain.
PROVERBS 30:5, 8–9

O my Lord, in Thine arms I am safe; keep me and I have nothing to fear; give me up, and I have nothing to hope for. I know nothing about the future, but I rely upon Thee. I pray Thee to give me what is good for me; I pray Thee to take from me whatever may imperil my salvation. I leave it all to Thee, because Thou knowest and I do not. If Thou bringest pain or sorrow on me, give me grace to bear it well, keep me from fretfulness and selfishness. If Thou givest me health and strength and success in this world, keep me ever on my guard lest these great gifts carry me away from Thee. Give me to know Thee, to believe on Thee, to love Thee, to serve Thee, to live to and for Thee. Give me to die just at that time and in that way which is most for Thy glory. Amen.

JOHN HENRY NEWMAN

DAY 181

Because you have the Bible, you know Jesus' full story. How He spent His life doing good, helping others, giving His Father God all the glory. Jesus wants you to do the same, to continue His Father's business. So don't get discouraged or become weary of doing good. Continue to follow Jesus' pattern. Do what God has called you to do until He at last calls you home to be with the Holy Three.

And his mother said unto him, Son, why hast thou thus dealt
with us? behold, thy father and I have sought thee sorrowing.
And he said unto them, How is it that ye sought me?
wist ye not that I must be about my Father's business?
LUKE 2:48–49

O Lord Jesus Christ, who when on earth wast ever about
thy Father's business: Grant that we may not grow weary in
well-doing. Give us grace to do all in thy name. Be thou the
beginning and the end of all: the pattern whom we follow,
the redeemer in whom we trust, the master whom we serve,
the friend to whom we look for sympathy. May we never shrink
from our duty from any fear of man. Make us faithful unto death;
and bring us at last into thy eternal presence, where with the
Father and the Holy Ghost thou livest and reignest for ever.
EDWARD B. PUSEY

DAY 182

Every day is a good day to give your hope a boost. To remember that this life here is not the end. To remember that there's a better place awaiting you in the new heaven where Christ, the Alpha and Omega, the beginning and the end, resides. Because you are a believer, a child of God, one who follows God's edicts to love Him, yourself, and others, you are blessed. For someday you can and will enter the gates of that eternal city where the bright Morning Star awaits you.

Today, pray for Christ to awaken you from your lethargy, your indifference, and renew your hope for that world without end.

I am Alpha and Omega, the beginning and the end, the first and the last. Blessed are they that do his commandments, that they may have right to the tree of life, and may enter in through the gates into the city . . . . I Jesus have sent mine angel to testify unto you these things in the churches. I am the root and the offspring of David, and the bright and morning star. And the Spirit and the bride say, Come.

REVELATION 22:13–14, 16–17

O Christ, our Morning Star,
Splendour of Light Eternal,
shining with the glory of the rainbow,
come and waken us
from the greyness of our apathy
and renew in us your gift of hope. Amen.

SAINT BEDE THE VENERABLE

DAY 183

For a good night's sleep, rest easy knowing God has His angels watching over you. In fact, they have *charge* over you, are with you, defending and protecting you. They bear you up so that you won't stumble (Psalm 91:11–12). Have faith that God is with you and those you love. That He will reassure those who wake in the night, ease the watchful, comfort the crier, tend the sick, rest the weary, bless the dying, soothe the suffering, shield the joyful—all because He loves them.

And forget about tomorrow. Know that God will take all your work and efforts and make something good come out of them—including your prayers for others. So tonight, before your head hits the pillow, launch your prayers up to God, then fall asleep in His arms.

Except the LORD build the house, they labour in vain that build it: except the LORD keep the city, the watchman waketh but in vain. It is vain for you to rise up early, to sit up late, to eat the bread of sorrows: for so he giveth his beloved sleep.
PSALM 127:1–2

Watch thou, dear Lord, with those who wake, or watch, or weep tonight, and give thine angels charge over those who sleep. Tend thy sick ones, O Lord Christ; rest thy weary ones; bless thy dying ones. Soothe thy suffering ones; shield thy joyous ones; and all for thy Love's sake. Amen.
SAINT AUGUSTINE

DAY 184

In the Old Testament, Joseph never lost his faith in God. Even after his brothers put him into a pit then sold him to passing strangers. Even when Joseph became a slave in Egypt then a prisoner in a dark dungeon, still his faith held. Eventually he was lifted up to become a great ruler in Egypt, second only to Pharaoh. There he met up with his brothers again. Men who had once betrayed him cowered in fear. But Joseph told them, "Don't worry. The evil you'd meant has been transformed into something good. And now I'll be able to save you and many others. So don't fear."

No matter what bad things come into your life, no matter how dark your dungeon, have no worries or fears. Instead, have faith that God will make something good come out of it all.

But as for you, ye thought evil against me; but God meant it unto good, to bring to pass, as it is this day, to save much people alive. Now therefore fear ye not.
GENESIS 50:20–21

I will not doubt, though all my ships at sea
Come drifting home with broken masts and sails;
I shall believe the Hand which never fails,
From seeming evil worketh good for me;
And though I weep because those sails are battered,
Still will I cry, while my best hopes lie shattered,
"I trust in Thee."

ELLA WHEELER WILCOX

DAY 185

God saved you, not because of anything you did but because of His mercy. And He did so by washing you, renewing you with the Holy Spirit that has come upon you. But this renewal is not just a once-and-done thing. It's a power you have access to every day as you offer yourself up to God.

So put yourself on God's altar today. Pray for Him to renew all of you—heart, body, mind, and soul—in the power of the Holy Spirit. When you do, your fear will be replaced by courage, your unknowing by knowing, and your discouragement with hope so that, in His strength and power, you will carry out the work God has put your hand to.

According to his mercy he saved us, by the washing of regeneration, and renewing of the Holy Ghost; which he shed on us abundantly through Jesus Christ our Saviour; that being justified by his grace, we should be made heirs according to the hope of eternal life.
TITUS 3:5–7

O God our Father, who sent your Son to be our Savior:
renew in us day by day the power of your Holy Spirit;
that with knowledge and zeal, with courage and love,
with gratitude and hope, we may strive powerfully in your
service: may he keep our vision clear, our aspiration high,
our purpose firm and our sympathy wide; that we may live
as faithful soldiers and servants of our Lord Jesus Christ.
WILLIAM TEMPLE

DAY 186

How wonderful life can be when you truly give yourself up to the Lord, when you give over your will to God's will. For then you no longer have to worry about anything. When all you have, are, and expect are in His hands, when you let Him do what He thinks best, all the pressure falls off you.

So today, tell God that you're His servant and that, as such, you're prepared for whatever He has in mind. That you're ready to do and be as He pleases. Experience the reign of freedom such servanthood gives you!

O Lord, truly I am thy servant; I am thy servant, and the son of thine handmaid: thou hast loosed my bonds. I will offer to thee the sacrifice of thanksgiving, and will call upon the name of the Lord. . . . Praise ye the Lord.
Psalm 116:16–17, 19

O Lord, Thou knowest what is best for us, let this or that be done, as Thou shalt please. Give what Thou wilt, and how much Thou wilt, and when Thou wilt. Deal with me as Thou thinkest good, and as best pleaseth Thee. Set me where Thou wilt, and deal with me in all things just as Thou wilt. Behold, I am Thy servant, prepared for all things; for I desire not to live unto myself, but unto Thee; and Oh that I could do it worthily and perfectly! Amen.

Thomas à Kempis

DAY 187

Just as God was with Moses wherever He sent him, whatever He asked him to do, God is also with you. Not only that but, regardless of how big or small your duty today, God also goes before you, preparing your path and removing any obstacles that stand in your way. Because you know He'll give you the tools, the strength, the means, and the grace to fulfill your task, there's no need to stress. Simply pray, follow, and listen for God's voice, and He'll clear your way.

———————————————————

Come now therefore, and I will send thee unto Pharaoh, that thou mayest bring forth my people the children of Israel out of Egypt. And Moses said unto God, Who am I, that I should go unto Pharaoh, and that I should bring forth the children of Israel out of Egypt? And he said, Certainly I will be with thee. . .I have sent thee.
EXODUS 3:10–12

———————————————————

Give us grace, O Lord, to work while it is day: fulfilling diligently and patiently whatever duty Thou appointest us, doing small things in the day of small things, and great labors if Thou summon us to any: rising and working, sitting still and suffering, according to Thy word. Go with me and I will go, but if Thou go not with me, send me not; go before me if Thou put me forth; let me hear Thy voice when I follow. Amen.
CHRISTINA ROSSETTI

DAY 188

Children are very precious, especially to God. As recent arrivals, they have a close connection to Him. In fact, they have angels who look upon God's face continually (Matthew 18:10)!

Yet because children are so innocent and vulnerable, they need your support and protection. And the best way to provide that is to pray for the young ones in your care. Pray for their health. Pray they would find their way to God, be open to His Spirit, and discover the light of Jesus.

Go to your Father God today, as a little child yourself. Ask Him to look out for all the little ones you know. Be secure in the knowledge that although they are on loan to you in this world, a temporary gift for you to love and learn from, they are always safe in God's hands.

Lo, children are an heritage of the LORD: and the fruit of the womb is his reward. As arrows are in the hand of a mighty man; so are children of the youth. Happy is the man that hath his quiver full of them: they shall not be ashamed, but they shall speak with the enemies in the gate.

PSALM 127:3–5

Bless my children with healthful bodies, with good understandings, with the graces and gifts of your Spirit, with sweet dispositions and holy habits, and sanctify them throughout in their bodies and souls and spirits, and keep them unblamable to the coming of the Lord Jesus.

JEREMY TAYLOR

DAY 189

When Zerubbabel led Jews back to Jerusalem after the exile, he took on the arduous task of governing the land and rebuilding God's temple. Although many forces and numerous delays came up against the Israelites, their leaders, and their rebuilding efforts, the prophet Haggai, speaking for God, told Zerubbabel, the high priest, and the people to be strong. To go ahead with the work. That God was with them.

When you feel you are lacking in wisdom and power, that you need strength, go to God. And like Zerubbabel and his people, you'll get that and more!

Yet now be strong, O Zerubbabel, saith the LORD; and be strong, O Joshua, son of Josedech, the high priest; and be strong, all ye people of the land, saith the LORD, and work: for I am with you, saith the LORD of hosts. . .my spirit remaineth among you: fear ye not.
HAGGAI 2:4–5

Almighty God, of Thy fulness grant to us who need so much, who lack so much, who have so little, wisdom and strength. Bring our wills unto Thine. Lift our understandings into Thy heavenly light; that we thereby beholding those things which are right, and being drawn by Thy love, may bring our wills and our understanding together to Thy service, until at last, body and soul and spirit may be all Thine, and Thou be our Father and our Eternal Friend. Amen.
GEORGE DAWSON

DAY 190

When you're in the midst of darkness, feeling weak and helpless, pray for Jesus' warm light and presence to rest upon you. Feel His love and strength filling you from head to toe. Ask Jesus to build up your trust in His love and power so that your frets and fears would dissipate. For when you live close to Jesus Christ, when you abide in His presence, when you trust in Him alone, you'll see His hand, will, and purpose in everything that comes into your life—His purpose being for you to have so much confidence in Him that you bring praise and glory to God in all ways!

In [Christ] whom also we have obtained an inheritance, being predestinated according to the purpose of him who worketh all things after the counsel of his own will: That we should be to the praise of his glory, who first trusted in Christ. In whom ye also trusted, after that ye heard the word of truth, the gospel of your salvation.
EPHESIANS 1:11–13

O Christ Jesus, when all is darkness
and we feel our weakness and helplessness,
give us the sense of Your presence,
Your love, and Your strength. Help us to have perfect
trust in Your protecting love and strengthening power,
so that nothing may frighten or worry us,
for, living close to You, we shall see Your hand,
Your purpose, Your will through all things.
SAINT IGNATIUS OF LOYOLA

DAY 191

When the Israelites begged for a king, God gave them Saul (1 Samuel 9:17–21). At first, he saw himself as insignificant, hiding among the baggage when his kingship was announced to the people (1 Samuel 10:22). Yet Saul later became too big for his britches. The prophet Samuel confronted him, saying, "When thou wast little in thine own sight, wast thou not made the head of the tribes of Israel, and the LORD anointed thee king over Israel?" (1 Samuel 15:17). Because Saul had begun following his own wisdom instead of God's, God rejected him as king (1 Samuel 15:23).

It can be easy to lose your perspective when you become "big enough to reach the world." Today, pray for God's love and power to keep you small enough to stay one with Him.

———————————

As thou, Father, art in me, and I in thee, that they also may be one in us: that the world may believe that thou hast sent me. And the glory which thou gavest me I have given them; that they may be one, even as we are one: I in them, and thou in me, that they may be made perfect in one; and that the world may know that thou hast sent me, and hast loved them, as thou hast loved me.

JOHN 17:21–23

———————————

Grant that with your love, I may be big enough to reach the world, and small enough to be one with you.

MOTHER TERESA

DAY 192

Do you refresh the people with whom you come in contact?

When the apostle Paul was journeying to Italy as a prisoner, the centurion in charge of guarding him allowed him to go to his friends to be cared for. If only we all would be as kind as that centurion, as caring as those friends!

Today, pray God would give you the compassion to refresh and befriend your fellow sojourners.

Julius courteously entreated Paul, and gave him
liberty to go unto his friends to refresh himself.
ACTS 27:3

Once more a new day lies before us, our Father. As we go out among men to do our work, touching the hands and lives of our fellows, make us, we pray Thee, friends of all the world. Save us from blighting the fresh flower of any heart by the flare of sudden anger or secret hate. May we not bruise the rightful self-respect of any by contempt or malice. Help us to cheer the suffering by our sympathy, to freshen the drooping by our hopefulness, and to strengthen in all the wholesome sense of worth and the joy of life. Save us from the deadly poison of class-pride. Grant that we may look all men in the face with the eyes of a brother. If any one needs us, make us ready to yield our help ungrudgingly, unless higher duties claim us, and may we rejoice that we have it in us to be helpful to our fellow-men.

WALTER RAUSCHENBUSCH

DAY 193

Imagine being in a boat upon the sea. At first, it's wonderful. You're awed by all the amazing things the Lord has created. The power of the wind and waves is glorious. The sunrises and sunsets upon the water are magnificent. But then the wind begins to gust, the waves to rage. You and your boat are thrown about. You become terrified. Then you cry out to God and He brings you out of trouble. He calms the storm and stills the waves.

Today's prayer is a powerful one to help you rise above the storm. To remind you that God, your Protector, will bring you to a good place.

They that go down to the sea in ships, that do business in great waters; these see the works of the LORD, and his wonders in the deep. For he commandeth, and raiseth the stormy wind, which lifteth up the waves thereof. They mount up to the heaven, they go down again to the depths: their soul is melted because of trouble. They reel to and fro, and stagger like a drunken man, and are at their wit's end. Then they cry unto the LORD in their trouble, and he bringeth them out of their distresses. He maketh the storm a calm, so that the waves thereof are still.

PSALM 107:23–29

Dear God, be good to me;
The sea is so wide,
and my boat is so small.

PRAYER USED BY BRETON FISHERMEN

DAY 194

Have you been tapping your foot recently? Waiting for Jesus to lead you somewhere?

Be patient. You're one of His sheep. He calls you by name and leads you out where He wants you to go. All you need to do as He clears the way ahead is follow Him. You'll know His voice.

Today, go to the Good Shepherd. Be still before Him. Listen for His voice. You'll know it when you hear it, for it is unlike any other. His powerful and loving words will give you the comfort and patience to either stay where you are or walk forward in and with Him.

But he that entereth in by the door is the shepherd of the sheep.
To him the porter openeth; and the sheep hear his voice: and he calleth
his own sheep by name, and leadeth them out. And when he putteth
forth his own sheep, he goeth before them, and the sheep follow him:
for they know his voice. And a stranger will they not follow,
but will flee from him: for they know not the voice of strangers.
JOHN 10:2–5

O Lord, who call your own sheep by name, grant, we beg
you, that all whom you call by the voice of conscience
may straightway arise to do your most compassionate will,
or abide patiently to suffer for it. Amen.
CHRISTINA ROSSETTI

DAY 195

When you sow peace, you reflect God's character to others. And there's a bonus—you're also rewarded for being considered a son or daughter of God.

Today's prayer asks God to make you a messenger of God's peace. To be the seed of love amid hatred, forgiveness amid hurt, faith amid doubt, hope amid despair, light amid darkness, joy amid grief—and to not stop there but go *looking* to help others instead of yourself.

Wear and spread your godly light, and you'll get so much more in return.

And he opened his mouth, and taught them, saying. . .
Blessed are the peacemakers: for they shall be called the children
of God. . . . Let your light so shine before men, that they may
see your good works, and glorify your Father which is in heaven.
MATTHEW 5:2, 9, 16

Lord, make me an instrument of your peace.
Where there is hatred, let me sow love;
Where there is injury, pardon; Where there is doubt, faith;
Where there is despair, hope; Where there is darkness, light;
Where there is sadness, joy.
O Divine Master, grant that I may not so much seek
To be consoled as to console;
To be understood as to understand; To be loved as to love.
For it is in giving that we receive;
It is in pardoning that we are pardoned;
And it is in dying that we are born to eternal life.
SAINT FRANCIS OF ASSISI

DAY 196

God is with you through thick and thin, sadness and joy, imprisonment and freedom. Today, defeat your discouragement by prayerfully praising God and affirming His presence, knowing that He won't give you more than you can bear, that His Son, Jesus, seeks you every moment.

[The Lord] hath sent me to bind up the brokenhearted, to proclaim liberty to the captives, and the opening of the prison to them that are bound. . .to give unto them. . .the garment of praise for the pirit of heaviness; that. . .[the Lord] might be glorified.
Isaiah 61:1, 3

O heav'nly Father, I praise and thank Thee for the peace
of the night. I praise and thank Thee for this new day.
I praise and thank Thee for all Thy goodness and faithfulness
throughout my life. Thou hast granted me many blessings:
now let me accept tribulation from Thy hand. Thou wilt not
lay on me more than I can bear. Thou makest all things work
together for good for Thy children. Lord Jesus Christ, Thou
wast poor and in misery, a captive and forsaken as I am. Thou
knowest all Man's distress; Thou abidest with me when all others
have deserted me. Thou dost not forget me but seekest me.
Thou willest that I should know Thee and turn to Thee. Lord,
I hear Thy call and follow Thee; do Thou help me. . . . Lord,
whatever this day may bring, Thy name be praised.
Dietrich Bonhoeffer

DAY 197

Oh to be like Christ. Offer your entire self to Jesus to obtain His light of life. Rejoice that He is in your mind, arranging your thoughts, aligning them with His own. Thank Him for being in your heart, reigning over your emotions, filling you with His love. Invite Jesus into your body, allowing Him to recreate it in the pattern of His perfect health and energy. As you do so, your mental, emotional, and physical power will strengthen, molding you more and more into His image each day. Become the light of His light, the life of His life.

Then spake Jesus again unto them, saying, I am the light
of the world: he that followeth me shall not walk
in darkness, but shall have the light of life.
JOHN 8:12

Let us praise Him then, for His life in our spirits, increasing in us the consciousness of being His children, light of His light, life of His life. And let us rejoice in His life in our minds, directing and arranging our thoughts, increasing our mental powers, giving us a better grasp of business and more wisdom in every line of work we undertake. Let us thank Him for His life in our hearts, ordering and controlling our emotions and filling us with His own love. And let us give thanks for His life in our bodies, recreating them after the image of His perfect health and strength.
AGNES SANFORD

DAY 198

Thank God for His Word, for His Good News, for the voice that speaks to you and becomes part of your very being, shoring up your faith in the Father, Son, and Spirit. Pray that God would bless what you read and hear from Him today through His Word. Pray that God would help you, that as you wait upon Him, He would strengthen you so that your faith would mount up with wings like an eagle. That your trust in the Holy Three would stretch its wings and soar so high that nothing of this world would be able to pull it back down to earth.

But they that wait upon the LORD shall renew their strength; they shall mount up with wings as eagles.
ISAIAH 40:31

Father, we pray Thy blessings upon the Word given. We pray that Thou wilt help us, that our faith might mount up like an eagle, stretch its broad wings and soar so high that nothing can pull it down, and as the eagle can look upon the son, we pray that we may look upon Thy Holy Son at the right hand of the Majesty, and that we may be grateful to the point of cheers and tenderness, that He who was God and very God, of very God, gave Himself and hung on yonder tree. Bless us. . . . In Christ's name. Amen.

A. W. TOZER

When troubles assail, when temptation comes knocking, run to God. He is your refuge, your strong tower. Know that God is standing with you. Make Him your very present help when you're shaken, in distress, losing ground. Behind His thick walls you can ignore the feel of earth quaking, the sound of waves churning, the sight of waters rising.

Today, pray God would so deeply engrave His name upon your heart that nothing will be able to move you when you stand in Him. That nothing would remove you from His love. Know that God will not only be your fortress but guide you out of and away from dangers that threaten within and without.

God is our refuge and strength, a very present help in trouble. Therefore will not we fear, though the earth be removed, and though the mountains be carried into the midst of the sea; though the waters thereof roar and be troubled, though the mountains shake with the swelling thereof. . . . The LORD of hosts is with us.
PSALM 46:1–3, 7

Write thy blessed name, O Lord, upon my heart, there to remain so indelibly engraved, that no prosperity, no adversity, shall ever move me from Thy love. Be Thou to me a strong tower of defence, a comforter in tribulation, a deliverer in distress, a very present help in trouble, and a guide to heaven through the many temptations and dangers of this life.
THOMAS À KEMPIS

DAY 200

To a child, few things are scarier than being alone in the dark, uncertain of how to find her way back to Mom or Dad, the person who loves her more than anyone else. Without light, the child feels lost, afraid of taking the next step in the blackness, frightened of going the wrong way.

The same is true of the child of God. At times, you may find yourself trembling in the darkness, afraid of taking the wrong path, uncertain of the next step. That's when you need to remember that Father God is not just your strength and fortress, your defender and rescuer, but your light and guide.

Today, pray that God would stretch His hand into your darkness. That He would shine His light upon your path, guiding you back to Him, His love, and His way.

Blessed be the LORD my strength. . .My goodness, and my fortress; my high tower, and my deliverer; my shield, and he in whom I trust. . . . Send thine hand from above; rid me, and deliver me out of great waters, from the hand of strange children.

PSALM 144:1–2, 7

O God our Father, hear me, who am trembling in this darkness, and stretch forth thy hand unto me; hold forth thy light before me; recall me from my wanderings; and, thou being my guide, may I be restored to myself and to thee.

SAINT AUGUSTINE

DAY 201

You were born not just to be saved by Jesus, who suffered and died for you, but to live your life as He lived His. He's your example, the pattern for you to follow. He was right with God, truthful. When injured with threats and insults, He did not return them but bore them. He fully committed Himself to God—heart, mind, body, spirit, and soul.

Today's prayer begins with thanks to Jesus for all He's done for you. It reminds you of who Jesus is to you—not just your Redeemer but your Friend who loves you unconditionally, your Brother who guides you to a better place. And it ends with asking Jesus for help to know Him better, love Him more, follow Him more closely—and to do so progressively, day by day.

For even hereunto were ye called: because Christ also suffered for us, leaving us an example, that ye should follow his steps: Who did no sin, neither was guile found in his mouth: Who, when he was reviled, reviled not again; when he suffered, he threatened not; but committed himself to him that judgeth righteously.

1 PETER 2:21–23

Thanks be to thee, my Lord Jesus Christ,
for all the benefits thou hast given me,
for all the pains and insults thou hast borne for me.
O most merciful Redeemer, Friend and Brother,
May I know thee more clearly,
Love thee more dearly,
Follow thee more nearly, day by day.

SAINT RICHARD OF CHICHESTER

DAY 202

One of the best ways to endure afflictions is to prepare your heart before they come your way. That means reaching out to God; it means putting away anything that stands between you and Him. Of course, you'll need help from God to do those things. But that's what He's there for, to give you the strength you need, the power to overcome, the passion to seek His face.

If thou prepare thine heart, and stretch out thine hands toward him; If iniquity be in thine hand, put it far away. . .For then shalt thou lift up thy face without spot; yea, thou shalt be stedfast, and shalt not fear: Because thou shalt forget thy misery, and remember it as waters that pass away: And thine age shall be clearer than the noonday. . .And thou shalt be secure.
JOB 11:13–18

O God, Who seest all our weaknesses, and the troubles we labour under, have regard unto the prayers of Thy servant, who stands in need of Thy comfort, Thy direction, and Thy help. Thou alone knowest what is best for us; let me never dispute Thy wisdom or Thy goodness. Lord, so prepare my heart, that no affliction may ever so surprise as to overbear me. Dispose me at all times to a readiness to suffer what Thy Providence shall order or permit. Grant that I may never murmur at Thy appointments, nor be exasperated at the ministers of Thy Providence. Amen.
THOMAS WILSON

DAY 203

God is looking for you (Psalm 14:2). He wants you to seek Him (Acts 17:27–28) with all your being (Psalm 63:1). He'll reward you for doing so (Hebrews 11:6), giving you all the guidance you need when you find Him (1 Kings 22:5).

Ask God to teach you how and where to find Him. Perhaps begin with looking for Him amid His creation, in His Word, in your praises and prayers. Seek Him with your entire being and before all other things (Matthew 6:33)—no matter what's happening in your life (2 Chronicles 30:18–20). Be open to God's teaching on how to seek Him. And be assured you'll find Him (Deuteronomy 4:29).

Let the heart of them rejoice that seek the LORD.
Seek the LORD and his strength, seek his face continually.
1 CHRONICLES 16:10–11

O Lord my God.
Teach my heart this day where and how to find you.

You have made me and re-made me, and you
have bestowed on me all the good things I possess,
and still I do not know you. I have not yet done
that for which I was made.

Teach me to seek you, for I cannot seek
you unless you teach me, or find you
unless you show yourself to me.

Let me seek you in my desire;
let me desire you in my seeking.
Let me find you by loving you;
let me love you when I find you.
SAINT ANSELM

DAY 204

No matter if you're little or big, young or old, God will support you. When you walk in His strength, you've got His true power. So turn to your Maker today. Know He will forever hold you. Your Deliverer will save you for Himself. Rise to God. Lean on Him, count on Him, for all things in this age, at your age, as you age. For when you trust in your Creator, you'll find yourself transported into the loving arms of one who has carried, is carrying, and will continue to carry you—here and beyond.

Hearken unto me. . .which are borne by me from the belly,
which are carried from the womb: And even to your old age
I am he; and even to hoar hairs will I carry you: I have made,
and I will bear; even I will carry, and will deliver you.
ISAIAH 46:3–4

O Lord, our God, under the shadow of Thy wings let us
hope. Thou wilt support us, both when little, and even to
gray hairs. When our strength is of Thee, it is strength; but,
when our own, it is feebleness. We return unto Thee, O Lord,
that from their weariness our souls may rise towards Thee,
leaning on the things which Thou hast created, and passing
on to Thyself, who hast wonderfully made them; for with
Thee is refreshment and true strength. Amen.
SAINT AUGUSTINE

DAY 205

Everything you have and are comes from the hand of God, the one who knows your heart. Surrender all of yourself to the Lord of your life today. Give yourself as a willing and living sacrifice, and He'll give you the mind of Christ and all the joy that comes with it.

Hear thou in heaven thy dwelling place, and forgive, and do, and give to every man according to his ways, whose heart thou knowest; (for thou, even thou only, knowest the hearts of all the children of men).
1 KINGS 8:39

Searcher of all hearts, Thou knowest my heart, and how it stands with me. Thou has made it, Thou knowest whether I love Thee. All I am or have that has any goodness in it, I am or have alone through Thee, for it is all Thy work in me; but it must be Thine also by the free surrender of my heart. In Thy service, and fulfilling Thy will, I would fain spend every minute of my life. The thought of Thee shall be the sweetest to me of all thoughts; to speak of Thee the dearest and best of all I speak or hear; the joy of Thy love shall be the inmost joy of my soul. Gladly would I devote my whole being to Thee; accept me, then, as a living sacrifice, and give me the mind that was in Christ Jesus, to the glory of God the Father. Amen.
MICHAEL SAILER

DAY 206

Sometimes, without even realizing it, our feelings of self-sufficiency may sap our desire for God. That's when it's time to humbly draw near to God, confident in His goodness and mercy. To come as the blind came to the Giver of sight. As the hungry and thirsty came to the God who satiates. As the afflicted came to the Comforter.

Know that in God you will find anything you could possibly desire. Make your being in the presence of Him—your Savior, Source, Provider, Redeemer, Helper, Defender, Protector, Fortress, and Strength—your only desire. And as you draw near to Him, He will draw ever so near to you.

God resisteth the proud, but giveth grace unto the humble.
Submit yourselves therefore to God. . . . Draw nigh to God,
and he will draw nigh to you. . . . Humble yourselves in
the sight of the Lord, and he shall lift you up.
JAMES 4:6–8, 10

In the confidence of your goodness and great mercy, O Lord,
I draw to you, as a sick person to the healer, as one hungry and
thirsty to the fountain of life, a creature to the creator, a desolate
soul to my own tender comforter. Behold, in you is everything
that I can or ought to desire. You are my salvation and my
redemption, my helper and my strength.

THOMAS À KEMPIS

DAY 207

Jesus wants you to abide, live, dwell in Him. To have a personal relationship with Him, one full of obedience to, dependence upon, and trust in Him. For only then will you experience the full workings of His power and realize your full potential *through* Jesus. Only then will you become the full person God created you to be *in* Jesus.

Place yourself before Jesus today. Look up into His face. Ask Him to take you out of yourself and into Him. For then you will find your thankfulness, safety, life, reward, and abundance as He becomes your all in all.

Abide in me, and I in you. As the branch cannot bear fruit of itself, except it abide in the vine; no more can ye, except ye abide in me. I am the vine, ye are the branches: He that abideth in me, and I in him, the same bringeth forth much fruit: for without me ye can do nothing.

JOHN 15:4–5

Sever me from myself that I may be grateful to you;
may I perish to myself that I may be safe in you;
may I die to myself that I may live in you;
may I wither to myself that I may blossom in you;
may I be emptied of myself that I may abound in you;
may I be nothing to myself that I may be all to you.

ERASMUS

Joy in the Lord empowers you spiritually, emotionally, mentally, and physically. Not there yet? No worries. Where there's a will, there's a way.

Your first step is knowing God. Loving Him before all others. Rejoicing in Him because He rejoices in you. The second step is praying for that knowledge of Him, love of Him, and delight in Him, knowing that your attainment of those three and the joy that follows is a progressive thing. You *will* get there. Begin now with today's prayer.

Thou wilt shew me the path of life: in thy presence is fulness of joy; at thy right hand there are pleasures for evermore.
PSALM 16:11

Grant me, even me, my dearest Lord, to know Thee, and love Thee, and rejoice in Thee. And if I cannot do these perfectly in this life, let me at least advance to higher degrees every day, till I can come to do them in perfection. Let the knowledge of Thee increase in me here, that it may be full hereafter. Let the love of Thee grow every day more and more here, that it may be perfect hereafter; that my joy may be great in itself, and full in Thee. I know, O God, that Thou art a God of truth. O make good Thy gracious promises to me, that my joy may be full. Amen.
SAINT AUGUSTINE

DAY 209

There's a story in Luke about a woman who for eighteen years had a sickness that kept her bent over double and she "could in no wise lift up herself" (Luke 13:11). But then Jesus saw her. And said one sentence: "Woman, thou art loosed from thine infirmity" (Luke 13:12). After He laid His hands on her, "immediately she was made straight, and glorified God" (Luke 13:13).

The Greek adverb for Luke 13:11's "in no wise" (meaning the woman *could not completely* straighten herself) is only used again in the New Testament; and it's found in Hebrews 7:25 in a positive sense with the word *uttermost*, meaning "completely, wholly, entirely."

The point is that just as Jesus helped the woman, the one who could in no wise completely straighten herself, Jesus helps you, who cannot completely straighten yourself, to the uttermost.

Pray for Jesus to help you today. Know that He alone can save you, lift you up, straighten you out—completely. Know that with one act, one sentence, one touch you are being saved. Your job? To glorify God—to the uttermost!

But this man [Jesus], because he continueth ever, hath an unchangeable priesthood. Wherefore he is able also to save them to the uttermost that come unto God by him, seeing he ever liveth to make intercession for them.
HEBREWS 7:24–25

Lord, keep us from sinning, and make us living witnesses of Thy mighty power to save to the uttermost.
HANNAH WHITALL SMITH

DAY 210

When caught up in the anxiety the world presents, you may begin to lose your footing. Yet that's when the light and power of Christ within can really shine out to that same world.

When stress threatens to overcome your faith, lean back into God. Pray for the strength, power, and endurance you need to face daily challenges. Commit to knowing God more, to increasing your awareness of the Holy Spirit within, to embracing the calmness of Jesus. As you do so, in prayer, you'll find your faith overcoming anything stress can pit against you.

But in all things approving ourselves as the ministers
of God, in much patience, in afflictions, in necessities,
in distresses. . .by pureness, by knowledge, by long suffering,
by kindness, by the Holy Ghost, by love unfeigned, by the word
of truth, by the power of God, by the armour of righteousness.
2 CORINTHIANS 6:4, 6–7

O gracious Father, keep me through Thy Holy Spirit; keep my heart soft and tender now in health and amidst the bustle of the world; keep the thought of Thyself present to me as my Father in Jesus Christ; and keep alive in me a spirit of love and meekness to all men, that I may be at once gentle and active and firm.
O strengthen me to bear pain, or sickness, or danger, or whatever Thou shalt be pleased to lay upon me, as Christ's soldier and servant; and let my faith overcome the world daily.

THOMAS ARNOLD

DAY 211

You gain so much when you give every bit of yourself to Jesus. When you give Him your hands, He gives you His work to do. When you give Him your feet, He gives you your path. When you give Him your eyes, He shows you what He sees. And the list goes on and on.

Today, give Christ every part of your being. As you do so, He'll give you all He has, all you need to serve Him.

For this cause I bow my knees unto the Father of our Lord Jesus Christ, of whom the whole family in heaven and earth is named, that he would grant you, according to the riches of his glory, to be strengthened with might by his Spirit in the inner man; that Christ may dwell in your hearts by faith.
EPHESIANS 3:14–17

Lord Jesus,
I give you my hands to do your work.
I give you my feet to go your way.
I give you my eyes to see as you do.
I give you my tongue to speak your words.
I give you my mind that you may think in me.
I give you my spirit that you may pray in me.
Above all, I give you my heart that you may
love in me your Father and all mankind.
I give you my whole self that you may grow in me,
so that it is you, Lord Jesus, who live and work and pray in me.
THE GRAIL PRAYER

DAY 212

At some point in your life, you may have heard the expression "Mother knows best." Or, "Father knows best." *You* may have even said to someone, "I know best." But in reality none of these statements are valid. For, in truth, only Father *God* knows best. He is your true guide to the right path. He knows your needs better than you do. Only He sees what lies before you, the total plan for your life, the road He has laid out, the one only you can walk for Him.

Trust that God has the right ideas, the right guidance for you. He has led servants, prophets, disciples, kings, and His Son. Let Him lead you.

In thee, O LORD, do I put my trust; let me never be ashamed:
deliver me in thy righteousness. Bow down thine ear to me;
deliver me speedily: be thou my strong rock, for an house
of defence to save me. For thou art my rock and my fortress;
therefore for thy name's sake lead me, and guide me.
PSALM 31:1–3

Lord God Almighty, I charge thee of thy great mercy and by the token of thy holy rood [cross] that thou guide me to thy will and to my soul's need better than I can myself, that above all things I may inwardly love thee with a clean mind and clean body; for thou art my Maker, my help and my hope.
ALFRED THE GREAT

DAY 213

Tradition says Ireland's Saint Patrick wrote his Breastplate prayer in AD 433. It served him as a means of divine protection.

A breastplate is a metal vestlike plate worn to protect the breast or chest. In the Old Testament, part of the high priest Aaron's wardrobe was a breastplate, which he wore when he went into the Holy Place before the Lord (Exodus 28:29–30). In the New Testament, a breastplate is part of the armor of God we're to wear so we can stand firm before dark spiritual forces.

Part 1 of Saint Patrick's Breastplate prayer appears below. Pray it as you arise, taking up God's strength, might, wisdom, power, protection, and more.

Wherefore take unto you the whole armour of God, that ye may be able to withstand in the evil day, and having done all, to stand. Stand therefore, having your loins girt about with truth, and having on the breastplate of righteousness.
EPHESIANS 6:13–14

I arise today, through God's strength to pilot me,
God's might to uphold me, God's wisdom to guide me,
God's eye to look before me, God's ear to hear me,
God's word to speak for me, God's hand to guard me,
God's shield to protect me, God's host to save me
From snares of devils, From temptation of vices,
From everyone who shall wish me ill, afar and near.
SAINT PATRICK'S BREASTPLATE—PART 1

DAY 214

God your Father is light. In Him there's no darkness (1 John 1:5). Because God is your Father, you're a child of light. As such, you need to be spiritually alert, putting on the breastplate of faith and love. And your best protection is Christ and His presence imbuing you—to the point that when others see and hear you, they see and hear Him.

Part 2 of Saint Patrick's Breastplate prayer appears below. Pray the power, light, and protection of Christ to be with you in all ways today.

Ye are all the children of light, and the children of the day. . . . Let us, who are of the day, be sober, putting on the breastplate of faith and love; and for an helmet, the hope of salvation. For God hath not appointed us to wrath, but to obtain salvation by our Lord Jesus Christ, who died for us, that. . .we should live together with him.

1 THESSALONIANS 5:5, 8–10

Christ with me, Christ before me,
Christ behind me, Christ in me,
Christ beneath me, Christ above me,
Christ on my right, Christ on my left,
Christ when I lie down, Christ when I sit down,
Christ when I arise,
Christ in the heart of every man who thinks of me,
Christ in the mouth of everyone who speaks of me,
Christ in every eye that sees me,
Christ in every ear that hears me.

SAINT PATRICK'S BREASTPLATE—PART 2

DAY 215

When you make it your aim in life to please God rather than other people or yourself, God notices. And so do the people you come into contact with. They begin to smell the sweet fragrance of Christ all around you. It permeates the very air, leaving His light, presence, and essence behind.

After praying today's prayer, make it your quest to be the best *in Christ*. To preach to others not by what you say but by what you do. To influence others by your Christlikeness—your love, kindness, gentleness, forbearance, grace, mercy, and forgiveness. To be so unlike the world that others see a new door opening to them, one from which Christ shines through.

Do all this for the love of Christ.

Now thanks be unto God, which always causeth us to triumph in Christ, and maketh manifest the savour of his knowledge by us in every place. For we are unto God a sweet savour of Christ, in them that are saved, and in them that perish: To the one we are the savour of death unto death; and to the other the savour of life unto life.
2 CORINTHIANS 2:14–16

Help me to spread your fragrance everywhere I go—let me preach you without preaching, not by words but by my example— by the catching force, the sympathetic influence of what I do, the evident fullness of the love my heart bears to you.
JOHN HENRY NEWMAN

DAY 216

Although today's prayer is called "Collect for Club Women," it can be prayed by both sexes.

As you speak these words into God's ears, you'll be reminded of the power of love (translated as "charity" in the verse below) and of the beauty exuded by one exhibiting a Christlike character.

Charity suffereth long, and is kind; charity envieth not; charity vaunteth not itself, is not puffed up, doth not behave itself unseemly, seeketh not her own, is not easily provoked, thinketh no evil; rejoiceth not in iniquity, but rejoiceth in the truth; beareth all things, believeth all things, hopeth all things, endureth all things.

1 Corinthians 13:4–7

"Collect for Club Women"

Keep us, O God, from pettiness;
let us be large in thought, in word, in deed.
Let us be done with fault-finding and leave off self-seeking.
May we put away all pretense and meet each other
face to face, without self-pity and without prejudice.
May we never be hasty in judgment and always be generous.
Let us take time for all things; make us to grow calm, serene, gentle.
Teach us to put into action our better impulses,
straightforward and unafraid.
Grant that we may realize it is the little things that create
differences; that in the big things of life we are at one.
And may we strive to touch and to know the great,
common [human]-heart of us all.
And, O Lord God, let us forget not, to be kind!

Mary Steward

DAY 217

At times, we can make a mess out of our lives. Thank God He can work all things out for His good—and ours. Today, pray for and trust God to take the tangled threads out of your hands, sort them out, and weave them into something beautiful.

But I trusted in thee, O LORD: I said, Thou art my God. My times are in thy hand: deliver me. . . . Oh how great is thy goodness, which thou hast laid up for them that fear thee; which thou hast wrought for them that trust in thee before the sons of men!

PSALM 31:14–15, 19

Some things have not gone well today. We have had our troubles. Our hearts have been hurt. You are the healer—will You heal us? Take the tangled threads out of our clumsy hands, disentangle them and weave them into a web of beauty! Take the dark things of the day's providences, the things that seem wrong, and by the power of Your grace, transmute them into blessing. Help us indeed to keep our hands off the strange, complex affairs of our lives—for we would only spoil the pattern which You are fashioning in us, if we attempted to adjust these complicated affairs. May You take entire charge of the myriad things of our lives that are beyond our managing, and bring good and only good out of them.

J. R. MILLER

DAY 218

Your thoughts can easily lead you astray. But take heart! Since accepting Jesus, you have a new inner being, a new spirit within.

Every day you are to awaken that new inner being. To allow the truth of Jesus to change up your thoughts, renewing your mind. And today's prayer will help you do just that.

You begin by asking God to be all that you love, all that you hope, all that you are striving for. From there, you ask Him to allow His thoughts to flow into your mind, His words to be the ones that come from your lips. For your daily life to be lived in Him. For every breath you take to be for Him.

Speak today's prayer slowly, meditatively. Feel God transforming you, His Spirit infusing you, and Christ's love emanating from you.

If so be that ye have heard him, and have been taught by him, as the truth is in Jesus: That ye put off concerning the former conversation the old man, which is corrupt according to the deceitful lusts; and be renewed in the spirit of your mind; and that ye put on the new man, which after God is created in righteousness and true holiness.

EPHESIANS 4:21–24

O God,
be all my love,
all my hope,
all my striving;
let my thoughts and words flow from You,
my daily life be in You,
and every breath I take be for You.

JOHN CASSIAN

God directed Abraham, telling him to leave home and go to a place he'd never seen before. In faith, Abraham went, not knowing where he was going. By faith, he lived in that land of promise and was rewarded for doing so.

Just as God directed Abraham, God's directing you. Today, ask God to fix your steps and strengthen your determination to abide here as a pilgrim, knowing heaven is your true home.

These all died in faith, not having received the promises, but having seen them afar off, and were persuaded of them, and embraced them, and confessed that they were strangers and pilgrims on the earth. . . . But now they desire a better country, that is, an heavenly: wherefore God is not ashamed to be called their God: for he hath prepared for them a city.
HEBREWS 11:13, 16

Fix thou our steps, O Lord, that we stagger not at the uneven motions of the world, but steadily go on to our glorious home; neither censuring our journey by the weather we meet with, nor turning out of the way for anything that befalls us. The winds are often rough, and our own weight presses us downwards. Reach forth, O Lord, thy hand, thy saving hand, and speedily deliver us. Teach us, O Lord, to use this transitory life as pilgrims returning to their beloved home, that we may take what our journey requires, and not think of settling in a foreign country.
JOHN WESLEY

DAY 220

There are some things within us—grudges, habits, tendencies, bitterness, fears, and negative thoughts—that we hide not only from God but from ourselves. Next thing we know, such hidden sins are bringing an impenetrable darkness into our lives.

Today, pray for God to shine His light into your hidden corners. As you do so, yield your secrets up to Him and allow His truth to transform you.

God is light, and in him is no darkness at all. If we say that we have fellowship with him, and walk in darkness, we lie, and do not the truth: But if we walk in the light, as he is in the light, we have fellowship one with another, and the blood of Jesus Christ his Son cleanseth us from all sin.
1 John 1:5–7

Penetrate those murky corners where we hide memories, and tendencies on which we do not care to look, but which we will not yield freely up to you, that you may purify and transmute them. The persistent buried grudge, the half-acknowledged enmity which is still smouldering; the bitterness of that loss we have not turned into sacrifice, the private comfort we cling to, the secret fear of failure which saps our initiative and is really inverted pride; the pessimism which is an insult to your joy, Lord, we bring all these to you, and we review them with shame and penitence in your steadfast light.

Evelyn Underhill

DAY 221

God's Word is powerful, God-breathed, alive, and active. It penetrates, judging your heart and mind (see Hebrews 4:12). And your Bible is full of prayers you can use to pray back to God! What power you unleash when you do so!

Not sure where to start? Begin with today's Lord's Prayer. It's bursting with power! From there, try the prayer of Jabez (1 Chronicles 4:10). If you're in dire straits, pray the prayer of Jonah (Jonah 2:2–9). For comfort, dip into one of the many prayers of David (Psalm 23). For praising, try Hannah's (1 Samuel 2:1–10). For direction on finding and abiding in that secret place of God, delve deeply into the prayer of an unknown author (Psalm 91).

Your job: pray. God will answer.

The holy scriptures. . .are able to make thee wise unto
salvation through faith which is in Christ Jesus.
All scripture is given by inspiration of God.
2 Timothy 3:15–16

After this manner therefore pray ye: Our Father which art in heaven, Hallowed be thy name. Thy kingdom come, Thy will be done in earth, as it is in heaven. Give us this day our daily bread. And forgive us our debts, as we forgive our debtors. And lead us not into temptation, but deliver us from evil: For thine is the kingdom, and the power, and the glory, for ever. Amen.

Matthew 6:9–13

DAY 222

In *My Utmost for His Highest*, Oswald Chambers wrote, "Keep your life so constant in its contact with God that His surprising power may break out on the right hand and on the left. Always be in a state of expectancy, and see that you leave room for God to come in as He likes."

That's just what King Jehoshaphat did when armies were knocking on the door of his kingdom (2 Chronicles 20). He began by seeking God's face. He went before Him, reminding himself and God of His supreme power. Then Jehoshaphat cried to God for help, admitting that he was weak. He didn't know what to do. Not only were his eyes upon God, but his expectation was in Him. As a result, God moved in a powerful way on his and his people's behalf!

Today, get into constant contact with God. Seek His face. Put your expectations in Him. And watch His power break through on *your* behalf!

For surely there is an end; and thine expectation shall not be cut off.
PROVERBS 23:18

O LORD God of our fathers, art not thou God in heaven?
and rulest not thou over all the kingdoms of the heathen?
and in thine hand is there not power and might, so that
none is able to withstand thee? . . . We have no might
against this great company that cometh against us;
neither know we what to do: but our eyes are upon thee.

2 CHRONICLES 20:6, 12

DAY 223

When your heart is focused on God's faithfulness to you—relying on the fact that He does not change and will constantly and consistently love you—you can abide any storm that comes your way. Because your trust is solid in Him, you'll be able to walk wherever He leads and be loving and kind to others you meet along the way.

Today, ask God for that staying power in Him. And rise with a soul quieted by the knowledge that God will turn all your troubles into something terrific.

God is not a man, that he should lie; neither the son of man, that he should repent: hath he said, and shall he not do it? or hath he spoken, and shall he not make it good?
NUMBERS 23:19

Almighty God, Lord of the storm and of the calm, the vexed sea and the quiet haven, of day and of night, of life and of death— grant unto us so to have our hearts stayed upon Thy faithfulness, Thine unchangingness and love, that, whatsoever betide us, however black the cloud or dark the night, with quiet faith trusting in Thee, we may look upon Thee with untroubled eye, and walking in lowliness towards Thee, and in lovingkindness towards one another, abide all storms and troubles of this mortal life, beseeching Thee that they may turn to the soul's true good. We ask it for Thy mercy's sake, shown in Jesus Christ our Lord. Amen.
GEORGE DAWSON

DAY 224

Nothing can separate you or your loved ones—whether in life or in death—from Christ and His love. Because you trust in the inseparableness of His unending love, you are constantly and consistently united with loved ones in this world and the next. Take comfort from this. Embrace this fact, knowing that as you fellowship with Christ, you also fellowship with those who are here on earth and those who reside in the heavenly realms.

As Christ lives in you and you in Him, take courage that on this day Christ is with you, as He will be tomorrow, in this world and the one that follows.

According to my earnest expectation and my hope, that in nothing I shall be ashamed, but that with all boldness, as always, so now also Christ shall be magnified in my body, whether it be by life, or by death. For to me to live is Christ, and to die is gain.
PHILIPPIANS 1:20–21

O Lord our God, from whom neither life nor death can separate those who trust in thy love, and whose love holds in its embrace thy children in this world and in the next: So unite us to thyself that in fellowship with thee we may always be united to our loved ones whether here or there: give us courage, constancy and hope; through him who died and was buried and rose again for us, Jesus Christ our Lord.
WILLIAM TEMPLE

DAY 225

Temptations come our way when we're weakened by doubts and fears, when we feel as if the forces of evil are more powerful than those of good. Yet Jesus has overcome all evil. Believe He will give you the strength to have victory over things that threaten you.

Today, pray for God to come to your aid, to bless you, to increase your resistance through the power of Christ Jesus.

For we have not an high priest which cannot be touched with the feeling of our infirmities; but was in all points tempted like as we are, yet without sin. Let us therefore come boldly unto the throne of grace, that we may obtain mercy, and find grace to help in time of need.
HEBREWS 4:15–16

Strong Son of God, who was tried and tempted to the uttermost, yet without sin; be near me now with Thy strength and give me the victory over this evil desire that threatens to ruin me. I am weak, O Lord, and full of doubts and fears. There are moments when I am afraid of myself, when the world and the flesh and the devil seem more powerful than the forces of good. But now I look to Thee in whom dwelleth all the fulness of grace and might and redemption. Blessed Saviour! I take Thee afresh to be my Refuge, my Covert, my Defence, my strong Tower from the enemy.
Hear me and bless me now and ever. Amen.
SAMUEL McCOMB

DAY 226

When this day, with all its joys and challenges, is over, God will be watching over you. For He is your keeper.

The Hebrew word for "keeper" is *samar*, which *Strong's Concordance* translates as "to *hedge* about (as with thorns), i.e. *guard*; generally to *protect*, *attend to*, etc."

Tonight, as you lie in bed, imagine the Lord who made heaven and earth guarding you, planting thorns around your bed so nothing will be able to get through to touch you, harm you. He'll be awake all night, watching, protecting, loving, as you drift into a soft and sweet sleep.

My help cometh from the LORD, which made heaven and earth. He will not suffer thy foot to be moved: he that keepeth thee will not slumber. Behold, he that keepeth Israel shall neither slumber nor sleep. The LORD is thy keeper.
PSALM 121:2–5

The day is past and over; All thanks, O Lord, to Thee;
I pray Thee now that sinless The hours of dark may be:
O Jesus, keep me in Thy sight
And guard me through the coming night.

The joys of day are over; I lift my heart to Thee
And ask Thee that offenseless The hours of dark may be.
O Jesus, keep me in Thy sight
And guard me through the coming night.
SAINT ANATOLIUS, TRANSLATED BY J. M. NEALE;
"THE DAY IS PAST AND OVER," HYMN

DAY 227

When your strength fails, when you're experiencing pain and despair, when you're as low as you can go, it becomes even clearer that without God, you're lost. Without Him, you are and can do nothing.

Today, banish whatever darkness and depression is obscuring God's light by praising Him with your whole heart. Know that as you cry out, He's giving you strength. Then rise in His power alone and watch Him work.

In the day when I cried thou answeredst me, and strengthenedst me with strength in my soul. . . . Though the LORD be high, yet hath he respect unto the lowly: but the proud he knoweth afar off. Though I walk in the midst of trouble, thou wilt revive me. . .and thy right hand shall save me. The LORD will perfect that which concerneth me: thy mercy, O LORD, endureth for ever: forsake not the works of thine own hands.
PSALM 138:3, 6–8

My strength fails;
I feel only weakness, irritation, and depression.
I am tempted to complain and to despair.
What has become of the courage I was so proud of
and that gave me so much self-confidence?
In addition to my pain,
I have to bear the shame of my fretful feebleness.
Lord, destroy my pride; leave it no resource.
How happy I shall be if you can teach me by these terrible trials
that I am nothing, that I can do nothing and that you are all!
FRANÇOIS FÉNELON

DAY 228

You may be most familiar with the first four lines of today's prayer, knowing them as the Serenity Prayer. But the lines that follow are even better! For they speak of taking life one day at a time. Of accepting hardships as the path to peace. Of taking the world as it is, not as you would like it to be. Of trusting that, as you surrender to Jesus' will, He'll make all things right. Of knowing that you'll be reasonably happy here but extraordinarily happy in your next life with God.

Enjoy this great and powerful prayer—not just today but every day!

Through the tender mercy of our God. . .the dayspring from on high hath visited us, to give light to them that sit in darkness and in the shadow of death, to guide our feet into the way of peace.
LUKE 1:78–79

God grant me the serenity
To accept the things I cannot change;
Courage to change the things I can;
And wisdom to know the difference.
Living one day at a time;
Enjoying one moment at a time;
Accepting hardships as the pathway to peace;
Taking, as Jesus did, this sinful world as it is,
not as I would have it;
Trusting that he will make all things right if I surrender to his will;
That I may be reasonably happy in this life
And supremely happy with him forever in the next.
REINHOLD NIEBUHR

DAY 229

If you're humble and open enough, you can find wisdom all around you. The place to begin is with the Bible, a treasure trove of wisdom—and not just in Proverbs. From Genesis to Revelation, you'll find stories of people who made mistakes you can learn from; in fact, that's one reason their tales are there (Romans 15:4). But you can also learn from your own mistakes, once the dust has settled of course. And you can learn from the mistakes of others, especially the children, in your life. For out of the mouths of babes. . .

After praying today's prayer, look to read the lessons in your own life.

The proverbs of Solomon the son of David, king of Israel; to know wisdom and instruction; to perceive the words of understanding; to receive the instruction of wisdom, justice, and judgment, and equity; to give subtilty to the simple, to the young man knowledge and discretion. A wise man will hear, and will increase learning; and a man of understanding shall attain unto wise counsels.

PROVERBS 1:1–5

Grant to us, O Father, the wisdom that is necessary in all the conduct of life. And grant that even our mistakes may rise up to guide us and when we behold the mistakes of others, while we seek to rescue them and to sympathize with them, grant that we may read likewise the lessons which they make for us.

HENRY WARD BEECHER

DAY 230

Ah, that God would grant you such grace that you might do what He's calling you to do, take on the work He wants you to perform, and gain the attitude He wants you to have toward Him, yourself, and others. That God would give you the grace to speak what He would have you speak, to walk before Him as He would have you walk. When you have that grace, when He so favors you, you will find a calmness like no other.

Before praying today's prayer, consider the calmness Christ showed in dire situations. How unruffled He remained when confronted with those who wanted His life. Think about the peace He exuded to those troubled, ill, and possessed by demons, those quaking for lack of faith.

Then pray today's prayer, taking on Jesus Christ's persona, making His grace, power, and peace your own. So that you too, no matter what your day brings, remain "calm like waters deep and still" as did He.

Grace and peace be multiplied unto you through the knowledge of God, and of Jesus our Lord, According as his divine power hath given unto us all things that pertain unto life and godliness, through the knowledge of him that hath called us to glory and virtue.
2 PETER 1:2–3

Grant us such grace that we may work Thy will,
And speak Thy words, and walk before Thy face,
Profound and calm like waters deep and still;
Grant us such grace.
CHRISTINA ROSSETTI

DAY 231

It's easy to have courage when your surroundings are familiar and your task routine. But what happens when God calls you to step out of that comfort zone? Do you react in fear or confidently step out of the boat and walk to Him across the water?

Today, pray for God to give you the courage you need to go wherever He leads.

And when the disciples saw him walking on the sea, they were troubled, saying, It is a spirit; and they cried out for fear. But straightway Jesus spake unto them, saying, Be of good cheer; it is I; be not afraid. And Peter answered him and said, Lord, if it be thou, bid me come unto thee on the water. And he said, Come. And when Peter was come down out of the ship, he walked on the water, to go to Jesus.
MATTHEW 14:26–29

May he give us all the courage that we need to go the way he shepherds us, that when he calls we may go unfrightened. If he bids us come to him across the waters, that unfrightened we may go. And if he bids us climb the hill, may we not notice that it is a hill, mindful only of the happiness of his company. He made us for himself, that we should travel with him and see him at his last in his unveiled beauty in the abiding city, where he is light and happiness and endless home.
BEDE JARRETT

DAY 232

When your spirit is quieted by God, your thoughts fixed on His will for you, and your heart steadily trusting Him, there is nothing God cannot do through you. For with such quietness, focus, and determination, you will be able to *see* what God would have you do. And you'll be able to perform that task without being self-conscious or overexcited. Without haste, yet without delay. Without fear of what others may say and without worry about results. You'll simply and easily be working God's will out in His way, with calmness, faith, and love in the doing. And in the end, you'll discover your only true pathway to unsurpassed peace is living and doing God's will.

Praise ye the LORD. Blessed is the man that feareth the LORD, that delighteth greatly in his commandments. His seed shall be mighty upon earth: the generation of the upright shall be blessed. . . . His heart is fixed, trusting in the LORD. His heart is established, he shall not be afraid.

PSALM 112:1–2, 7–8

Dear Lord, quiet my spirit and fix my thoughts on thy will, that I may see what thou wouldst have done, and contemplate its doing without self-consciousness or inner excitement, without haste and without delay, without fear of other people's judgments or anxiety about success, knowing only that it is thy will and therefore must be done quietly, faithfully and lovingly, for in thy will alone is our peace.

GEORGE APPLETON

DAY 233

It's difficult to feel safe in this tumultuous world. But there's an otherworldly place of protection for you in God. When you commit your will and your way to Him, when you put all of yourself—mind, body, spirit, and soul—into His hands, you're safe for all time. For no one will ever be able to pluck you out of His hands. It's His foolproof protection plan!

In thee, O Lord, do I put my trust. . . . For thou art my rock and my fortress; therefore for thy name's sake lead me, and guide me. . . . for thou art my strength. Into thine hand I commit my spirit: thou hast redeemed me, O Lord God of truth. . . . O love the Lord. . .for the Lord preserveth the faithful.
PSALM 31:1, 3–5, 23

O my dear Heavenly Father, God and Father of my Lord Jesus Christ, God of all consolation, I give Thee thanks that Thou hast revealed to me Thy dear Son, Jesus Christ, in Whom I have lived and glorified. I pray Thee, my Lord Jesus Christ, to take my poor soul under Thy protection. O my dear Heavenly Father, though I may be obliged to quit this body and quit this life, I am sure I shall dwell forever with Thee, and no one shall pluck me out of Thy hands. Father, into Thy hands I commit my spirit, for Thou hast redeemed me, O Lord God of Truth. Amen.

MARTIN LUTHER

DAY 234

When you have a real desire to please God instead of people, you'll never get lost. For the God you trust, the one you live to please above all, will give you continual guidance. In fact, He and His light will be with you, navigating you even when you seem to be lost in the shadows.

For do I now persuade men, or God? or do I seek to please men?
for if I yet pleased men, I should not be the servant of Christ.
GALATIANS 1:10

My Lord God, I have no idea where I am going. I do not see the road ahead of me. I cannot know for certain where it will end. Nor do I really know myself, and the fact that I think that I am following your will does not mean that I am actually doing so. But I believe that the desire to please you does in fact please you. And I hope I have that desire in all that I am doing. I hope that I will never do anything apart from that desire. And I know that if I do this you will lead me by the right road, though I may know nothing about it. Therefore will I trust you always, though I may seem to be lost and in the shadow of death. I will not fear, for you are ever with me, and you will never leave me to face my perils alone.

THOMAS MERTON

Whatever you want, Jesus has the supply. Whatever your question, Jesus is the answer. All you need to do is two things: *trust* in His goodness and mercy, then *go* to Him and ask. If you're sick, go to Jesus your Great Physician. If you're thirsty, go to Jesus your Water. If you're hungry, go to Jesus your Bread. If you're needy, go to Jesus, the King of heaven. And it doesn't stop there. Jesus is also your Light, Door, Shepherd, Friend, Way, Truth, Life, and Vine.

Know that Jesus will never fail you. He is all you need no matter what your need! And expect that He will go beyond your simple request, giving you so much more than you ever asked for because He is the God of abundance! He gives till you're overflowing with supply!

Just trust Jesus. He's only a prayer away.

But whosoever drinketh of the water that I shall give him
shall never thirst; but the water that I shall give him shall be
in him a well of water springing up into everlasting life. . . .
I am the living bread which came down from heaven:
if any man eat of this bread, he shall live for ever.
JOHN 4:14; 6:51

Trusting in your goodness
and great mercy, Lord, I come;
sick—I come to my Saviour;
hungry and thirsty—to the well of Life;
needy—to the King of Heaven.
THOMAS À KEMPIS

DAY 236

God is love. And you are His child. As such, the greatest act He wants you to perform is to love Him. With all of your being. From the depths of your heart. With all of your soul. And with all of your mind.

Do that today. Give the God of love all your love. Give Him your soul, living only through Him. Give Him your will, loving only for Him. Because God is your source, life, breath, and cause. When you put God first on your list, when you make loving Him your aim, you'll find the rest you are craving, the peace you are desiring. As He becomes your all in all, you find that's all you need.

Jesus said unto him, Thou shalt love the Lord thy God with all thy heart, and with all thy soul, and with all thy mind. This is the first and great commandment.
MATTHEW 22:37–38

My soul is yours,
and must live only through you.
My will is yours,
and must love only for you.
I must love you as my first cause,
since I am from you.
I must love you as my goal and rest,
since I am for you.
I must love you more than my own being,
since my being comes from you.
I must love you more than myself,
since I am all yours and all in you. Amen.

SAINT FRANCIS DE SALES

DAY 237

Sometimes it can be hard to wait. Remember Sarah? God promised she'd have a son by Abraham. But it had yet to happen. Time was ticking by and she wasn't getting any younger. So Sarah came up with a plan, one that had disastrous results. Eventually, in accordance with God's timing, Sarah did have a son named Isaac. Yet the repercussions of her impatience remained.

Years later, Isaac begat Jacob, who waited seven years to get his wife Rachel. Yet those years "seemed unto him but a few days, for the love he had to her" (Genesis 29:20).

The point is, when you hope for what you don't yet see, God will give you the hope and patience you need to wait for it. And all things will turn out well! But when you give up hope, when you lose your patience, you'll likely take things into your own hands with disastrous results.

Today, ask God to take away your impatience. To fill you with hope. To help you wait for all the good He's already planned for you!

For we are saved by hope: but hope that is seen is not hope:
for what a man seeth, why doth he yet hope for? But if we
hope for that we see not, then do we with patience wait for it.
ROMANS 8:24–25

Take from us, O God, all tediousness of spirit,
all impatience and unquietness. Let us possess
ourselves in patience: through Jesus Christ our Lord.
JEREMY TAYLOR

DAY 238

Too down to rise up? Pray to God for one word. He'll speak. You'll be comforted.

Save me, O God; for the waters are come in unto my soul. . . .
I am come into deep waters, where the floods overflow me. I am
weary of my crying. . . . I am poor and sorrowful: let thy salvation,
O God, set me up on high. I will praise the name of God with a song.
PSALM 69:1–3, 29–30

Gracious and most merciful God! thou seest how my heart is
filled with sorrow—a stone which I cannot throw off, a load
of affliction too heavy to be borne, presses me to the earth—
Therefore, I come to thee, almighty God! I pour out my heart
into thy bosom, for those art my refuge and my salvation. I cast
my troubles from myself upon thee, and beseech thee to save and
to assist me. The little bark, driven by fearful winds and waves, is
held by the anchor; and so my soul clings to thee, thou living and
almighty God. The timid roe [doe] pursued in the chase hastens
to the mountains for deliverance, and I lift my eyes to thee, my
Rock, my Rescuer, and mighty Defender! I will not despair, for I
know that thou art an almighty God—thou canst help me.
O send deliverance now, and I am helped; speak but a
single word, and my help has come.
JOHANN FRIEDRICH STARCK

DAY 239

The disciple Philip is a great example of obedience not just to Jesus and God, but to the Holy Spirit. After Jesus' resurrection and His giving of the Holy Spirit, an angel of God tells Philip to head in a certain direction. He does, then discovers a eunuch there, reading God's Word. When the Spirit tells Philip to join the man, he *runs* to obey. Talk about obedience! Later, when Philip is baptizing the eunuch, "the Spirit of the Lord caught away Philip" (Acts 8:39).

Today, realize the power of obedience and pray for God to give you understanding so that you will *run* to obey the Spirit's promptings. You'll find yourself swept away, growing ever closer to God!

And the angel of the Lord spake unto Philip, saying, Arise, and go toward the south unto the way that goeth down from Jerusalem unto Gaza, which is desert. And he arose and went: and, behold, a man of Ethiopia, an eunuch. . .[who] had come to Jerusalem for to worship, was returning, and sitting in his chariot read Esaias the prophet. Then the Spirit said unto Philip, Go near, and join thyself to this chariot. And Philip ran thither to him.

Acts 8:26–30

Make us of quick understanding and tender conscience, O Lord; that understanding, we may obey every word of thine this day, and discerning, may follow every suggestion of thine indwelling Spirit. Speak, Lord, for thy servant heareth, through Jesus Christ our Lord. Amen.

Christina Rossetti

DAY 240

The world's problems can seem so huge, so complex. It's difficult to get our minds around them, much less our hands. This is when we need to remember we have a God so much bigger than any troubles this world can present!

Today, ask God to help you love Him and others, even your enemies, and to be with you as you come and go, rise up and lie down, until His new day dawns.

The LORD is thy keeper: the LORD is thy shade upon thy right hand. The sun shall not smite thee by day, nor the moon by night. The LORD shall preserve thee from all evil: he shall preserve thy soul. The LORD shall preserve thy going out and thy coming in from this time forth, and even for evermore.
PSALM 121:5–8

God, we thank you for the inspiration of Jesus. Grant that we will love you with all our hearts, souls, and minds, and love our neighbors as we love ourselves, even our enemy neighbors. And we ask you, God, in these days of emotional tension, when the problems of the world are gigantic in extent and chaotic in detail, to be with us in our going out and our coming in, in our rising up and in our lying down, in our moments of joy and in our moments of sorrow, until the day when there shall be no sunset and no dawn. Amen.

MARTIN LUTHER KING JR.

DAY 241

You want to spend time in God's presence. But as you begin seeking such a blessed communion with Him, thoughts begin to creep in about your missteps, faults, and more. Yet you know God is there, ready to lead, to advise, to whisper in your ear.

Today, ask God to renew you as you sense Him. Then sit at His feet, having chosen the better part, with no thought of distraction.

Mary. . .sat at Jesus' feet, and heard his word. . . . And Jesus. . . said. . .One thing is needful: and Mary hath chosen that good part, which shall not be taken away from her.
LUKE 10:39, 41–42

Source of all good! Day by day are Your blessings renewed to us, and again we come with thankful hearts to seek the sense of Your presence. O that we could be reborn like the morning. For even as we seek to commune with You, shadows from our past dim the joy of our aspiration. We remember our thoughtless lives, our impatient tempers, our selfish aims; and yet we know that You have neither made us blind nor left us without the guidance of Your still, small voice speaking in our inmost conscience, and Your open word, appealing to us to choose the better part. Take us now to serve You in newness of spirit, and sweep away every dust of care, every trace of unjustified fear, and every trace of an uncharitable mind.
JAMES MARTINEAU

DAY 242

Think back to all the blessings you've received from God this week. How things turned out better than you had imagined. How your fears turned to naught. How you endured the things you didn't think you had the strength for. How you had food, shelter, and clothing.

Thank God today for His never-ending, unfailing blessings to you and yours.

Be strong and of good courage, and do it: fear not, nor be dismayed:
for the LORD God, even my God, will be with thee;
he will not fail thee, nor forsake thee.
1 CHRONICLES 28:20

Our Father. . . We thank You for all Your mercies. Blessings have come to us in abundant measure. The evils we dreaded when the week began, have not come. The clouds we thought we saw gathering, and which we feared would bring darkness and storm—were either blown away from our sky, or coming, brought only gentle rains which have blessed our fields, leaving them more fertile. The labors we feared would be too great for our strength, have been endured, and we have had strength for them as they came. We thank You, too, for all the blessings of the week, which came to us in so many ways—through Your providences, through our friends, through our work. We have had bread to eat, and clothing to wear. We have had health and life's comforts.
You have not once failed us! Amen.

J. R. MILLER

DAY 243

You may have issues. . .but, with faith, God can make you whole!

There was a woman who had an issue of blood (Matthew 9:20–22; Mark 5:25–34; Luke 8:43–48). For twelve years she had been hemorrhaging. She'd seen numerous doctors, but none of them could cure her. Then she heard Jesus was coming. Although unclean, she crept through a crowd and managed to touch the hem of Jesus' robe. She said to herself, "If I can only touch His robe, I will be made whole." She did—and she was!

The same thing can happen to you. Take your unresolved issues, even if they've been hanging around for years. Tell yourself that contact with Jesus can make you complete. Reach out to Him. Touch Him. His power will go out from Him and complete you. He will make you whole! Will yourself to believe. And you will believe!

And, behold, a woman, which was diseased with an issue of blood twelve years, came behind him, and touched the hem of his garment: For she said within herself, If I may but touch his garment, I shall be whole. But Jesus turned him about, and when he saw her, he said, Daughter, be of good comfort; thy faith hath made thee whole. And the woman was made whole from that hour.
MATTHEW 9:20–22

Lord, I will believe; I do believe.
HANNAH WHITALL SMITH

DAY 244

You're a citizen of God's kingdom, of heaven. You need not fear death for yourself or your loved ones. Instead, you can have peace in the hope of believing God is good. He has new mercies and compassion for you every morning. He is forever faithful—in life and in death. Strengthen your heart with this belief today.

This I recall to my mind, therefore have I hope. It is of the LORD's mercies that we are not consumed, because his compassions fail not. They are new every morning: great is thy faithfulness. The LORD is my portion, saith my soul; therefore will I hope in him.

LAMENTATIONS 3:21–24

Father in heaven, draw our hearts to you, that our hearts may be where our treasures ought to be, that our minds and thoughts may look to your kingdom, whose citizens we are. Thus, when you shall call us hence, our departure may not be a painful separation from this world, but a joyous meeting with you. Perhaps a long road still lies before us. Yet sometimes our strength is taken from us, a faintness overcomes us, like a mist before our eyes, so that we are in darkness of the night; restless desires stir within us, impatient, wild longings, and the heart groans in anxious anticipation of what is to come: O Lord our God, do teach us then, and strengthen in our hearts the conviction that in life as in death we belong to you.

SØREN KIERKEGAARD

DAY 245

Because Jesus died for you, you look "right" in God's eyes—and you're a member of His kingdom! But it doesn't end there. You've also been given the Holy Spirit and all the peace, joy, and hope found in Him!

So on those days when you feel weak, have fears, and are downcast, lift your soul up to God. Ask the Holy Spirit for the strength to face today's work. Ask for the courage to step upon the road God has laid before you. Ask the Spirit for the optimism to bear your load. And ask Him to give you constant inner joy, not just when hearing and seeing the good things in life, but when witnessing the tough things as well.

For the kingdom of God is not meat and drink; but righteousness,
and peace, and joy in the Holy Ghost. . . . Let us therefore follow
after the things which make for peace, and things wherewith one
may edify another. . . . Now the God of hope fill you with all
joy and peace in believing, that ye may abound in hope,
through the power of the Holy Ghost.
ROMANS 14:17, 19; 15:13

These are the gifts I ask
Of Thee, Spirit serene;
Strength for the daily task,
Courage to face the road,
Good cheer to help me bear the traveler's load;
And for the hours that come between,
An inward joy in all things heard and seen.
HENRY VAN DYKE

DAY 246

According to Jewish tradition, a Jew entering a Gentile's house would be ceremonially defiled. That's why the centurion didn't feel worthy of Jesus coming home with him.

At times, you may feel the same way, as if your soul is unworthy of inviting Jesus in. Yet that's exactly where He wants to be!

Today, pray for Jesus to enter your soul—no matter how unworthy you deem it. Boldly go to Him—and He will lovingly come to you.

There came unto him [Jesus] a centurion, beseeching him, and saying,
Lord, my servant lieth at home sick. . . . And Jesus saith unto him,
I will come and heal him. The centurion answered and said,
Lord, I am not worthy that thou shouldest come under my roof:
but speak the word only, and my servant shall be healed.
MATTHEW 8:5–8

I am not worthy, Master and Lord, that You should come beneath the roof of my soul; yet since in Your love towards all, You wish to dwell in me, in boldness I come. Open the gates which You alone have made and enlighten my darkened reasoning. I believe that You will do this; for You did not send away the harlot who came to You with tears. You did not cast out the repenting tax-collector, nor reject the thief who acknowledged Your kingdom. But You counted all of these as members of Your band of friends. You are blessed for evermore.
JOHN CHRYSOSTOM

DAY 247

God created everything that surrounds you. And He loves what He's created, calling it not just good but "very good" (Genesis 1:31). The things that God has made and that you are to care for (Genesis 1:28–30) are an extension of Him who "is love" (1 John 4:8).

Look around you. Take in the wonder of God's plants, animals, sand, sky, and air. Praise His gift of things visible *and* invisible. And love God's creation as you love your Creator.

The earth is full of the goodness of the LORD. By the word of the LORD were the heavens made; and all the host of them by the breath of his mouth. He gathereth the waters of the sea together as an heap: he layeth up the depth in storehouses.

PSALM 33:5–7

Lord, may we love all your creation, all the earth and every grain of sand in it. May we love every leaf, every ray of your light. May we love the animals: you have given them the rudiments of thought and joy untroubled. Let us not trouble it; let us not harass them, let us not deprive them of their happiness, let us not work against your intent. For we acknowledge unto you that all is like an ocean, all is flowing and bending, and that to withhold any measure of love from anything in your universe is to withhold that same measure from you.

FYODOR DOSTOEVSKY, ADAPTED FROM
A PASSAGE IN *THE BROTHERS KARAMAZOV*

DAY 248

No matter where you are—spiritually, physically, mentally, emotionally, or physically—God hears your cry. When you go to Him, He will give you His peace and heal you. He will relieve you of your stress, calm your fears, take you out of yourself and into Him.

Today, pray and listen for God's deep voice, one that assures you Jesus lives and all is well.

---

*Peace, peace to him that is far off, and to him
that is near, saith the LORD; and I will heal him.*
ISAIAH 57:19

Ever Blessed God, whose word is, "Peace, peace to him that is far off and to him that is near," fulfil Thy promise to this Thy servant for whom we pray. Rescue him from the misery of groundless fears and restless anxieties. Take him more and more out of himself, that duty may be no longer a drudgery but a delight. Lead him into the secret of Thy peace which quiets every misgiving and fills the heart with joy and confidence. Save him from the shame and emptiness of a hurried life. Grant him to possess his soul in patience. Amid the storms and stress of life, let him hear a deeper voice assuring him that Thou livest and that all is well. Strengthen him to do his daily work in quietness and confidence, fearing no tomorrow, nor the evil that it brings, for Thou art with him. And this we ask for Jesus Christ's sake. Amen.

SAMUEL MCCOMB

DAY 249

Although *faith* and *hope* are two separate concepts, they're linked. *Faith* is what you believe in at the present time. *Hope* is your confidence in the future, your expectation of something you desire. Hebrews 11:1 says, "Now faith is the substance of things hoped for, the evidence of things not seen." In other words, faith is the certainty you've received what you hope for, even if you don't actually see it in the present.

Yet sometimes we need to shore up our faith, which in turn lifts our hope.

When you need a faith boost, go to Jesus using today's prayer. Ask Him to remind you that all things *are possible* to those who believe.

And one of the multitude answered and said, Master, I have brought unto thee my son, which hath a dumb spirit. . . . And ofttimes it hath cast him into the fire, and into the waters, to destroy him: but if thou canst do any thing, have compassion on us, and help us. Jesus said unto him, If thou canst believe, all things are possible to him that believeth. And straightway the father of the child cried out, and said with tears, Lord, I believe; help thou mine unbelief.

MARK 9:17, 22–24

Lord, perfect for me what is lacking in Thy gifts;
of faith, help Thou mine unbelief; of hope, establish
my trembling hope; of love, kindle its smoking flax.

LANCELOT ANDREWES

Think back on all the blessings you've received from God. Consider those you're enjoying in this moment. Imagine all the good He has in store for you tomorrow.

Although you can never repay God for all He has done for you, you can offer Him your praise for all your blessings today—and every day.

What shall I render unto the Lord for all his benefits toward me?...
I will offer to thee the sacrifice of thanksgiving, and will
call upon the name of the Lord. . . . Praise ye the Lord.
Psalm 116:12, 17, 19

O Lord, my God, for life and reason, nurture, preservation, guidance, education; for Thy gifts of grace and nature, for Thy calling, recalling, manifold recalling me again and again, for Thy forbearance, long-suffering, and long long-suffering toward me, even until now; for all from whom I have received any good or help; for the use of Thy present good things; for Thy promise, and my hope, of good things to come. For all these things and for all other, which I know, which I know not, manifest or secret, remembered or forgotten by me, I praise Thee, I bless Thee, I give Thee thanks; and I will praise, and bless, and give Thee thanks all the days of my life. What shall I render unto the Lord for all His benefits to me? Thou art worthy, O Lord, to receive glory, and honor, and power. Amen.

Lancelot Andrewes

DAY 251

God is your wellspring of life, your Fountain of Joy. He's the source of your ultimate pleasure. That's why you can have deep, abiding joy no matter where your path leads. Use God, the light of your spirit and body, to find your way to Him. Know that at the end of your days, Jesus will be standing at the open gate, ready to usher you in. Oh what joy!

O God! . . .the children of men put their trust under the shadow of thy wings. They shall be abundantly satisfied with the fatness of thy house; and thou shalt make them drink of the river of thy pleasures. For with thee is the fountain of life: in thy light shall we see light.
PSALM 36:7–9

O God, Who has commanded that no man should be idle, give us grace to employ all our talents and faculties in the service appointed for us; that, whatsoever our hand findeth to do, we may do it with all our might. Cheerfully may we go in the road which Thou has marked out, not desiring too earnestly that it should be either more smooth or wise; but daily seeking our way by Thy light, may we trust ourselves and the issue of our journey to Thee, the Fountain of Joy, and sing songs of praise as we go along. Then, O Lord, receive us at the gate of life which Thou has opened for us in Christ Jesus. Amen.
JAMES MARTINEAU

DAY 252

Something extraordinary happens when you commune with Father God. For He's not just your Lord and Master but your Daddy, your Abba. In Him you experience an unfathomable love enveloping you, infusing you. Such love banishes every fear, replacing it with your supernatural Protector's warmth and light.

Today, use the power of the prayer below to experience your Abba as you never have before.

For as many as are led by the Spirit of God, they are the sons of God. . . . Ye have received the Spirit of adoption, whereby we cry, Abba, Father. The Spirit itself beareth witness with our spirit, that we are the children of God: And if children, then heirs; heirs of God, and joint-heirs with Christ.

ROMANS 8:14–17

Eternal God, lead us into the blessedness of the mystery of communion with Thee. Bow our spirits in deepest reverence before Thee, yet uplift us into a sense of kinship. Send the spirit of Thy Son into our hearts, crying "Abba, Father," that all unworthy fear may be banished by the gladness of Thy perfect love. Thy love is like the luminous heaven, receiving only to purify the foulest breath of earth. Thy gentleness is like the sun, seeking to cheer and warm the chilled hearts of men. Touch us, O our Father, with a feeling of Thy great realities, for though our thought about Thee is better than our words, our experience of Thee is better than our thought.

SAMUEL MCCOMB

DAY 253

Truly believing God is your Protector drastically changes your perspective. At least it did for two out of twelve men sent to spy out the Promised Land.

Ten said that the land of Canaan ate up its inhabitants and that the men living there were giants: "And we were in our own sight as grasshoppers, and so we were in their sight" (Numbers 13:33). But Joshua and Caleb said the land was good and, because God was with them, they'd be able to conquer its people.

Today, pray to God your Protector. He'll change your perspective.

And Joshua the son of Nun, and Caleb the son of Jephunneh. . . spake unto. . .Israel, saying, The land, which we passed through to search it, is an exceeding good land. If the LORD delight in us, then he will bring us into this land, and give it us; a land which floweth with milk and honey. Only rebel not ye against the LORD, neither fear ye the people of the land; for they are bread for us: their defence is departed from them, and the LORD is with us: fear them not.
NUMBERS 14:6–9

O Lord, give us grace, I pray Thee, so to realize Thine Almighty succor pledged to us, Thy protecting Presence surrounding us, Thine all-seeing eye fixed upon us, that we may cease to tremble at man's anger, or shrink from man's ridicule, but may with a good courage perform the work Thou givest us to do.
CHRISTINA ROSSETTI

DAY 254

When you truly love someone, you want to do anything that person asks and give him or her all you have. With that person in your life, nothing's too hard to bear.

It's the same when you truly love and are loved by God. When you're filled with His love, light, and life, there's no task you cannot perform for Him, no situation unbearable.

Imagine sitting down with God, basking in His adoration. He gently puts His left hand under your head. His right hand embraces you. He's yours and you're His. Oh such love! There's no greater power than that mutual love between you and your Creator.

Today, pray for that love. Then, "Rise up, my love, my fair one, and come away" (Song of Solomon 2:10), able to do all you're asked.

I sat down under his shadow with great delight, and his fruit was sweet to my taste. . . . His banner over me was love. . . . His left hand is under my head, and his right hand doth embrace me. . . . My beloved is mine, and I am his.
SONG OF SOLOMON 2:3–4, 6, 16

Fill us, we pray, Lord, with your light and life that we may show forth your wondrous glory. Grant that your love may so fill our lives that we may count nothing too small to do for you, nothing too much to give and nothing too hard to bear.
SAINT IGNATIUS OF LOYOLA

DAY 255

It's only when you can fully trust God that you can give yourself, body, spirit, soul, and heart, completely over to Him. When you have such trust to abandon yourself to God and His will, you will find Him giving you all the strength you need to carry it out.

Today, be as Jesus, the one in whose footsteps you are to follow. Kneel down, pray, and allow the Father's will to be done in you. As you do, you will rise again in strength.

And he was withdrawn from them about a stone's cast, and kneeled down, and prayed, saying, Father, if thou be willing, remove this cup from me: nevertheless not my will, but thine, be done. And there appeared an angel unto him from heaven, strengthening him.

LUKE 22:41–43

Father,
I abandon myself into your hands; do with me what you will.
Whatever you may do, I thank you: I am ready for all, I accept all.

Let only your will be done in me, and in all your creatures—
I wish no more than this, O Lord.

Into your hands I commend my soul:
I offer it to you with all the love of my heart,
for I love you, Lord, and so need to give myself,
to surrender myself into your hands without reserve,
and with boundless confidence, for you are my Father.

CHARLES DE FOUCAULD

DAY 256

Forgiveness of others can be difficult, especially if they've grievously wounded you. Yet if you do not fully forgive others, you block God's forgiveness to you (Matthew 6:14–15). Not only that, but by holding on with closed fists to the bitterness and resentment attached to your unforgiveness, you cannot open your hands to blessings God is so wanting to give!

Today, think about any unforgiveness, bitterness, or resentment you may have stored up in your heart. Turn it over to God and ask Him to help you handle what you cannot.

Dearly beloved, avenge not yourselves, but rather give place unto wrath: for it is written, Vengeance is mine; I will repay, saith the Lord. Therefore if thine enemy hunger, feed him; if he thirst, give him drink: for in so doing thou shalt heap coals of fire on his head. Be not overcome of evil, but overcome evil with good.
ROMANS 12:19–21

Lord, You have plainly told me that all vengeance is thine, not my business at all. You have said that I must forgive. I am willing to, but I've tried over and over, and the resentments keep surging back. Now I will this bitterness over to You. Here—I hold it out to You in my open hand. I promise only that I will not again close my fist and reclaim the resentment. Now I ask You to take it and handle these emotions that I cannot handle.

CATHERINE MARSHALL, *BEYOND OUR SELVES*

DAY 257

God grants you so much mercy, grace, and blessings. He's constantly thinking of you, caring for you.

With those thoughts in mind, go to God, asking Him to broaden your heart so you can understand His will for you and walk in the path He's designed for you. All to His glory and praise.

I will run the way of thy commandments, when thou shalt enlarge my heart. . . . Make me to go in the path of thy commandments; for therein do I delight.
PSALM 119:32, 35

O most merciful and gracious God, Thou Fountain of all mercy and blessing, Thou hast opened the hand of Thy mercy to fill me with blessings, and the sweet effects of Thy loving-kindness. Thou feedest us like a shepherd. . .Thou lovest us as a friend, and thinkest on us perpetually, as a careful mother on her helpless babe, and art exceeding merciful to all that fear Thee. . . . As Thou hast spread Thy hand upon me for a covering, so also enlarge my heart with thankfulness. . .and let Thy gracious favors and loving-kindness endure for ever and ever upon Thy servant. . .and let Thy grace so strengthen my purposes that I may sin no more. . .but. . .walk in the paths of Thy commandments; that I, living here to the glory of Thy name, may at last enter into the glory of my Lord, to spend a whole eternity in giving praise to Thy ever glorious name. Amen.
JEREMY TAYLOR

DAY 258

Three times Balaam's donkey saw God's angry angel standing in her master's way. The first time, she silently turned away into a field. The second time, "she thrust herself unto the wall, and crushed Balaam's foot against the wall" (Numbers 22:25). The third time, "she fell down under Balaam" (Numbers 22:27)!

May you have the patience of a donkey, uncomplaining, remaining silent when slandered, unfed, forgotten, and ill used, as you stand before God. As did Jesus.

Then the LORD opened the eyes of Balaam, and he saw the angel of the LORD standing in the way, and his sword drawn in his hand: and he bowed down his head, and fell flat on his face. And the angel of the LORD said unto him, Wherefore hast thou smitten thine ass these three times? behold, I went out to withstand thee, because thy way is perverse before me: And the ass saw me, and turned from me these three times: unless she had turned from me, surely now also I had slain thee, and saved her alive.
NUMBERS 22:31–33

Every time I do not behave like a donkey, it is the worse for me. How does a donkey behave? If it is slandered, it keeps silent; if it is not fed, it keeps silent; if it is forgotten, it keeps silent; it never complains, however much it is beaten or ill-used, because it has a donkey's patience. That is how the servant of God must be. I stand before you, Lord, like a donkey.
SAINT PETER CLAVER

DAY 259

Jesus. Oh what love He showered upon you, laying down His life to save yours! Enduring beatings, mocking, rejection so you could be reunited with and reconciled to God.

Today, allow Jesus to fill you with His infinite love. Imagine it infusing and surrounding you so that you can see all things in life through the light of His compassion for you and extend His undying love to others.

Hereby perceive we the love of God, because he laid down his life for us: and we ought to lay down our lives for the brethren. But whoso hath this world's good, and seeth his brother have need, and shutteth up his bowels of compassion from him, how dwelleth the love of God in him? My little children, let us not love in word, neither in tongue; but in deed and in truth.

1 JOHN 3:16–18

Good Jesus, Fountain of Love,
Fill us with thy love.
Absorb us into thy love;
Compass us with thy love,
That we may see all things in the light of thy love,
Receive all things as the token of thy love,
Speak of all things in words breathing of thy love,
Win through thy love others for thy love,
Be kindled day by day with a new glow of thy love,
Until we be fitted to enter into thine everlasting love,
To adore thy love and love to adore thee, our God and all.
Even so come, O Lord Jesus.

EDWARD B. PUSEY

DAY 260

When you began believing in Jesus, you took on a new life. You were transformed within to speak, think, and act like Jesus. Now you need to act in a way without that matches your new identity within! That means actually speaking words that are God's words, thinking thoughts that are God's thoughts, and doing things that God would have you do!

And there's only one way to do all that. You must have God always with you, giving you the strength, energy, love, thoughts, and words to do as Jesus would do.

Before praying today's prayer, reflect upon the life of Jesus. Take note of His character—giving, loving, forgiving, blessing, healing, watching, waiting, serving. Then ask God to stick with you so that you can find the will and power to put on the wardrobe tailored by Jesus.

Put off all these; anger, wrath, malice, blasphemy, filthy communication out of your mouth. Lie not one to another, seeing that ye have put off the old man with his deeds; and have put on the new man, which is renewed in knowledge after the image of him that created him.
COLOSSIANS 3:8–10

O God, stay with me; let no word cross my lips that is not your word, no thoughts enter my mind that are not your thoughts, no deed ever be done or entertained by me that is not your deed.
MALCOLM MUGGERIDGE

DAY 261

We all have hidden faults or sins, ones we either don't remember or committed unknowingly. Yet just as nothing is hidden from the sun's heat, so is nothing hidden from the illuminating light of God (Psalm 19:6). And we are called to walk in that light (1 John 1:7). To do so, we must admit we've erred in our ways, knowingly and unknowingly.

Today, confess your errors to God, asking His light to illuminate them, knowing Christ will forgive and cleanse you (1 John 1:9), making you right with and pleasing to God again.

Who can understand his errors? cleanse thou me from secret faults. Keep back thy servant also from presumptuous sins; let them not have dominion over me: then shall I be upright, and I shall be innocent from the great transgression. Let the words of my mouth, and the meditation of my heart, be acceptable in thy sight, O LORD, my strength, and my redeemer.
PSALM 19:12–14

Forgive me my sins, O Lord—the sins of my present and the sins of my past, the sins of my soul and the sins of my body, the sins which I have done to please myself and the sins which I have done to please others. Forgive me my casual sins and my deliberate sins and those which I have laboured so to hide that I have hidden them even from myself. Forgive me them, O Lord, forgive them all; for Jesus Christ's sake.
THOMAS WILSON

DAY 262

Sometimes you may feel as if you're walking in the dark. But with God, you have light, because "in him is no darkness at all" (1 John 1:5). Some days you may feel lonely, but you have a God who will never leave or forsake you (Hebrews 13:5). You may be feeling restless, but in Jesus you have peace (John 16:33). You may feel bitterness, but in God you learn the joy of patience (James 5:11). And although you may not understand God's ways, you know He knows *your* way (Proverbs 3:5–7).

Today, reaffirm God as the light, companion, peace, patience, and guide upon your life path. And walk in the power of that knowledge.

O the depth of the riches both of the wisdom and knowledge of God! how unsearchable are his judgments, and his ways past finding out! For who hath known the mind of the Lord? or who hath been his counsellor? Or who hath first given to him, and it shall be recompensed unto him again? For of him, and through him, and to him, are all things: to whom be glory for ever. Amen.

ROMANS 11:33–36

In me there is darkness.
But with Thee there is light.
I am lonely, but Thou leavest me not.
I am restless, but with Thee there is peace.
In me there is bitterness, but with Thee there is patience.
Thy ways are past understanding,
but Thou knowest the way for me.

DIETRICH BONHOEFFER

DAY 263

The first four of the Ten Commandments concern your relationship to God: you shall have no other gods, not make a graven image, not curse using God's name, and keep the Sabbath (Exodus 20:3–11). The last five concern what you shall not do as it affects others: you shall not murder, commit adultery, steal, lie, or covet (Exodus 20:13–17). Between those two categories is the commandment about honoring your parents (Exodus 20:12). And it's the only one with a promise: honor your folks that you may live long and prosper!

Both Jesus and Paul stress the importance of this command (Mark 7:1–13; Ephesians 6:1–3; 1 Timothy 5:4). Tap into the power of today's prayer to help you on your way to obeying this directive from God.

Honour thy father and thy mother, as the Lord *thy God hath commanded thee; that thy days may be prolonged, and that it may go well with thee, in the land which the* Lord *thy God giveth thee.*
Deuteronomy 5:16

O Lord God, whose will it is that, next to yourself, we should hold our parents in highest honour; it is not the least of our duties to beseech your goodness towards them. Preserve, I pray, my parents and home, in the love of your religion and in health of body and mind. Grant, that through me no sorrow may befall them; and finally, as they are kind to me, so may you be to them, O supreme Father of all.

Erasmus

DAY 264

Jesus wants you to come to Him as a little child. To be simple and helpless in His presence, having a trusting dependence upon Him alone. When you approach Him as a child, you admit you have no resources of your own, have done nothing to recommend yourself to Him, have no accomplishments or attainments to offer. For only then, as humble as a little one, can you truly see Christ and enter His kingdom.

Today, ask Christ to give you the humbleness of a child as you come to Him in prayer. Ask Jesus to give you a childlike love of Him, the perfect love that will cast out all fears (1 John 4:18) that may be troubling you. And experience the peace and love He gives you in return.

At the same time came the disciples unto Jesus, saying, Who is the greatest in the kingdom of heaven? And Jesus called a little child unto him, and set him in the midst of them, and said, Verily I say unto you, Except ye be converted, and become as little children, ye shall not enter into the kingdom of heaven. Whosoever therefore shall humble himself as this little child, the same is greatest in the kingdom of heaven. And whoso shall receive one such little child in my name receiveth me.
MATTHEW 18:1–5

Most loving Lord, give me a childlike love
of Thee, which may cast out all fear. Amen.
EDWARD B. PUSEY

DAY 265

God's Word gives you comfort, strength, guidance, and wisdom (see verses below). It also gives you light for your path (Psalm 119:105), joy (Psalm 119:111), refuge and protection (Psalm 119:114), delight (Psalm 119:143)—and so much more!

Be sure to pray today's prayer before launching into God's Word. May its power help transform your mind into that of Christ's.

Strengthen thou me according unto thy word. . . . Give me understanding, and I shall keep thy law. . . . Make me to go in the path of thy commandments; for therein do I delight. . . . This is my comfort in my affliction: for thy word hath quickened me. . . . I thought on my ways, and turned my feet unto thy testimonies. . . . The entrance of thy words giveth light; it giveth understanding unto the simple.

Psalm 119:28, 34–35, 50, 59, 130

As we read Your word, may its lessons be made plain to us. Help us to receive its instruction into our hearts, so that our lives shall be controlled by it. As we pray, may Heaven's blessings be given to us: comfort for our sorrow, strength for our weakness, guidance for our feet, and wisdom for our ignorance. As we seek to be a blessing to others—may we receive the mind that was in Christ Jesus. We ask all in Jesus' precious name. Amen.

J. R. Miller

DAY 266

Sometimes it's good to talk to yourself—especially to your heart through prayer.

In the verses below, the Hebrew word for "heart" is *lēb*, which literally means the heart. Figuratively, says *Strong's Concordance*, it's used "very widely for the feelings, the will and even the intellect; likewise for the *centre* of anything."

To find true rest, today's prayer has you speaking to your heart, encouraging it to turn aside from all things and rest awhile in God. Pray it from your core—and you'll find true rest in God's presence.

One thing have I desired of the Lord, that will I seek after; that I may dwell in the house of the Lord all the days of my life, to behold the beauty of the Lord, and to enquire in his temple. . . . When thou saidst, Seek ye my face; my heart said unto thee, Thy face, Lord, will I seek.

Psalm 27:4, 8

Come now, little one, turn aside for a while from your daily employment, escape for a moment from the tumult of your thoughts. Put aside your weighty cares, let your burdensome distractions wait, free yourself awhile for God and rest awhile in him. Enter the inner chamber of your soul, shut out everything except God and that which can help you in seeking him. And when you have shut the door, seek God. Now, my whole heart, say to God, "I seek your face, Lord, it is your face I seek."

Saint Anselm

DAY 267

God is looking for you to look to Him as you serve Him. That means following "the least indications" of His will, allowing Him to rule your inner being and pervade all your thoughts.

Today, pray God would help you serve Him. Then go and do so, in His power.

If any man serve me, let him follow me; and where I am, there shall also my servant be: if any man serve me, him will my Father honour.
JOHN 12:26

O Lord, we acknowledge Thy dominion over us; our life, our death, our soul and body, all belong to Thee. Oh, grant that we may willingly consecrate them all to Thee, and use them in Thy service. Let us walk before Thee in childlike simplicity, steadfast in prayer; looking ever unto Thee, that whatsoever we do or abstain from we may in all things follow the least indications of Thy will. Become Lord of our hearts and spirits; that the whole inner man may be brought under Thy rule, and that Thy life of love and righteousness may pervade all our thoughts and energies and the very ground of our souls; that we may be wholly filled with it. Come, O Lord and King, enter into our hearts, and live and reign there for ever and ever. O faithful Lord, teach us to trust Thee for life and death, and to take Thee for our All in All. Amen.
GERHARD TERSTEEGEN

DAY 268

Life can be scary. Sometimes you don't know what your next step should be, which direction you should go. At other times, although you began on the right track, you have somehow lost your way. And then there are the distractions, attention grabbers, and time consumers that stall you where you stand.

Thank God you have Jesus. He has already given you the two most important commandments (Matthew 22:37–40) to abide by. And He's lived His life as an example for you to follow. Thus, you need not ever feel as if you've lost your way. You haven't! Jesus has got your pathway covered!

Today, pray that nothing would distract you from following Jesus and the course, the plans, He has laid out for you. Doing so will keep your feet on the right path.

For I have given you an example, that ye should do as I have done to you. Verily, verily, I say unto you, The servant is not greater than his lord; neither he that is sent greater than he that sent him. If ye know these things, happy are ye if ye do them.
JOHN 13:15–17

O Lord, let nothing divert our advance towards you, but in this dangerous labyrinth of the world and the whole course of our pilgrimage here, your heavenly dictates be our map and your holy life be our guide.
JOHN WESLEY

DAY 269

David was in a tough spot. When he and his men came back from warring, they found their homes burned and families taken captive. First, they wept. Then "David encouraged himself in the LORD his God" (1 Samuel 30:6) and "enquired at the LORD" (1 Samuel 30:8).

When you meet with discouragement, it's fine to grieve. But don't linger there, nor react in a way against God's will for you, nor look for comfort elsewhere. Instead, go to God. Use today's prayer to ask Him what your next step should be. Know He will encourage you, bring good out of your disappointment, and prepare you for the next step.

David and the people that were with him lifted up their voice and wept, until they had no more power to weep. . . . And David was greatly distressed. . .but David encouraged himself in the LORD his God. . . . And David enquired at the LORD.
1 SAMUEL 30:4, 6, 8

O God, the Father of Consolation, let me neither desire anything against Thy will, nor in disappointment seek comfort away from Thee; but, knowing Thy will to comprehend what is best, in both my own life and my neighbor's, and in that of all creatures, let me ever resign myself to Thy disposal, who out of evil bringest good, and to whom our prayer should be in perfect peace. Give us what Thou seest fit, only fit us for what Thou givest. Amen.
ROWLAND WILLIAMS

DAY 270

The disciple Peter admired Jesus. In fact, he proclaimed He was "the Christ, the Son of the living God" (Matthew 16:16). And he vowed to lay down his life for Jesus (John 13:37–38). Yet Peter was also the one who didn't have enough faith in Jesus to stay afloat on the water (Matthew 14:28–31). And he denied knowing Jesus three times (John 18:15–17, 25–27), just as Jesus predicted.

Yet Jesus didn't want Peter to just respect and appreciate Him. He wanted him to follow and resemble Him. And in spite of all Peter's shortcomings, Jesus gave him a second chance, and Peter leaped at it (John 21:7, 15–17).

Today's prayer invites you to tap into the power found in willingly following and resembling Jesus. Leap at this chance.

Whither I go, ye cannot come; so now I say to you. A new commandment I give unto you, That ye love one another; as I have loved you, that ye also love one another. By this shall all men know that ye are my disciples, if ye have love one to another. Simon Peter said unto him, Lord, whither goest thou? Jesus answered him, Whither I go, thou canst not follow me now; but thou shalt follow me afterwards.

JOHN 13:33–36

O Lord Jesus Christ. . .save us from the error of wishing to admire Thee instead of being willing to follow Thee and to resemble Thee.

SØREN KIERKEGAARD

DAY 271

People prayed for a bound and imprisoned Peter. As a result, God's angel came, shined a light into the prison, woke Peter, and raised him up. After Peter's chains fell off, the angel led him through the city gates and then departed. When Peter realized what had happened, he made his way to the house where people had been praying for him.

Today, experience the power of praying for others.

Peter therefore was kept in prison: but prayer was made without ceasing of the church unto God for him. . . . When Peter was come to himself, he said, Now I know of a surety, that the LORD hath . . . delivered me. . . . When he had considered the thing, he came to the house of Mary the mother of John, whose surname was Mark; where many were gathered together praying.

ACTS 12:5, 11–12

O Lord of love, who art not far from any of thy children, watch with thy care those who are far away from us; be thou about their path; be thou within their hearts; give them unfailing trust in thee; grant them power against temptation; qualify them for whatever task thou givest them to do; make it their joy to do thy will. Let not distance break the bonds of love which bind them to us and to thee, but unite us closer in thy love; for the sake of Jesus Christ our Lord.

WILLIAM BOYD CARPENTER

DAY 272

Every opportunity to do good and walk right, every success and victory within and without, you owe to God. Thank Him for all that and more, knowing the best thanks you can offer to Him is to live according to, and grow in the knowledge of, His will for you.

I pray, that your love may abound yet more and more in knowledge and in all judgment; that ye may approve things that are excellent; that ye may be sincere and without offence till the day of Christ. Being filled with the fruits of righteousness.
PHILIPPIANS 1:9–11

Father, with thankful and humble hearts we appear before Thee. We would thank Thee for all the benefits that we have received from Thy goodness: It is to Thy blessing we owe what success we have found. Every opportunity for doing good; every impulse in the right way; each victory we have gained over ourselves; every thought of Thy presence, O Father; every silent but loving glance on the example of our Pattern, Thy Son our Lord—all are alike. Thy gifts to us. Give us strength and wisdom to walk faithfully and joyfully in the way of willing obedience to Thy laws, and cheerful trust in Thy love. The best thanksgiving we can offer to Thee is to live according to Thy holy will; grant us every day to offer it more perfectly, and to grow in the knowledge of Thy will and the love thereof for evermore. Amen.

MICHAEL SAILER

DAY 273

Elisha was a man of God. When his servant saw that "an host compassed the city both with horses and chariots" (2 Kings 6:15), he panicked. Elisha told him not to fear. That "they that be with us are more than they that be with them" (v. 16). Then Elisha said, "LORD, I pray thee, open his eyes, that he may see" (v. 17). And the servant saw that "the mountain was full of horses and chariots of fire round about Elisha" (v. 17).

Child of God, use today's prayer to ask the Lord to open your spiritual eyes so that you can see not the visible things coming against you but His unseen chariots that will save you.

The chariots of God are twenty thousand, even thousands of angels: the Lord is among them. . . . Blessed be the Lord, who daily loadeth us with benefits, even the God of our salvation. . . . To him that rideth upon the heavens of heavens, which were of old; lo, he doth send out his voice, and that a mighty voice. Ascribe ye strength unto God: his excellency is over Israel, and his strength is in the clouds. . . . The God of Israel is he that giveth strength and power unto his people. Blessed be God.
PSALM 68:17, 19, 33–35

Lord, open my eyes that I may see, not the visible enemy,
but Thy unseen chariots of deliverance.
HANNAH WHITALL SMITH

DAY 274

Elijah was on his way to being swept up in a whirlwind, taken up by horses and chariots to God. He told his friend and pupil Elisha to wait in Gilgal. Elisha said, "As God and my soul lives, I will not leave you." So they went to Bethel. When they got to Bethel, Elijah again told Elisha to stay behind. He again refused, and they went to Jericho together. And at Jericho Elijah repeated his request and Elisha again refused. Three times Elisha declared he wouldn't leave his friend.

Today, thank God for the joy your worthy friends bring you—and pray that you might be such a worthy, joy-bringing friend to them, at every turn of the road.

And it came to pass, when the LORD would take up Elijah into heaven by a whirlwind, that Elijah went with Elisha from Gilgal. And Elijah said unto Elisha, Tarry here, I pray thee; for the LORD hath sent me to Bethel. And Elisha said unto him, As the LORD liveth, and as thy soul liveth, I will not leave thee. So they went down to Bethel.

2 KINGS 2:1–2

It is my joy in life to find
At every turning of the road,
The strong arm of a comrade kind
To help me onward with my load.
And since I have no gold to give,
And love alone must make amends,
My only prayer is, while I live,—
God make me worthy of my friends!

FRANK DEMPSTER SHERMAN

DAY 275

When you feel as if your life is parched, dry like a desert, that's a signal it's time to change up your thoughts. To get a new perspective. To get a *God* perspective.

Today, ask God to fill you with thoughts of Him so you can make the very desert bloom—and His beauty be upon and surround you.

Remember ye not the former things, neither consider the things of old. Behold, I will do a new thing; now it shall spring forth; shall ye not know it? I will even make a way in the wilderness, and rivers in the desert. . . . This people have I formed for myself; they shall shew forth my praise.

ISAIAH 43:18–19, 21

O Lord of life, and Lord of love! Love us into life, and give us life to love Thee. Grant us life enough to put life into all things, that when we travel through this part of our life, and it seems but dust and barrenness, we may be full of hope in Thee. Touch this barrenness, till all things bloom. Lord, forgive us that our life is so poor, and grant us thoughts of God that we may be enabled for the time to come to make this very desert blossom. Grant that the Spirit of God may so come and so dwell, that the beauty of the Lord may be upon us: through Jesus Christ our Lord. Amen.

GEORGE DAWSON

DAY 276

When God called Jonah, telling him to go to Nineveh with His message, Jonah ran off in another direction. He boarded a ship he thought would take him away from God. So the Lord created a storm that threatened to break up the ship. Jonah, realizing he was the cause of all this tumult, told the sailors to throw him into the sea. Reluctantly, they did. And the sea calmed. Yet Jonah's troubles weren't over, because God sent a great fish to swallow him.

After three days and three nights in the belly of the fish, Jonah finally prayed to God. He began by recognizing God as his supreme ruler, and ended with giving his life to God. Hearing Jonah's prayer, God had the fish vomit Jonah onto dry land.

Although you may not be physically running from God's will for you, you may be doing so emotionally, mentally, or spiritually. Today's prayer will help you come out of yourself so you can give yourself fully to God. No great fish necessary.

---

*Submit yourselves therefore to God. . . . Draw nigh to God,
and he will draw nigh to you. . . . Humble yourselves
in the sight of the Lord, and he shall lift you up.*
JAMES 4:7–8, 10

O Lord, help us to go out of ourselves,
so that we may give ourselves over to Thee, with all
our powers, with all that we are and all that we have.
JAKOB BÖHME

DAY 277

It's one thing for a child to have an adult in his life who provides him with food, clothing, shelter, love, compassion, help, teachings, security, protection, joy, and more so that he can grow up to adulthood. It's a whole nother thing for that child to have God in his life to provide him with supernatural food, clothing, shelter, love, compassion, etc. A God who can save him and bring out the best in him!

Kids surround us, whether they are our children, grandchildren, nieces, nephews, siblings, fosters, or church kids. And they all deserve the opportunity to grow up in God. But how will they know of Him unless you tell them?

Today, thank God there are children in your life. Ask Him for the grace to lovingly train them up in the way He wants them to go so that they will find a firm foundation in Christ.

Train up a child in the way he should go:
and when he is old, he will not depart from it.
PROVERBS 22:6

Almighty God and heavenly Father, we thank you for the children which you have given us; give us also grace to train them in your faith, fear, and love; that as they advance in years they may grow in grace, and may hereafter be found in the number of your children; through Jesus Christ our Lord. Amen.
JOHN COSIN

DAY 278

The Bible is full of paradoxes, statements that seem to be contradictory but are in fact true (see Mark 8:35; John 12:24; Acts 20:35; Romans 6:18; 2 Corinthians 12:10; Philippians 3:7–8; James 4:10).

Today, pray God would help you learn to see the world through His eyes.

He that findeth his life shall lose it: and he
that loseth his life for my sake shall find it.
MATTHEW 10:39

Lord, high and holy, meek and lowly,
Thou hast brought me to the valley of vision,
where I live in the depths but see thee in the heights;
hemmed in by mountains of sin I behold thy glory.
Let me learn by paradox that the way down is the way up,
that to be low is to be high, that the broken heart is the healed
heart, that the contrite spirit is the rejoicing spirit,
that the repenting soul is the victorious soul,
that to have nothing is to possess all,
that to bear the cross is to wear the crown,
that to give is to receive, that the valley is the place of vision.
Lord, in the daytime stars can be seen from deepest wells,
and the deeper the wells the brighter thy stars shine;
Let me find thy light in my darkness,
thy life in my death, thy joy in my sorrow,
thy grace in my sin, thy riches in my poverty, thy glory in my valley.
PURITAN PRAYER

DAY 279

Following certain rules in our own power takes us nowhere in our relationship with Christ, our right standing with God. By doing so, we're cutting ourselves off from God's grace. But if we rely on the Spirit to help us, and in faith wait for a good connection with Him, then we find true faith activated, generated by, and expressed through love.

Today, pray that God would increase your trust in Him so you can rise up in and glorify Him in true faith.

For we through the Spirit wait for the hope of righteousness by faith. For in Jesus Christ neither circumcision availeth any thing, nor uncircumcision; but faith which worketh by love.
GALATIANS 5:5–6

We desire, O Lord, that You will, to all Your other mercies, add that gift by which we shall trust in You—faith that works by love; faith that abides with us; faith that transforms material things, and gives them to us in spiritual meanings; faith that illumines the world by a light that never sets, that shines brighter than the day, and that clears the night quite out of our experience . . . . We beg You to grant us this faith, that shall give us victory over the world and over ourselves; that shall make us valiant in all temptation and bring us off conquerors and more than conquerors through Him that loved us. Amen.
HENRY WARD BEECHER

DAY 280

Today's prayer is wrapped up in love. It acknowledges that "love is of God" (1 John 4:7) and "God *is* love" (1 John 4:8, emphasis added). And the deeper we get into God, the more we realize these truths.

Jesus felt, lived, and personified God's love. He admitted God loved Him before the world was ever created, before the Spirit of God hovered over the waters. He prays that the love of God for Him would be in His followers, and He Himself in them.

What's with all the love that keeps circling back? It's God Himself. For when you have the grace of love and God who is love, all your days will empty into the fullness of His eternal love. It's a love fest!

Father, I will that they also, whom thou hast given me, be with me where I am; that they may behold my glory, which thou hast given me: for thou lovedst me before the foundation of the world. O righteous Father, the world hath not known thee: but I have known thee, and these have known that thou hast sent me. And I have declared unto them thy name, and will declare it: that the love wherewith thou hast loved me may be in them, and I in them.

JOHN 17:24–26

You who are love itself,
give me the grace of love,
give me yourself,
so that all my days may finally empty
into the one day of your eternal life.

KARL RAHNER

DAY 281

Esther was a Jewish orphan who, through providence, ended up being Persia's queen. When her cousin Mordecai refused to bow to Haman, one of the king's officials, Haman had the king sign an edict to destroy the Jews.

When Mordecai heard of the plot, he told Esther she needed to do something about it, saying, "Perhaps this is why you have become queen during such a time." Esther instituted a fast of her people then thwarted the plot, and Haman was destroyed instead of the Jews.

Why are you here for such a time as this? Today, pray, asking that God would give you the faith and determination to work out your part in His plan and make a creative contribution to this world.

Who knoweth whether thou art come
to the kingdom for such a time as this?
ESTHER 4:14

O God, we thank you for the lives of great saints and prophets in the past, who have revealed to us that we can stand up amid the problems and difficulties and trials of life and not give in. We thank you for our foreparents, who've given us something in the midst of the darkness of exploitation and oppression to keep going.

Grant that we will go on with the proper faith and the proper determination of will, so that we will be able to make a creative contribution to this world. In the name and spirit of Jesus we pray.

MARTIN LUTHER KING JR.

DAY 282

Jesus was an untiring worker in the kingdom. Even as a twelve-year-old boy He stayed behind, instead of accompanying His parents home from Jerusalem. After three days of searching for Him, they finally found Him "in the temple, sitting in the midst of the doctors, both hearing them, and asking them questions. And all that heard him were astonished" (Luke 2:46–47). He was about His Father's business.

When you find yourself weary of doing good for God, ask Jesus for the encouragement and grace to continue being about your Father's business. You'll get that and more.

Son, why hast thou thus dealt with us? behold, thy father and I have sought thee sorrowing. And he said unto them, How is it that ye sought me? wist ye not that I must be about my Father's business?
Luke 2:48–49

O Lord Jesus Christ, who when on earth wast ever about thy Father's business: Grant that we may not grow weary in well-doing. Give us grace to do all in thy name. Be thou the beginning and the end of all: the pattern whom we follow, the redeemer in whom we trust, the master whom we serve, the friend to whom we look for sympathy. May we never shrink from our duty from any fear of man. Make us faithful unto death; and bring us at last into thy eternal presence, where with the Father and the Holy Ghost thou livest and reignest for ever.

Edward B. Pusey

DAY 283

At times, we might not feel very generous toward others, or even God. We might be tired of continually serving and giving, wondering how much more energy or resources we can expend. Or we're tired of fighting and only want rest. Or we work and work and work but seem to find no thank-yous or benefits in doing so.

Yet we *can* find the generous heart, energy in serving, strength to fight, and determination to work when we go to God, realizing that simply *knowing* we do the Lord's will *is* our reward. For in doing His will, we find our joy in the Lord!

Whatever you do, do it as if you are working for and serving God alone, not your fellow humans. Seek the reward of joy in the Lord. Look no other place. Today's prayer will help get you there.

And whatsoever ye do, do it heartily, as to the Lord, and not unto men; knowing that of the Lord ye shall receive the reward of the inheritance: for ye serve the Lord Christ.
Colossians 3:23–24

Dearest Lord, teach me to be generous;
Teach me to serve thee as thou deserves;
To give and not to count the cost,
To fight and not to seek for rest,
To labour and not to seek reward,
Save that of knowing that I do thy will.
Saint Ignatius of Loyola

DAY 284

So often we wake up, read the Bible, pray, and then go about our day, trying to live and work in our own power instead of tapping into God's. Doing so can become exhausting, taxing our bodies, minds, and spirits! As a result, we can wind up being laid up (or laid down) because we've been trying to do too much in our own strength.

Today's prayer reminds us that God's power is the strongest when we're at our weakest. That whether we're sick or well, it's wiser to learn to live in God's power, rather than our own.

There was given to me a thorn in the flesh, the messenger of Satan to buffet me, lest I should be exalted above measure. For this thing I besought the Lord thrice, that it might depart from me. And he said unto me, My grace is sufficient for thee: for my strength is made perfect in weakness. Most gladly therefore will I rather glory in my infirmities, that the power of Christ may rest upon me.

2 Corinthians 12:7–9

Lord, teach me the art of patience whilst I am well, and give me the use of it when I am sick. In that day either lighten my burden or strengthen my back. Make me, who so often in my health have discovered my weakness presuming on my own strength, to be strong in my sickness when I solely rely on Thy assistance.

Thomas Fuller

Whatever you're requesting of God, know that what He has in mind for you is better than you can imagine.

Now unto him that is able to do exceeding abundantly above all that we ask or think, according to the power that worketh in us, unto him be glory.
EPHESIANS 3:20–21

Thou hast called us to Thyself, most merciful Father, with love and with promises abundant; and we are witnesses that it is not in vain that we draw near to Thee. We bear witness to Thy faithfulness. Thy promises are Yea and Amen. Thy blessings are exceeding and abundant more than we know or think. We thank Thee for the privilege of prayer, and for Thine answers to prayer; and we rejoice that Thou dost not answer according to our petitions. We are blind, and are constantly seeking things which are not best for us. If Thou didst grant all our desires according to our requests, we should be ruined. In dealing with our little children, we give them, not the things which they ask for, but the things which we judge to be best for them; and Thou, our Father, art by Thy providence overruling our ignorance and our headlong mistakes, and are doing for us, not so much the things that we request of Thee as the things that we should ask; and we are, day by day, saved from peril and from ruin by Thy better knowledge and Thy careful love. Amen.

HENRY WARD BEECHER

DAY 286

You may think you have control of your life, that you are in charge, that you own yourself. But such thinking is false. For, as a believer, you are joined to God. You are one with Him. As such, your body belongs to the Lord, is a part of Christ, and is the temple of the Holy Spirit.

So, you are God's property, having been bought with the precious blood of Christ. Today's prayer invites you into that reality. It asks you to acknowledge to God that He owns you and all that you are—spirit, heart, body, soul, gifts, and personality. And it's up to Him to send you where He will, to do with and use you as He wills. Be willing.

But he that is joined unto the Lord is one spirit. . . . What?
know ye not that your body is the temple of the Holy Ghost
which is in you, which ye have of God, and ye are not your
own? For ye are bought with a price: therefore glorify
God in your body, and in your spirit, which are God's.
1 CORINTHIANS 6:17, 19–20

Heavenly Father, here I am. I am Thy property. Thou hast bought
me with a price. I acknowledge Thine ownership, and surrender
myself and all that I am absolutely to Thee. Send me where
Thou wilt; do with me what Thou wilt; use me as Thou wilt.

R. A. TORREY

DAY 287

It can be hard, if not downright impossible, to find peace in this world. Thank God for Jesus! In Him, you can find true peace. The peace He has left you guarantees calm in the face of trouble, takes away your fear, and reigns over your heart. Such peace has been promised to those who believe! And it can never be taken away!

Today's prayer brings you to the place of Christ's peace. It asks you to invite that promised peace into your heart, mind, spirit, and soul so that God can act in you.

No longer look elsewhere for peace. Look to God alone, and you'll find His calm. That's a promise!

Peace I leave with you, my peace I give unto you:
not as the world giveth, give I unto you. Let not
your heart be troubled, neither let it be afraid.

JOHN 14:27

O Lord, calm the waves of this heart; calm its tempest! Calm thyself, O my soul, so that the divine can act in thee! Calm thyself, O my soul, so that God is able to repose in thee, so that his peace may cover thee! Yes, Father in heaven, often have we found that the world cannot give us peace. O but make us feel that thou art able to give peace; let us know the truth of thy promise: that the whole world may not be able to take away thy peace.

SØREN KIERKEGAARD

DAY 288

Have you ever tried to count the number of times you have done wrong, have grieved someone else, including God? Chances are, keeping track of those stats would be impossible, not to mention somewhat depressing. Yet God has forgiven you for all these sins—*if* you've forgiven everyone else who has sinned against you. Thus, God's forgiveness to you is conditional. You only gain it *after* you've forgiven all others.

Today, ask God to help you forgive. And to do so as He requires: "from your hearts" (Matthew 18:35). To forgive that deeply means to not mention old offenses committed against you and to not dwell on them, turning them over in your mind. It also means to then love those who have wronged you, just as God loves you even with your missteps.

That may sound like a tall order, but with God's help, it *can* be filled.

And when ye stand praying, forgive, if ye have ought against any: that your Father also which is in heaven may forgive you your trespasses. But if ye do not forgive, neither will your Father which is in heaven forgive your trespasses.

MARK 11:25–26

O Lord, because we often sin and have to ask for
pardon, help us to forgive as we would be forgiven;
neither mentioning old offences committed against us,
nor dwelling upon them in thought, but loving our
brother freely as you freely love us; for your name's sake.

CHRISTINA ROSSETTI

DAY 289

Many heroes have gone before you (see Hebrews 11). Consider Moses, born of brave parents who, defying the king's edict that all newborn Jewish males were to be killed, kept him hidden. Later, even though Moses could have lived a privileged life as the pharaoh's adopted grandson, he chose instead to take up the challenge of leading his own people to freedom.

God will give you the courage to take on the adventures He's planned for you. Through Jesus. If you'll only ask.

By faith Moses, when he was born, was hid three months of his parents, because they saw he was a proper child; and they were not afraid of the king's commandment. By faith Moses, when he was come to years, refused to be called the son of Pharaoh's daughter. . . . By faith he forsook Egypt, not fearing the wrath of the king: for he endured, as seeing him who is invisible. . . . By faith they passed through the Red sea as by dry land.
HEBREWS 11:23–24, 27, 29

O thou who art heroic love, keep alive in our hearts that adventurous spirit which makes men scorn the way of safety, so that thy will be done. For so only, O Lord, shall we be worthy of those courageous souls who in every age have ventured all in obedience to thy call, and for whom the trumpets have sounded on the other side; through Jesus Christ our Lord.
JOHN OLDHAM

DAY 290

When God called Moses, telling him to confront Pharaoh and free the Israelites from Egypt, Moses had lots of questions. After all, who was he to lead the Israelites? Why would they believe his message was from God? How would he know what to say? But God told Moses not to worry about any of that. The Lord, the one who had made his mouth, eyes, mind, etc., would be in him, helping him every step of the way.

What God said to Moses pertains to you as well. There is "one God and Father of all, who is above all, and through all, and in you all" (Ephesians 4:6). Today, ask God to be in every part of you on your journey to freedom.

———

And Moses said unto the LORD, O my LORD, I am not eloquent. . .but I am slow of speech, and of a slow tongue. And the LORD said unto him, Who hath made man's mouth? or who maketh the dumb, or deaf, or the seeing, or the blind? have not I the LORD? Now therefore go, and I will be with thy mouth, and teach thee what thou shalt say.

EXODUS 4:10–12

———

God be in [my] head and in my understanding;
God be in my eyes and in my looking;
God be in my mouth and in my speaking;
God be in my heart and in my thinking;
God be at my end and at my departing.

OLD SARUM PRAYER

DAY 291

When you're looking for love, look no further than God—for He *is* love! And He loves you so much more than you could ever imagine. When you take into account that He loved you so much He sacrificed His one and only Son, and that Jesus loved you so much He willingly went along with that plan, you will find yourself overflowing with love. So much so that you will have the love you need to love anyone—and everyone!

Today, pray that God would help you love others—from the depths of your heart.

Beloved, let us love one another: for love is of God; and every one that loveth is born of God, and knoweth God. He that loveth not knoweth not God; for God is love. . . . Beloved, if God so loved us, we ought also to love one another.
1 JOHN 4:7–8, 11

Grant unto us, O Lord God, that we may love one another unfeignedly; for where love is, there art Thou; and he that loveth his brother is born of Thee, and dwelleth in Thee, and Thou in him. And where brethren do glorify Thee with one accord, there dost Thou pour out Thy blessing upon them. Love us, therefore, O Lord, and shed Thy love into our hearts, that we may love Thee, and our brethren in Thee and for Thee, as all children to Thee, through Jesus Christ our Lord. Amen.

ANONYMOUS

DAY 292

As dew was one of the main sources of water for arid Israel, so is the Holy Spirit a key source of refreshment for you.

Today, awaken the sense of the Holy Spirit within you, asking Him to renew you, to restore your energy and vitality. To refill you with the light, joy, strength, direction, power, and protection that comes with His presence.

I will be as the dew unto Israel: he shall grow as the lily, and cast forth his roots as Lebanon. His branches shall spread, and his beauty shall be as the olive tree, and his smell as Lebanon. They that dwell under his shadow shall return; they shall revive as the corn, and grow as the vine.

HOSEA 14:5–7

O Holy Spirit, Love of God, infuse Thy grace, and descend plentifully into my heart; enlighten the dark corners of this neglected dwelling, and scatter there Thy cheerful beams; dwell in that soul that longs to be Thy temple; water that barren soil, over-run with weeds and briars, and lost for want of cultivating, and make it fruitful with Thy dew from heaven. O come, Thou refreshment of them that languish and faint. Come, Thou Star and Guide of them that sail in the tempestuous sea of the world; Thou only Haven of the tossed and shipwrecked. Come, Thou Glory and Crown of the living, and only Safeguard of the dying. Come, Holy Spirit, in much mercy, and make me fit to receive Thee. Amen.

SAINT AUGUSTINE

DAY 293

It's easy to get caught up in praying only for ourselves. Yet we are called to pray for others, to be intercessors "for all men"—and women. But how can we do that if we're not exactly sure how to or what to pray for others?

First, pray today's prayer, asking God to help you remember to pray for others, to make you so bound up in love for them that you feel their needs as much as you do your own.

Second, try coming up with creative ideas on how to pray for someone else. One idea may be to find a psalm that you can personalize and pray for another. Try Psalm 23. Perhaps something like, "Lord, You are Jane's good shepherd. Help her not to feel lack. . ." Ask God for more ideas to make your intercessions incredible!

I exhort therefore, that, first of all, supplications, prayers, intercessions, and giving of thanks, be made for all men. . . . For this is good and acceptable in the sight of God our Saviour.
1 TIMOTHY 2:1, 3

Lord, save us from being self-centered in our prayers and teach us to remember to pray for others. May we be so bound up in love with those for whom we pray, that we may feel their needs as acutely as our own, and intercede for them with sensitivity, with understanding and with imagination.
JOHN CALVIN

DAY 294

True contentment is found not in the things you possess or in what God has given you but in surrendering all to Jesus and freely receiving His love and grace.

Today's prayer asks you to give to the Lord all your freedom, memory, understanding, and will. To restore to Him all He has given you, surrendering it to His will and for His direction. And at the end, to ask for the love of the Lord only. For that love, with His grace, makes you rich enough. After all, what more do you really need?

Again, the kingdom of heaven is like unto treasure hid in a field; the which when a man hath found, he hideth, and for joy thereof goeth and selleth all that he hath, and buyeth that field. Again, the kingdom of heaven is like unto a merchant man, seeking goodly pearls: Who, when he had found one pearl of great price, went and sold all that he had, and bought it.
MATTHEW 13:44–46

Take, Lord, all my liberty. Receive my memory, my understanding, and my whole will. Whatever I have and possess, you have given to me; to you I restore it wholly, and to your will I utterly surrender it for your direction. Give me the love of you only, with your grace, and I am rich enough; nor ask I anything beside.
SAINT IGNATIUS OF LOYOLA

DAY 295

Not many things are better than a really good night's sleep. And it is attainable when you lift yourself to God just before you close your eyes.

Know that you need not be afraid. For God promises you a night of sweet sleep as you rest in the knowledge that He's your guard, your guide, your protector. He's firm, strong, and will keep you from all dangers! Sleeping in His light, you need not be afraid of the dark. Pray today's prayer for that good night's sleep. And your dreams will be sweet!

When thou liest down, thou shalt not be afraid: yea, thou shalt lie down, and thy sleep shall be sweet. . . . For the LORD shall be thy confidence, and shall keep thy foot from being taken.
PROVERBS 3:24, 26

O Lord my God, I thank thee that thou hast brought this day to a close; I thank thee for giving me rest in body and soul. Thy hand has been over me and has guarded and preserved me. Forgive my lack of faith and any wrong that I have done today, and help me to forgive all who have wronged us. Let me sleep in peace under thy protection, and keep me from all the temptations of darkness. Into thy hands I commend my loved ones and all who dwell in this house; I commend to thee my body and soul. O God, thy holy name be praised.
DIETRICH BONHOEFFER

DAY 296

Jesus. The more you learn about Him, the greater you will trust Him. The closer you live by His Word, the nearer you will get to Him. And He will show Himself to you, if you will but knock and keep on knocking. He will answer your questions, if you will but ask and keep on asking. He will be found by you, if you will but seek and keep on seeking.

As you live your life in this constant and consistent asking, seeking, and knocking, you will awaken a love that knows no bounds. You will find your thoughts returning to Him alone.

Today, pray the prayer with the intention of seeking Jesus in all His wonder. And you will find Him and more.

Ask, and it shall be given you; seek, and ye shall find; knock, and it shall be opened unto you: For every one that asketh receiveth; and he that seeketh findeth; and to him that knocketh it shall be opened.

MATTHEW 7:7–8

O beloved Saviour, show yourself to us who knock,
that knowing you, we may love you alone, desire only you,
think always of you alone, meditating day and night on
your words. Awaken in us such a love as may be rightly
and fittingly rendered to you. O God, may your love take
possession of our whole being and make it totally yours.

SAINT COLUMBANUS

DAY 297

God is love. And Jesus taught us the way of that love, through His words and actions.

Even when the mob came to arrest Jesus, He did not strike out to protect Himself. But someone from the crowd surrounding Him did, cutting off the right ear of the high priest's servant. Jesus responded by saying, "Let them take Me." Then He "touched his ear, and healed him" (Luke 22:51).

Pray that God would make you willing to do what He wills, come what may. And to walk the way of peace in Jesus' love, just as He taught you through His words and deeds.

Ye have heard that it hath been said, An eye for an eye, and a tooth for a tooth: But I say unto you, That ye resist not evil: but whosoever shall smite thee on thy right cheek, turn to him the other also. . . . Love your enemies, bless them that curse you, do good to them that hate you, and pray for them which despitefully use you, and persecute you; that ye may be the children of your Father which is in heaven.

MATTHEW 5:38–39, 44–45

O God, make us willing to do your will, come what may. Increase the number of persons of good will and moral sensitivity. Give us renewed confidence in nonviolence and the way of love as taught by Christ. Amen.

MARTIN LUTHER KING JR.

After David cut off part of the robe of Saul (who was God's anointed) and later took a census, "David's heart smote him" (1 Samuel 24:5; 2 Samuel 24:10). Weighed down with a guilty conscience, David was "not able to look up" (Psalm 40:12). Yet he knew if he confessed to God, he'd be forgiven.

Because God has put His laws into our hearts and written them in our minds (Hebrews 10:16), we know when we've done wrong. And there's nothing like a guilty conscience to drag us down into a depression. But God has provided a remedy to lift us out.

To clear up matters between you and God, confess any wrongdoings to Him, taking refuge in His forgiveness. Afterward, as you look up, you'll be lifted up.

Let us draw near with a true heart in full assurance of faith, having our hearts sprinkled from an evil conscience, and our bodies washed with pure water.
HEBREWS 10:22

O God, animate us to cheerfulness. May we have a joyful sense of our blessings, learn to look on the bright circumstances of our lot, and maintain a perpetual contentedness under thy allotments. Fortify our minds against disappointment and calamity. Preserve us from despondency, from yielding to dejection. Teach us that no evil is intolerable but a guilty conscience, and that nothing can hurt us, if, with true loyalty of affection, we keep thy commandments and take refuge in thee; through Jesus Christ our Lord. Amen.
WILLIAM ELLERY CHANNING

DAY 299

Jesus says if you love Him, you'll obey His words. And as you obey, both Jesus and God will make Their home with you.

Are you obeying Jesus' words? Are you loving God with all your being and others as yourself? Are you forgiving others' debts as God forgives yours? Are you listening to the Spirit's promptings, God's directions, and Jesus' calls?

When you love and trust the Holy Three with all you are, you'll find obedience easier. To grow that love and trust, dig into the Word and allow it to permeate your whole being.

Today, pray to give God the love and obedience owed Him, just as a child owes love and obedience to a father, and as a servant to a lord. Be assured that when you're walking in obedience to God and following Jesus' Word, the Spirit will lead you to level ground (Psalm 143:10).

Jesus answered and said unto him, If a man love me,
he will keep my words: and my Father will love him,
and we will come unto him, and make our abode with him.
JOHN 14:23

Most gracious God and Father. . .inasmuch as it hath pleased Thee to remember us with Thy servants and children, grant that we may render unto Thee the love and obedience which we owe Thee, as children to their father and servants to their lord. We ask all for the sake of Jesus Christ our only Saviour. Amen.
JOHN CALVIN

DAY 300

When trouble arrives, your first reaction may not be to smile. Yet Jesus wants you to make a conscious effort to face all trials with joy! And you *can have* that joy when you trust He's with you, knowing you'll be sustained by His presence.

Use today's prayer to let the comforts you find in Jesus' presence give you peace and patience no matter what comes your way.

Count it all joy when ye fall into divers temptations; knowing this, that the trying of your faith worketh patience. But let patience have her perfect work, that ye may be perfect and entire, wanting nothing.
JAMES 1:2–4

Holy Father. . .we rejoice that we can turn to Thee in the midst of great anxiety, and commit all our troubles to Thy sure help. As Thou art with us in the sunlight, oh, be Thou with us in the cloud. In the path by which Thou guidest us, though it be through desert and stormy sea, suffer not our faith to fail, but sustain us by Thy near presence, and let the comforts which are in Jesus Christ fill our hearts with peace. And, O God, grant that the fiery trial which trieth us may not be in vain, but may lead us to a cheerful courage, and a holy patience; and let patience have her perfect work, that we may be perfect and entire, wanting nothing, wholly consecrate to Thee, through Jesus Christ our Lord. Amen.
HENRY W. FOOTE

DAY 301

The words *meek* and *weak* may rhyme, but that's the only thing they have in common. For meekness is not weakness. *Meek*, as Jesus used it, is strength and power under control. And that's just what He exhibited when He was arrested, beaten, questioned, and crucified. As the Son of God, He could have fought back, annihilated all who came against Him. But that was neither His message nor His mission. So He stayed meek, an example of extreme power under control, for you.

Jesus wants you, His follower, to display that same meekness. When you do, you will be blessed, inheriting the earth (Matthew 5:5). So ask Jesus today to pour out not just His spirit of meekness but His spirit of love upon you. To wipe out the ego in you, replacing it with His gentle nature. To guide your hand as it rests upon the Rock of ages, trusting in "the Lord Jehovah [who] is everlasting strength" (Isaiah 26:4).

Put on therefore, as the elect of God, holy and beloved, bowels of mercies, kindness, humbleness of mind, meekness, longsuffering; forbearing one another, and forgiving one another. . . .
And above all these things put on charity.
Colossians 3:12–14

O Savior, pour upon me thy spirit of meekness and love, annihilate the selfhood in me, be thou all my life. Guide thou my hand which trembles exceedingly upon the rock of ages.
William Blake

DAY 302

Although you may get so caught up in your duties, so enmeshed in the busyness of your day that you forget about God, be assured He won't forget about you.

God isn't a parent who has so many kids He needs to do a head count. He's always aware of you, what you're doing, thinking, and saying. He knows where you are and when. He knows your every movement, understands your every thought, is familiar with all your habits, good and bad.

Today's prayer helps you rest easy in the assurance that God will not forget about you even though you may forget about Him.

O LORD, thou hast searched me, and known me. Thou knowest my downsitting and mine uprising, thou understandest my thought afar off. Thou compassest my path and my lying down, and art acquainted with all my ways. For there is not a word in my tongue, but, lo, O LORD, thou knowest it altogether. Thou hast beset me behind and before, and laid thine hand upon me. . . . Thine eyes did see my substance, yet being unperfect; and in thy book all my members were written, which in continuance were fashioned, when as yet there was none of them. How precious also are thy thoughts unto me, O God! how great is the sum of them!

PSALM 139:1–5, 16–17

O Lord, Thou knowest how busy
I must be this day.
If I forget Thee,
do not forget me.

JACOB ASTLEY

DAY 303

When you get right down to the heart of the matter, "God is love" (1 John 4:8). He loved you before you loved Him (1 John 4:19). He chose you, picked you out in Christ, before He made the world (Ephesians 1:4). And, as His child, a child of Love, He wants you to walk in love, as Christ loved you and gave Himself up for you (Ephesians 5:1–2). What love for you to build your faith on!

Today, get down on your knees. Pray God would strengthen you with His Spirit so that the Son of Love would live in your heart by faith, and that you, finding security in that love, would be able to grasp and experience the enormity of that magnificent love and so understand the love of Christ and be filled with the presence of God.

I bow my knees unto the Father of our Lord Jesus. . .that he would grant you, according to the riches of his glory, to be strengthened with might by his Spirit in the inner man; that Christ may dwell in your hearts by faith; that ye, being rooted and grounded in love, may be able to comprehend with all saints what is the breadth, and length, and depth, and height; And to know the love of Christ, which passeth knowledge, that ye might be filled with all the fulness of God.
EPHESIANS 3:14, 16–19

God, thou art Love. I build my faith on that!
ROBERT BROWNING

DAY 304

Take yourself and all that's weighing you down to Jesus. In Him alone will you find true rest, release, relief, and refreshment for your soul.

Come unto me, all ye that labour and are heavy laden, and I will give you rest. Take my yoke upon you, and learn of me; for I am meek and lowly in heart: and ye shall find rest unto your souls. For my yoke is easy, and my burden is light.
MATTHEW 11:28–31

O Lord, Thy hands have formed us, and Thou hast sent us into this world, that we may walk in the way that leads to heaven and Thyself, and may find a lasting rest in Thee, Who art the Source and Centre of our souls. Look in pity on us poor pilgrims in the narrow way; let us not go astray, but reach at last our true home where our Father dwells. Guide and govern us from day to day, and bestow on us food and strength for body and soul, that we may journey on in peace. Forgive us for having hitherto so often wavered or looked back, and let us hence-forward march straight on in the way of Thy laws, and may our last step be a safe and peaceful passage to the arms of Thy love, and the blessed fellowship of the saints in light. Hear us, O Lord, and glorify Thy name in us, that we may glorify Thee for ever and ever. Amen.
GERHARD TERSTEEGEN

DAY 305

The word *charity* in the verses below means "love." It's love that endures, is kind, doesn't envy, is not self-seeking, etc. Today, pray to become that love to others so you can be a blessing of love to them. When you do so, you become like Christ. You become love on earth. Today, love.

Charity suffereth long, and is kind; charity envieth not; charity vaunteth not itself, is not puffed up, doth not behave itself unseemly, seeketh not her own. . .beareth all things, believeth all things, hopeth all things, endureth all things.
1 Corinthians 13:4–5, 7

O Thou, Whose name is Love, Who never turnest away from the cry of Thy needy children, give ear to my prayer this morning. Make this a day of blessings to me, and make me a blessing to others. Keep all evil away from me. Preserve me from outward transgression and from secret sin. Help me to control my temper. May I check the first risings of anger or sullenness. If I meet with unkindness or ill-treatment, give me that charity which suffereth long and beareth all things. Make me kind and gentle towards all, loving even those who love me not. Let me live this day as if it were to be my last. O my God, show me the path that Thou wouldest have me to follow. May I take no step that is not ordered by Thee, and go nowhere except Thou, Lord, go with me. Amen.
Ashton Oxenden

DAY 306

As you cheerfully give of your material resources to others, God pays you back and then some! In Malachi 3:10, God asks you to prove Him in this. See if He "will not open you the windows of heaven, and pour you out a blessing, that there shall not be room enough to receive it"! God's blessing of you prompts you to do more and more to bless others.

Today's prayer leads you into asking God for more grace and more gratitude for what you have and for what you willingly and joyfully give to others as God has willingly and joyfully given to you. Bless and be blessed.

And God is able to make all grace abound toward you; that ye, always having all sufficiency in all things, may abound to every good work: (As it is written, He hath dispersed abroad; he hath given to the poor: his righteousness remaineth for ever. Now he that ministereth seed to the sower both minister bread for your food, and multiply your seed sown, and increase the fruits of your righteousness;) being enriched in every thing to all bountifulness, which causeth through us thanksgiving to God. For the administration of this service not only supplieth the want of the saints, but is abundant also by many thanksgivings unto God.
2 CORINTHIANS 9:8–12

Lord, give me more grace and more gratitude,
now that You multiply Your favors.
CHARLES SPURGEON

DAY 307

God's love has created you, moved you, lit upon you. Seek His face with today's prayer. Know and reach out to Him so that you may feel Him rising up within you, shedding His light, life, healing, and peace into your being—for His glory and grace.

For God, who commanded the light to shine out of darkness, hath shined in our hearts, to give the light of the knowledge of the glory of God in the face of Jesus Christ.
2 CORINTHIANS 4:6

O God, Thou hast found us, and not we Thee. At times we but dimly discern Thee; the dismal mists of earth obscure Thy glory. Yet in other and more blessed moments, Thou dost rise upon our souls, and we know Thee as the Light of all our seeing, the Life of all that is not dead within us, the Bringer of health and cure, the Revealer of peace and truth. We will not doubt our better moments, for in them Thou dost speak to us. We rejoice that Thou hast created us in Thine image. Thy love has stirred us into being, has endowed us with spiritual substance. In the intellect, whose thoughts wander through eternity; in the conscience that bears witness to Thy eternal righteousness; in the affects that make life sweet, and reach forth to Thee, O Lover of Mankind—in these, we are made heirs to the riches of Thy grace.
SAMUEL MCCOMB

DAY 308

In the scripture verses below, Paul talks about how God delivered him figuratively "out of the mouth of the lion." Hopefully you were never literally in the mouth of a lion. Yet during times of trial, you may have *felt* as if you were.

The good news is that no matter what you're going through, God will stand with you and give you all the strength and comfort you need to see things through to the end. Use today's prayer to embed that knowledge deep within so you'll be able to stand up (with God) through anything and everything.

Notwithstanding the Lord stood with me, and strengthened me; that by me the preaching might be fully known, and that all the Gentiles might hear: and I was delivered out of the mouth of the lion. And the Lord shall deliver me from every evil work, and will preserve me unto his heavenly kingdom: to whom be glory for ever and ever. Amen.
2 TIMOTHY 4:17–18

Lord, do not permit my trials to be above my strength; and do thou vouchsafe to be my strength and comfort in the time of trial. Give me grace to take in good part whatever shall befall me; and let my heart acknowledge it to be the Lord's doing, and to come from thy providence, and not by chance. . . . May I receive everything from thy hand with patience and joy.
THOMAS WILSON

DAY 309

It's great to have friends in your life, people who share your interests and whom you get along with. But what's even more special is being with people who are not just friends but brothers and sisters in Christ. For with them you have a *spiritual* connection. You're actually siblings, related through your Brother Jesus and Father God!

Today, pray for your friends who may not be part of your spiritual family tree. Ask that the Holy Spirit sow Jesus in their hearts.

But he answered and said unto him that told him, Who is my mother? and who are my brethren? And he stretched forth his hand toward his disciples, and said, Behold my mother and my brethren! For whosoever shall do the will of my Father which is in heaven, the same is my brother, and sister, and mother.

MATTHEW 12:48–50

I shook hands with my friend, Lord,
And suddenly when I saw his sad and anxious face,
I feared that you were not in his heart.
I am troubled as I am before a closed tabernacle
when there is no light to show that you are there.
If you were not there, Lord, my friend and I would be separated.
For his hand in mine would be only flesh in flesh
And his love for me that of man for man.
I want your life for him as well as for me.
For it is only in you that he can be my brother.

MICHEL QUOIST

DAY 310

When you're feeling restless, consider working some applause for God into your day. For you won't find true peace and rest until you do so.

Know that God has called you by name. He created you for Himself, for His glory. He chose you before the foundation of the world, to be a part of Him and His family. He delights in you and is even more delighted when you delight in Him.

So use part of today to lift your voice in praise to the one who raised you up into His heavenly arms. Remember all He has done, is doing, and will continue to do for you. Wake up and thank Him with all your heart, mind, and soul.

Even every one that is called by my name: for I have created him for my glory, I have formed him; yea, I have made him. . . . Ye are my witnesses, saith the LORD, and my servant whom I have chosen: that ye may know and believe me, and understand that I am he: before me there was no God formed, neither shall there be after me. I, even I, am the LORD; and beside me there is no saviour. . . . This people have I formed for myself; they shall shew forth my praise.
ISAIAH 43:7, 10–11, 21

You awaken us to delight in your praises; for you made us for yourself, and our heart is restless until it reposes in you.
SAINT AUGUSTINE

DAY 311

Today, confess your shortcomings to God and receive the power to live the life you were designed to live.

This is my commandment, That ye love one another, as I have loved you. Greater love hath no man than this, that a man lay down his life for his friends. Ye are my friends, if ye do whatsoever I command you.
JOHN 15:12–14

Thou Eternal God, out of whose absolute power and infinite intelligence the whole universe has come into being, we humbly confess that we have not loved thee with our hearts, souls and minds, and we have not loved our neighbors as Christ loved us. We have all too often lived by our own selfish impulses rather than by the life of sacrificial love as revealed by Christ. We often give in order to receive. We love our friends and hate our enemies. We go the first mile but dare not travel the second. We forgive but dare not forget. And so as we look within ourselves, we are confronted with the appalling fact that the history of our lives is the history of an eternal revolt against you. But thou, O God, have mercy upon us. Forgive us for what we could have been but failed to be. Give us the intelligence to know your will. Give us the courage to do your will. Give us the devotion to love your will.
In the name and spirit of Jesus, we pray. Amen.
MARTIN LUTHER KING JR.

DAY 312

God knows we are but frail creatures, that we need Him and His strength to stand firm. That to turn *from* Him is to fall but to turn *to* Him is to rise up.

It's okay to go to God with a laundry list of what you need to stand strong. So today, go to God in prayer with that intention: to be renewed in every way. Ask for His help to carry out His will for upcoming duties. Ask for His guidance to clear up any confusion you may have. Ask for His protection from any dangers you may be facing. Ask Him for His peace to help you overcome any sorrows that have come to your door.

Ask for these things, knowing that as you ask, He's already answering, granting you all you need—and more.

Therefore, my brethren dearly beloved and longed for, my joy and crown, so stand fast in the Lord, my dearly beloved. . . . My God shall supply all your need according to his riches in glory by Christ Jesus.
PHILIPPIANS 4:1, 19

O Lord, to be turned from you is to fall, to be turned
to you is to rise, and to stand in you is to abide for ever;
grant us in all our duties your help, in all our perplexities
your guidance, in all our dangers your protection, and in
all our sorrows your peace; through Jesus Christ our Lord.
SAINT AUGUSTINE

DAY 313

Someone once said, "Worry is a thin stream of fear that trickles through the mind, which, if encouraged, will cut a channel so wide that all other thoughts will be drained out." Today's prayer aims to discourage the fear that leads to worry and to encourage your awe of God. When your eyes are on God and your trusting heart is quiet, God and His angels rush in to defend and deliver you! So pray away your worries and rest in God. He's got this.

I sought the LORD, and he heard me, and delivered me from all my fears. . . . This poor man cried, and the LORD heard him, and saved him out of all his troubles. The angel of the LORD encampeth round about them that fear him, and delivereth them.
PSALM 34:4, 6–7

Grant unto us, Almighty God, of Thy good Spirit, that quiet heart, and that patient lowliness to which Thy comforting Spirit comes; that we, being humble toward Thee, and loving toward one another, may have our hearts prepared for that peace of Thine which passeth understanding; which, if we have, the storms of life can hurt us but little, and the cares of life vex us not at all; in the presence of which death shall lose its sting, and the grave its terror; and we, in calm joy, walk all the days of our appointed time, until our great change shall come. Amen.
GEORGE DAWSON

DAY 314

Some occasions call for short and sweet SOS prayers to God. You need His direction so badly that you just start crying out for help. That's the prayer you have today, an SOS that asks God to teach you what to ask for, how to ask for it, and what to think and do next.

As you pray this prayer, do so with the knowledge that God is your most important guide in this life and the next. That if you ask, He will lead you. And when you follow, you'll have peace like a river and all the living water you need in those desert places.

Pray. God's help is already on its way.

Thus saith the LORD, thy Redeemer, the Holy One of Israel; I am the LORD thy God which teacheth thee to profit, which leadeth thee by the way that thou shouldest go. O that thou hadst hearkened to my commandments! then had thy peace been as a river, and thy righteousness as the waves of the sea. . . . And they thirsted not when he led them through the deserts: he caused the waters to flow out of the rock for them: he clave the rock also, and the waters gushed out.
ISAIAH 48:17–18, 21

Lord, help me! Lord, help me! Teach me what to ask for! Teach me how to ask for it! Teach me what to think of next! Teach me what to do next.
CHARLES SPURGEON

DAY 315

When you hand your work over to God for His results, doing your labors in His name, it no longer seems arduous. You become refreshed and forget worrying about outcomes. You suddenly have new strength, new goals, new joy. For you know you're working for God alone. Not your boss. Not yourself. Not your family. But God.

Today's prayer gives you the opportunity to change up your work attitude. To gain the courage to face whatever your tasks are today—and to complete them with joy in your heart and on your face. At the end of the day, you can go to bed tired but content, knowing you have done a good day's job for the Lord and expecting a peaceful night's sleep in Jesus' arms.

But thanks be to God, which giveth us the victory through our Lord Jesus Christ. Therefore, my beloved brethren, be ye stedfast, unmoveable, always abounding in the work of the Lord, forasmuch as ye know that your labour is not in vain in the Lord.

1 CORINTHIANS 15:57–58

The day returns and brings us the petty round of irritating concerns and duties. Help us to play the man, help us to perform them with laughter and kind faces, let cheerfulness abound with industry. Give us to go blithely on our business all this day, bring us to our resting beds weary and content and undishonoured, and grant us in the end the gift of sleep. Amen.

ROBERT LOUIS STEVENSON

DAY 316

We all experience stress in our lives. But God can lift us out of it. He reminds us that in Him we live, move, and have our being. He opens our eyes so that we see His presence all around us. He uses His love to draw our hearts to Him. He soothes us with His Word, telling us to be anxious for nothing, to put the work He's given us to do into His hands and leave it there. He removes our doubts, erases our mistrust.

Today, lift your thoughts to God and allow Him to relieve the burden of stress through prayer.

They should seek the Lord, if haply they might feel after him,
and find him, though he be not far from every one of us:
For in him we live, and move, and have our being.
ACTS 17:27–28

O Lord God, in whom we live, and move, and have our being, open our eyes that we may behold Thy Fatherly presence ever about us. Draw our hearts to Thee with the power of Thy love. Teach us to be anxious for nothing, and when we have done what Thou hast given us to do, help us, O God, our Saviour, to leave the issue to Thy wisdom. Take for us all doubt and mistrust. Lift our thoughts up to Thee in heaven, and make us to know that all things are possible to us through Thy Son our Redeemer. Amen.
BROOKE FOSS WESTCOTT

DAY 317

Even the most insignificant decisions or desires can turn into a wrestling match between God's will and our own will, the will of others, or the will of the world. That's when we need to remind ourselves that God can defeat any foe, that Jesus is the ultimate conqueror.

The "victory verses" below can shore up your confidence in God's overcoming power. Add in today's go-to prayer to strengthen you when you're on the mat and about to get pinned, and you'll be sure to win the day—God willing.

For the Lord your God is he that goeth with you, to fight for you against your enemies, to save you. . . . And the Lord said unto Joshua, Fear them not: for I have delivered them into thine hand; there shall not a man of them stand before thee. . . . If God be for us, who can be against us? . . . Thanks be to God, which giveth us the victory through our Lord Jesus Christ. . . . My brethren, be strong in the Lord, and in the power of his might. . . . For whatsoever is born of God overcometh the world.
Deuteronomy 20:4; Joshua 10:8; Romans 8:31;
1 Corinthians 15:57; Ephesians 6:10; 1 John 5:4

Victory in Jesus' name: victory in Jesus' name; to-day: to-day: Thy will be being done: the other will undone: victory in Jesus' name.
S. D. Gordon

DAY 318

Reduced levels of sunlight can mess up your biological clock (circadian rhythm) and drop your serotonin levels (a brain chemical that affects your mood), causing a type of depression called Seasonal Affective Disorder (SAD). Just as less sunlight can distress you physically and emotionally, less of the Son's light can affect you spiritually.

Today, rise up. The light of Jesus is here! Pray for God's illuminating presence to stick close to you and you'll find your joy—and power.

---

*Arise, shine; for thy light is come, and the glory of the L*ORD *is risen upon thee. . . . The sun shall be no more thy light by day; neither for brightness shall the moon give light unto thee: but the L*ORD *shall be unto thee an everlasting light, and thy God thy glory. Thy sun shall no more go down; neither shall thy moon withdraw itself: for the L*ORD *shall be thine everlasting light.*
ISAIAH 60:1, 19–20

Grant me, O Lord, the royalty of inward happiness and the serenity which comes from living close to thee. Daily renew the sense of joy, and let the eternal spirit of the Father dwell in my soul and body, filling every corner of my heart with light and grace, so that bearing about with me the infection of a good courage, I may be a diffuser of life and may meet all ills and crosses with gallant and high-hearted happiness, giving thee thanks always for all things.
ROBERT LOUIS STEVENSON

DAY 319

Someone once wrote, "Pray as though everything depended on God. Work as though everything depended on you." Praying, then just sitting back, waiting for God to provide with no effort on your part, may prove to not be very productive for Him or you. And to work as if you'll get no help from God will not only burn you out but may leave no room for God to work. Yet if you pray and leave it all up to God but work as if all depends on you, you will most likely be rewarded at both ends of the spectrum! For you'll be pleasing God *and* be pleased with God, all at the same time. It's a win-win!

———————————

For even when we were with you, this we commanded you,
that if any would not work, neither should he eat. For we hear
that there are some which walk among you disorderly, working not
at all, but are busybodies. Now them that are such we command and
exhort by our Lord Jesus Christ, that with quietness they work, and
eat their own bread. But ye, brethren, be not weary in well doing. . . .
The grace of our Lord Jesus Christ be with you all. Amen.
2 THESSALONIANS 3:10–13, 18

———————————

The things that we pray for, good Lord,
give us your grace to work for.
SIR THOMAS MORE

DAY 320

Both life and love are eternal. So when faced with the deaths of saved loved ones, keep in mind that you will see them again. And when you are in heaven with the Lord, you will be spending even more time with them and Him. For now, take comfort in the fact that the closer you are to the Lord, the closer you are to them.

For whether we live, we live unto the Lord; and whether we die, we die unto the Lord: whether we live therefore, or die, we are the Lord's. For to this end Christ both died, and rose, and revived, that he might be Lord both of the dead and living.
ROMANS 14:8–9

We give back to you, O God, those whom you gave to us. You did not lose them when you gave them to us, and we do not lose them by their return to you. Your dear Son has taught us that life is eternal and love cannot die. So death is only a horizon, and a horizon is only the limit of our sight. Open our eyes to see more clearly, and draw us closer to you that we may know that we are nearer to our loved ones, who are with you. You have told us that you are preparing a place for us: prepare for us also that happy place, that where you are we may also be always, O dear Lord of life and death.
WILLIAM PENN

DAY 321

When focused on things other than God and His Word, your vision can become clouded, causing you to stumble in your walk. Today's prayer invites you to clear up your eyesight. To look away from false idols, pride, and ego and turn to God.

As you pray, let all distractions fall away. Imagine yourself in God's presence, your eyes firmly fixed on Him. See all the light, power, majesty, strength, love, and compassion He exudes, which reach out to touch and envelop you. In so doing, you'll begin to understand what God is and what you are not.

Make me to go in the path of thy commandments; for therein do I delight. Incline my heart unto thy testimonies, and not to covetousness. Turn away mine eyes from beholding vanity; and quicken thou me in thy way. . . . I thought on my ways, and turned my feet unto thy testimonies.
PSALM 119:35–37, 59

Nothingness strives to be something, and the Omnipotent becomes nothing! I will be nothing with Thee, my Lord! I offer Thee the pride and vanity which have possessed me hitherto. Help Thou my will; remove from me occasions of my stumbling; turn away mine eyes from beholding vanity (Psalm 119:37); let me behold nothing but Thee and myself in Thy presence, that I may understand what I am and what Thou art.
FRANÇOIS FÉNELON

DAY 322

It's hard for a caregiver to see Jesus in the afflicted. They're often cranky, demanding, and irrational. Yet Jesus says you'll be blessed when you give the hungry and thirsty food and drink, when you take in strangers, clothe the unclothed, care for the sick, and visit the imprisoned. For when you do those things for others, you're really doing them for Jesus.

Today's prayer helps pave the way to you recognizing Jesus within those you minister to. Believe it—and you'll see it.

Come, ye blessed of my Father, inherit the kingdom prepared for you from the foundation of the world: For I was an hungred, and ye gave me meat: I was thirsty, and ye gave me drink: I was a stranger, and ye took me in: Naked, and ye clothed me: I was sick, and ye visited me: I was in prison, and ye came unto me. . . . Inasmuch as ye have done it unto one of the least of these my brethren, ye have done it unto me.
MATTHEW 25:34–36, 40

Dearest Lord, may I see you today and every day in the person of your sick, and, whilst nursing them, minister unto you. Though you hid yourself behind the unattractive disguise of the irritable, the exacting, the unreasonable, may I still recognize you, and say: "Jesus, my patient, how sweet it is to serve you." Lord, give me this seeing faith.
MOTHER TERESA

DAY 323

You have access to the greatest teacher, the one to whom God the Father has given all knowledge. And that teacher is the Holy Spirit. He has been sent in Jesus' name. He will instruct you in all things, including the power of prayer.

Invite the Holy Spirit in with prayer today. Ask Him to teach you how to pray, what to pray. He will search your heart. He will speak to God for you, translating your groans and moans, your sighs and tears, your laughter and smiles. He will make clear to God what you are feeling, thinking, hoping, desiring. What a gift of comfort, what an inspiring partner to have as you close your eyes, fold your hands, and seek the face and presence of God.

But the Comforter, which is the Holy Ghost, whom the Father will send in my name, he shall teach you all things, and bring all things to your remembrance, whatsoever I have said unto you. . . . Likewise the Spirit also helpeth our infirmities: for we know not what we should pray for as we ought: but the Spirit itself maketh intercession for us with groanings which cannot be uttered. And he that searcheth the hearts knoweth what is the mind of the Spirit, because he maketh intercession for the saints according to the will of God.
JOHN 14:26; ROMANS 8:26–27

Blessed Prayer-Spirit, Master-Spirit,
teach me how to pray.
S. D. GORDON

DAY 324

Wars and threats of wars, terrorist attacks, bombings, and the like seem to be more and more prevalent in this world we live in. But Jesus tells us not to panic (Matthew 24:6; Mark 13:7). Such things are part of this fallen world. Yet we can pray for peace. For world peace. For God to draw all people together, that they might then recognize we're all the same under the skin, sharing a common blood and destiny.

Today, pray God would step into the fray, wake people up to our commonality, so that peace would at last reign on earth and God's sun shine upon us all in brother- and sisterhood.

The people that walked in darkness have seen a great light: they that dwell in the land of the shadow of death, upon them hath the light shined. . . . For unto us a child is born, unto us a son is given: and the government shall be upon his shoulder: and his name shall be called Wonderful, Counsellor, The mighty God, The everlasting Father, The Prince of Peace. Of the increase of his government and peace there shall be no end.
ISAIAH 9:2, 6–7

O Thou strong Father of all nations, draw all Thy great family together with an increasing sense of our common blood and destiny, that peace may come on earth at last, and Thy sun may shed its light rejoicing on a holy brotherhood of peoples.
WALTER RAUSCHENBUSCH

DAY 325

Overcoming evil with good can be difficult when we're focused on and dragged down by the negativity surrounding us, such as falsehood, cheating, injustice, immorality, ugliness, and bad news reports. But when we fix our attention on and cling to truth, honesty, justice, purity, beauty, and good news, we're reenergized. We find ourselves overcoming the baseness of the world and becoming willingly obedient to God.

Today, ask God to move you, His servant, to see the worthy things in life. And in doing so, become an overcomer.

Whatsoever things are true, whatsoever things are honest, whatsoever things are just, whatsoever things are pure, whatsoever things are lovely, whatsoever things are of good report; if there be any virtue, and if there be any praise, think on these things. . . . and the God of peace shall be with you.
PHILIPPIANS 4:8–9

Almighty God, Who art over all things, Life of all life—stir in our souls, that we, being moved by Thy Spirit, may see those things which are fairest and truest in life, and clinging thereunto, be enabled to get the victory over that which is mean and base; that so at last, all evil passion and unholy desire, all self-will and contrariness to Thee, may be overcome, and we come at last to that sublime state of willing obedience, when Thy will shall be in us supreme. Of Thy mercy hear us, through Jesus Christ our Lord. Amen.
GEORGE DAWSON

DAY 326

The travelers on the road to Emmaus didn't realize they'd been talking with Jesus until He blessed their dinner, after which He vanished. "And they said one to another, Did not our heart burn within us, while he talked with us by the way, and while he opened to us the scriptures?" (Luke 24:32).

Jesus, the living Flame of love, is available to you. Ask that He would burn within you, setting you on fire to become more and more like Him.

[I saw] one like unto the Son of man. . . . And his eyes were as a flame of fire. . . . I saw heaven opened, and behold a white horse; and he that sat upon him was called Faithful and True. . . . His eyes were as a flame of fire, and on his head were many crowns; and he had a name written, that no man knew, but he himself. . . . And his name is called The Word of God.

REVELATION 1:13–14; 19:11–13

Enter my heart substantially and personally, and fill it with fervour by filling it with Thee. Thou alone canst fill the soul of man, and Thou hast promised to do so. Thou art the living Flame, and ever burnest with love of man: enter into me and set me on fire after Thy pattern and likeness.

JOHN HENRY NEWMAN

DAY 327

You're never lost, as long as you stick with Jesus. Why? Because He's the Way, the Truth, and the Life! He's your way to reconciling and being with God. He's got the truth of God that you need to hear and follow. He's able to give you eternal life.

With today's prayer, ask Jesus to keep you on track with Him, who is the Way. To trust in Him, who is the Truth. To rest in only Him, who is the Life. To teach you, via the Holy Spirit, what to believe and do and where to rest. In so doing, you'll find all the guidance you need.

And if I go and prepare a place for you, I will come again,
and receive you unto myself; that where I am, there ye may be also.
And whither I go ye know, and the way ye know. . . . I am the way,
the truth, and the life: no man cometh unto the Father, but by me.
JOHN 14:3–4, 6

O Lord Jesus Christ, who art the Way, the Truth, and the Life,
we pray thee suffer us not to stray from thee, who art the Way, nor
to distrust thee, who art the Truth, nor to rest in any other thing
than thee, who art the Life. Teach us, by thy Holy Spirit what to
believe, what to do, and wherein to take our rest. Amen.

ERASMUS

DAY 328

When trouble arises, your first reaction may be fear, grief, doubt, panic, or worry. That's when you need to go to Jesus in prayer.

Ask Jesus to be with your spirit, and He will do so instantly. Ask Him to live in your heart by faith, and He will enter in immediately, giving you the strength to face any challenge. But He doesn't stop there. With Jesus in your life, He will make whatever befalls you come out not just right—but good!

Know that you've got a Savior by your side. And He'll stick to you like glue!

———————

For this cause I bow my knees unto the Father of our Lord Jesus Christ. . .that he would grant you, according to the riches of his glory, to be strengthened with might by his Spirit in the inner man; that Christ may dwell in your hearts by faith.
EPHESIANS 3:14, 16–17

———————

Lord Jesus. . .be with my spirit, and dwell in my heart by faith. Be with me, O my Saviour, everywhere, and at all times. . . in all events and circumstances of my life; let thy presence sanctify and sweeten to me whatever befalls me. Never leave nor forsake me in my present pilgrimage, but abide with me till thou hast brought me safe, through all trials and dangers, to thy heavenly kingdom; that I may there dwell in thy sight, and enjoy thy love, and inherit thy glory for evermore. Amen.
BENJAMIN JENKS

DAY 329

Only God can break the spell of those things that blind your mind. Ask Him to do so today, and He'll be sure to show you what He wants you to see.

One thing I know, that, whereas I was blind, now I see.
JOHN 9:25

Most gracious and all wise God, before whose face the generations rise and fall; thou in whom we live, and move, and have our being. We thank thee [for] all of thy good and gracious gifts, for life and for health; for food and for raiment; for the beauties of nature and human nature. We come before thee painfully aware of our inadequacies and shortcomings. We realize that we stand surrounded with the mountains of love and we deliberately dwell in the valley of hate. We stand amid the forces of truth and deliberately lie. We are forever offered the high road and yet we choose to travel the low road. For these sins, O God, forgive. Break the spell of that which blinds our minds. Purify our hearts that we may see thee. O God, in these turbulent days when fear and doubt are mounting high give us broad visions, penetrating eyes, and power of endurance. Help us to work with renewed vigor for a warless world, for a better distribution of wealth and for a brother/sisterhood that transcends race or color. In the name and spirit of Jesus we pray. Amen.

MARTIN LUTHER KING JR.

DAY 330

God's words hold power. That's why Moses told his people to put them in their hearts, to teach them, and to talk about them at home, while walking, when lying down, and when rising (Deuteronomy 6:6–7). After Moses died, God told Joshua to meditate on His words day and night, that by doing so, Joshua would then be able to follow those words, which would make him prosperous and successful (Joshua 1:8).

Today, ask God to help you keep His words close, meditating on them day and night. To help you understand and implement them, growing closer to God and prospering for Him in the process.

[The blessed man's] delight is in the law of the LORD; and in his law doth he meditate day and night. And he shall be like a tree planted by the rivers of water, that bringeth forth his fruit in his season; his leaf also shall not wither; and whatsoever he doeth shall prosper.

PSALM 1:2–3

Lord God, let us keep your Scriptures in mind and meditate on them day and night, persevering in prayer; always on the watch. We beg you, Lord, to give us real knowledge of what we read and to show us not only how to understand it, but how to put it into practice, so that we may deserve to obtain spiritual grace, enlightened by the law of the Holy Spirit, through Jesus Christ our Lord, whose power and glory will endure throughout all ages.

ORIGEN

DAY 331

It's a mystery, this Holy Three. One we can hardly wrap our minds around. But although Three, They are yet One. And They and Their power reside within you. Prayerfully meditate upon this today.

And I will pray the Father, and he shall give you another Comforter,
that he may abide with you for ever; even the Spirit of truth; whom
the world cannot receive, because it seeth him not, neither knoweth
him: but ye know him; for he dwelleth with you, and shall be in you
. . . . For there are three that bear record in heaven, the Father,
the Word, and the Holy Ghost: and these three are one.

JOHN 14:16–17; 1 JOHN 5:7

Our God, God of all men,
God of heaven and earth, seas and rivers,
God of sun and moon, of all the stars,
God of high mountains and lowly valleys,
God over heaven and in heaven and under heaven,
He has a dwelling In heaven and earth and sea
And in all things that are in them.
He gives a being to all things, He gives life to all things,
He is Lord over all things, He nurtures all things.
He makes the light of the sun to shine.
He surrounds the moon and stars.
He has made wells in the arid earth
And placed islands in the sea
And stars to give light to the planets.
He has a Son co-eternal with Himself
Like Himself. . . And the Holy Spirit breathes in Them.
They are not separate beings, Father and Son and Holy Spirit.

SAINT PATRICK

DAY 332

It's true. We're imperfect. Some days more than others. Yet Jesus still died for us so that our missteps and mistakes would not become a barrier between us and God. And although we can neither erase what we've done nor carry the weighty load of our worries and cares, Jesus can. He and God are strong enough to roll not only our sins but our burdens away.

Leave all you are, all you've done, and all you're carrying at the foot of the cross today. Then take on the strength and power of the Spirit so you can live more like God would have you live. In Jesus' name.

[Mary Magdalene, Mary the mother of James, and Salome] came unto the sepulchre at the rising of the sun. And they said among themselves, Who shall roll us away the stone from the door of the sepulchre? And when they looked, they saw that the stone was rolled away: for it was very great.

MARK 16:2–4

When we think of ourselves and of the meanness and ugliness and weakness of our lives, we thank Thee for Jesus Christ our Saviour. Grant unto us a true penitence for our sins. Grant that at the foot of the Cross, we may find our burdens rolled away. And so strengthen us by Thy Spirit that in the days to come, we may live more nearly as we ought. Through Jesus Christ our Lord.

WILLIAM BARCLAY

DAY 333

There's a lot about Jesus that attracts us: His love, His scent, His pure life. Today, give in to His attraction. Allow Jesus to draw you deeply within to Him. For it is in Him that you live, move, and have your being (Acts 17:28). It is there, your spirit joined to His, that you find the secret power, the energy of your existence, a love that is better than wine.

Today, let all distractions of the world fall away. Close your eyes and allow yourself to be drawn deeply within. Follow the path of your spirit, the one that senses Jesus' presence. Follow the smell of His sweet perfume. Allow His purity to pour over you. Within that soul and spirit chamber you share with Him, revel and rejoice in His love.

Thy love is better than wine. Because of the savour of thy good ointments thy name is as ointment poured forth, therefore do the virgins love thee. Draw me, we will run after thee: the king hath brought me into his chambers: we will be glad and rejoice in thee, we will remember thy love more than wine: the upright love thee.
SONG OF SOLOMON 1:2–4

Lord, You attract us by the fragrance of Your very being, and You draw us so deeply within to Yourself! Draw me to Yourself, Oh my Divine Center, by the secret springs of my existence, and all my powers and senses will follow You!
JEANNE GUYON

DAY 334

God's grace is so much more powerful than your mistakes, your earthly urges, and the world's wiles. Not only that, but it's a free gift given to you by God, your Creator.

Today, put all fears aside. Reach out with all your heart to receive the grace that draws you into the presence of Jesus. Humbly allow God's gift of grace to supply all you need to face this day—physically, emotionally, mentally, and spiritually. Recognize that God will then do for you all those things you cannot do by yourself.

But he giveth more grace. Wherefore he saith, God resisteth the proud, but giveth grace unto the humble. Submit yourselves therefore to God. . . . Draw nigh to God, and he will draw nigh to you.
JAMES 4:6–8

I come to thee, O Lord, not only because I am unhappy without thee; not only because I feel I need thee, but because thy grace draws me on to seek thee for thy own sake, because thou art so glorious and beautiful. I come in great fear, but in greater love. Oh may I never lose, as years pass away, and the heart shuts up, and all things are a burden, let me never lose this youthful, eager, elastic love of thee. Make thy grace supply the failure of nature. Do the more for me, the less I can do for myself.
JOHN HENRY NEWMAN

DAY 335

The Bible has a lot to say about the tongue, the words you speak. In fact, the Word says, "Death and life are in the power of the tongue" (Proverbs 18:21). That's a pretty strong statement but oh so painfully true!

You cannot tame your tongue. You don't have enough power to do so. But God does.

Today, reflect on some of the things you've said but wish you hadn't. Then seek God's help and wisdom to speak as He would have you speak, bearing good fruit in all you say. Pray for His power to tame your tongue.

But the tongue can no man tame. . . . Out of the same mouth proceedeth blessing and cursing. My brethren, these things ought not so to be. . . . Who is a wise man and endued with knowledge among you? let him shew out of a good conversation his works with meekness of wisdom. . . . The wisdom that is from above is first pure, then peaceable, gentle, and easy to be intreated, full of mercy and good fruits, without partiality, and without hypocrisy.
JAMES 3:8, 10, 13, 17

We must praise your goodness that you have left nothing undone to draw us to yourself. But one thing we ask of you, our God, not to cease to work in our improvement. Let us tend towards you, no matter by what means, and be fruitful in good words, for the sake of Jesus Christ our Lord.
LUDWIG VAN BEETHOVEN

DAY 336

Attitudes of pride and self-sufficiency have no place in your walk or relationship with God. For all that you are and all that you have has been given to you *by* God.

Today, ask God to teach you to respect the earth. To help you remember it's by the efforts of others that you're fed and clothed. To give you compassion for those who are hungry and to help teach them how to harvest God's plenty. As you trust God to help you do this, you'll receive a full reward (Ruth 2:12).

Then said Boaz unto Ruth, Hearest thou not, my daughter?
Go not to glean in another field, neither go from hence, but abide
here fast by my maidens: Let thine eyes be on the field that they do
reap, and go thou after them. . .and when thou art athirst, go unto
the vessels, and drink of that which the young men have drawn.
RUTH 2:8–9

O God, from whose unfailing bounty we draw our life and
all that we possess, forgive our pride and self-sufficiency.
Teach us to reverence the earth, which thou hast made fruitful.
Help us to remember our unity with those by whose work we
are fed and clothed. Touch us with compassion for all who have
not enough to eat. As thou hast given us the knowledge which
can produce plenty, so give us also the wisdom to bring it
within the reach of all: through Jesus Christ our Lord.
JOHN OLDHAM

DAY 337

In this life, we will all have times of suffering. But Jesus took it upon Himself; He carried away our weakness, sickness, and disease—even death—so that someday we will be wholly healed.

In the meantime, although often faced with trouble, we have Jesus to shine within us. In fact, the weaker we are, the more His presence is revealed through us. And we can be encouraged knowing that, although we may be fading without, we're being renewed within day by day (2 Corinthians 4:16).

Today, pray for those who are burdened with cares, sorrows, and illness. Ask Jesus to reveal to them who He is—the God who loves them more than they can imagine.

But we have this treasure in earthen vessels, that the excellency of the power may be of God, and not of us. We are troubled on every side, yet not distressed; we are perplexed, but not in despair; persecuted, but not forsaken; cast down, but not destroyed; always bearing about in the body the dying of the Lord Jesus, that the life also of Jesus might be made manifest in our body. For we which live are always delivered unto death for Jesus' sake, that the life also of Jesus might be made manifest in our mortal flesh.
2 Corinthians 4:7–11

Lord, we pray for all those who are weighed down with the mystery of suffering. Reveal yourself to them as the God of love, who yourself bear all our suffering.
George Appleton

DAY 338

You're never lost if you're following in Christ's footsteps. He has left you an example, a pattern for you to follow so that you would know how God would have you live.

Look upon Jesus today. Allow His pierced heart to win your love for Him. Allow His torn hands to inspire you to do good work, His wounded feet to urge you to errands of mercy, His crown of thorns to move you out of idleness of thought. Most of all, allow His life to be your pattern as you live for Him.

Be ye followers of me, even as I also am of Christ. . . .
For even hereunto were ye called: because Christ also
suffered for us, leaving us an example, that ye should follow
his steps. . . . For ye were as sheep going astray; but are
now returned unto the Shepherd and Bishop of your souls.
1 Corinthians 11:1; 1 Peter 2:21, 25

By virtue of Thy victory, give us also, I entreat Thee, victory.
Let Thy pierced heart win us to love Thee, Thy torn hands
incite us to every good work, Thy wounded feet urge us on
errands of mercy, Thy crown of thorns prick us out of sloth,
Thy thirst draw us to thirst after the Living Water Thou
givest; let Thy life be our pattern while we live and Thy
death our triumph over death when we come to die.
Christina Rossetti

DAY 339

No one really knows what heaven will be like when we get there. But the Bible gives us a few hints, one of which is that it will be a city. Angels and God will be there. And so will lots of other people. Best of all, believers will be able to meet Jesus face-to-face. What's not to like?

This vision of heaven comforts us who remain behind when we think about the loved ones who have gone before. For we know we will one day meet them again in the company of God and angels and believers.

Today, ask God to welcome loved ones who have passed from this life into a better one filled with rest, calm, and peace, forever and ever, amen.

But ye are come unto mount Sion, and unto the city of the living God, the heavenly Jerusalem, and to an innumerable company of angels, To the general assembly and church of the firstborn, which are written in heaven, and to God the Judge of all, and to the spirits of just men made perfect, and to Jesus the mediator of the new covenant.

HEBREWS 12:22–24

Lord, welcome into your calm and peaceful kingdom those who have departed out of this present life to be with you. Grant them rest and a place with the spirits of the just. Give them the life that knows no age, the reward that passes not away, through Christ our Lord. Amen.

SAINT IGNATIUS OF LOYOLA

DAY 340

If you don't have love, you have and are nothing. In fact, love is greater and more powerful than faith and hope. So put aside all else and focus solely on love and loving today. Pray God would so fill you with love that you would be made completely His—in love.

And though I have the gift of prophecy, and understand all mysteries, and all knowledge; and though I have all faith, so that I could remove mountains, and have not charity, I am nothing. . . . And now abideth faith, hope, charity, these three; but the greatest of these is charity.

1 CORINTHIANS 13:2, 13

Lord, because you have made me, I owe you the whole of my love; because you have redeemed me, I owe you the whole of myself; because you have promised so much, I owe you my whole being. Moreover, I owe you as much more love than myself as you are greater than I, for whom you gave yourself and to whom you promised yourself. I pray you, Lord, make me taste by love what I taste by knowledge; let me know by love what I know by understanding. I owe you more than my whole self, but I have no more, and by myself I cannot render the whole of it to you. Draw me to you, Lord, in the fullness of your love. I am wholly yours by creation; make me all yours, too, in love.

SAINT ANSELM

DAY 341

Jesus wants you to be "clear as crystal" (Revelation 21:11) so that His light can shine through you (Matthew 5:16), so that you'll be a child of light (John 12:36).

To be clear, to be able to spread the light of Christ, the eye of your body (your conscience) needs to be healthy, swept clean of any guilt, distrust, greed, and other things that would make you murky, less than transparent.

Today's prayer is short and sweet. It asks God to make you clear as crystal so that His light can shine through. So that others would see Him alone. So that His light and love can be spread around, noticed, and others drawn to it and, thus, to Him.

This simple prayer is a good one to repeat every day. As you do so, you'll be doing a great deal to lighten up this dark world.

The light of the body is the eye: therefore when thine eye is single, thy whole body also is full of light; but when thine eye is evil, thy body also is full of darkness. Take heed therefore that the light which is in thee be not darkness. If thy whole body therefore be full of light, having no part dark, the whole shall be full of light, as when the bright shining of a candle doth give thee light.
LUKE 11:34–36

Lord, make me like crystal that your light may shine through me.
KATHERINE MANSFIELD

DAY 342

To have true companionship with Jesus, you need to bring to Him all your dirt—your misdeeds, your missteps, your mistakes. For only when you come to Him just as you are can He begin to clean you up, forgive you, and fellowship with you, heart to heart, spirit to spirit.

Today, ask Jesus to wash your feet. Then spend time basking in His presence and love.

[Jesus] riseth from supper, and laid aside his garments; and took a towel, and girded himself. After that he poureth water into a bason, and began to wash the disciples' feet, and to wipe them with the towel wherewith he was girded. . . . Peter saith unto him, Thou shalt never wash my feet. Jesus answered him, If I wash thee not, thou hast no part with me. . . . Ye also ought to wash one another's feet. For I have given you an example, that ye should do as I have done to you.

JOHN 13:4–5, 8, 14–15

Jesus, my feet are dirty. Come even as a slave to me, pour water into your bowl, come and wash my feet. In asking such a thing I know I am overbold, but I dread what was threatened when you said to me, "If I do not wash your feet I have no fellowship with you." Wash my feet then, because I long for your companionship.

ORIGEN

DAY 343

Some days you may feel naked, wounded, bleeding, left for dead, and ignored by people you thought would go out of their way to help you. That's when you need to go to Jesus. He's your Good Samaritan. He comes where you are, has compassion on you. He'll bind you, heal you, carry you to comfort, and take care of you there—to His praise and your joy.

But a certain Samaritan, as he journeyed, came where he was: and when he saw him, he had compassion on him, and went to him, and bound up his wounds, pouring in oil and wine, and set him on his own beast, and brought him to an inn, and took care of him. And on the morrow when he departed, he took out two pence, and gave them to the host, and said unto him, Take care of him; and whatsoever thou spendest more, when I come again, I will repay thee.

LUKE 10:33–35

O Lord, show Your mercy to me and gladden my heart. I am like the man on the way to Jericho who was overtaken by robbers, wounded and left for dead. O Good Samaritan, come to my aid. I am like the sheep that went astray. O Good Shepherd, seek me out and bring me home in accord with Your will. Let me dwell in Your house all the days of my life and praise You for ever and ever with those who are there. Amen.

SAINT JEROME

DAY 344

God has a plan for your life. He's steering your boat. He's with you through the raging waters and narrow currents. Nothing can stop His purposes for you.

Your job is to get so close to God and trust Him so much that you'll not be shaken, no matter what happens, because you're certain He'll eventually bring you to not just a safe harbor, but a good and wonderful haven. Pray you would reach that goal today.

But he is in one mind, and who can turn him? and what his soul desireth, even that he doeth. For he performeth the thing that is appointed for me: and many such things are with him.

JOB 23:13–14

Preserve my soul, O Lord, because it belongs to Thee, and preserve my body because it belongs to my soul. Thou alone dost steer my boat through all its voyage, but hast a more especial care of it, when it comes to a narrow current, or to a dangerous fall of waters. Thou hast a care of the preservation of my body in all the ways of my life; but, in the straits of death, open Thine eyes wider, and enlarge Thy Providence towards me so far that no illness or agony may shake and benumb the soul. Do Thou so make my bed in all my sickness that, being used to Thy hand, I may be content with any bed of Thy making. Amen.

JOHN DONNE

DAY 345

Speak to God and God will speak to you.

And the LORD. . .will not fail thee.
DEUTERONOMY 31:8

I do need thee, Lord. I need thee now. I needed thee when sorrow
came, when shadows were thrown across the threshold of my life,
and thou didst not fail me then. I needed thee when sickness laid
a clammy hand upon my family, and I cried to thee, and thou didst
hear. I needed thee when perplexity brought me to a parting of
the ways, and I knew not how to turn. Thou didst not fail me then,
but in many ways, big and little, didst indicate the better way. And
though the sun is shining around me today, I know that I need
thee even in the sunshine, and shall still need thee tomorrow. I give
thee my gratitude for that constant sense of need that keeps me
close to thy side. Help me to keep my hand in thine and my ears
open to the wisdom of thy voice. Speak to me, that I may hear thee
giving me courage for hard times and strength for difficult places;
giving me determination for challenging tasks. I ask of thee no
easy way, but just thy grace that is sufficient for every need, so that
no matter how hard the way, how challenging the hour, how dark
the sky, I may be enabled to overcome. In thy strength, who hast
overcome the world, I make this prayer. Amen.

PETER MARSHALL

DAY 346

So often we do things without thinking. We take on projects without realizing their ramifications. As a result, we may find ourselves stretching our resources or doing things God would rather us not do. But if we ask God to bless all our thoughts, if we ask His advice on what we should do and when, He'll open our eyes to His wisdom, plan, and intentions, and our work will be done in His way and strength. What peace of mind that will bring!

Know thou the God of thy father, and serve him with
a perfect heart and with a willing mind: for the LORD
searcheth all hearts, and understandeth all the imaginations
of the thoughts: if thou seek him, he will be found of thee.
1 CHRONICLES 28:9

Almighty God, Who alone gavest us the breath of life, and alone canst keep alive in us the breathing of our holy desires, we beseech Thee for Thy compassion's sake to sanctify all our thoughts and endeavors, that we may neither begin any action without a pure intention, nor continue it without Thy blessing; and grant that, having the eyes of our understanding purged to behold things invisible and unseen, we may in heart by inspired with Thy wisdom, and in work be upheld by Thy strength, and in the end be accepted of Thee, as Thy faithful servants, having done all things to Thy glory, and thereby to our endless peace. Grant this prayer, O Lord. Amen.

ROWLAND WILLIAMS

DAY 347

The stories of the Bible cover a span of about 1,500 years, from about 1450 BC to AD 100. And the complete volume we have today was canonized before AD 375. That means the form of the Bible you now read has been around for over 1,500 years. Yet God's story, and all the participants in it, are still relevant to you today! They still speak to your heart, mind, and soul.

God's promises continue to bear fruit, have power, and give hope. May that knowledge give you patience as you wait on the promises of the God that inspired the Word, the Christ that became the Word, and the Spirit that translates the Word that lives in you.

For whatsoever things were written aforetime were written for our learning, that we through patience and comfort of the scriptures might have hope. Now the God of patience and consolation grant you to be likeminded one toward another according to Christ Jesus: That ye may with one mind and one mouth glorify God, even the Father of our Lord Jesus Christ.

ROMANS 15:4–6

O God, by whose command the order of time runs its course: Forgive, we pray thee, the impatience of our hearts; make perfect that which is lacking in our faith; and, while we tarry the fulfilment of thy promises, grant us to have a good hope because of thy word; through Jesus Christ our Lord.

SAINT GREGORY OF NAZIANZUS

DAY 348

Jesus knew what lay before Him. That He would be rejected, despised, misunderstood, reviled, mocked, beaten, and killed by those He'd come to save. But none of those things deterred Him from His mission for you.

Just before His arrest, Jesus went into a garden. He put some distance between Himself and His disciples then got down on His knees and prayed. Not for His will but for God's will to be done. As He did so, an angel from heaven came to Him, giving Him the spiritual strength and courage He would need to face His duty, to prevail, to overcome all that was to come against Him. And to rise again.

Each day you have the same opportunity to ask God for His will to be done. And for the courage and strength to live out His will for you in your life. Know God will bless and empower you as you do so today.

And he was withdrawn from them about a stone's cast, and kneeled down, and prayed, Saying, Father, if thou be willing, remove this cup from me: nevertheless not my will, but thine, be done. And there appeared an angel unto him from heaven, strengthening him.

LUKE 22:41–43

Make us, O blessed Master, strong in heart, full of courage, fearless of danger, holding pain and danger cheap when they lie in the path of duty. May we be strengthened with all might by thy Spirit in our hearts.

F. B. MEYER

DAY 349

Disagreements with others can cause discomfort. You can't rest easy until you have another conversation to settle the matter. It's the same thing with God. When you're not walking in His way, you won't rest until you have a heart-to-heart, spirit-to-spirit conversation with Him. Do that today. Bring before Him whatever's standing between you delighting in Him and Him delighting in you. Then enjoy the peace that comes from doing so.

Trust in the LORD, and do good. . . . Delight thyself also in the LORD: and he shall give thee the desires of thine heart. Commit thy way unto the LORD; trust also in him; and he shall bring it to pass. . . . The steps of a good man are ordered by the LORD: and he delighteth in his way.

PSALM 37:3–5, 23

O God, Who puttest into our hearts such deep desire, that we cannot be at peace until we enjoy the feeling of Thy love; mercifully grant that the unspeakable sighing of our souls' need may not go unsatisfied because of any unrighteousness of heart, which must divide us from the All-holy One; but strengthen us to do right by whomsoever we have wronged in thought, word, or deed; to renounce all plans of wrong-doing for the future; to purify our thoughts and govern our appetites, so that we may have no bar between us and Thy glory, but enjoy Thy peace which passeth understanding. Amen.

ROWLAND WILLIAMS

Sometimes, having run ahead of God's plans for us, God begins to work on us. Then we come to our senses and slowly begin making our way back to Him. But God doesn't go slow. He sees us coming and runs to meet us. He hugs us to Himself and kisses us. When we begin to explain, He interrupts us to clothe, feed, and sup with us, to make merry.

Today, come to your senses. Use the prayer to run to God before He gets a chance to run to you. Allow Him to draw you into His loving arms. And make merry in His presence.

And when he came to himself. . .he arose, and came to his father. But when he was yet a great way off, his father saw him, and had compassion, and ran, and fell on his neck, and kissed him. And the son said unto him, Father, I have sinned against heaven, and in thy sight, and am no more worthy to be called thy son. But the father said to his servants, Bring forth the best robe. . .and let us eat, and be merry: For this my son was dead, and is alive again; he was lost, and is found. And they began to be merry.

LUKE 15:17, 20–24

Come, Lord, work upon us, set us on fire and clasp
us close, be fragrant to us, draw us to your
loveliness, let us love, let us run to you.

SAINT AUGUSTINE

DAY 351

Mary Magdalene was devastated. Jesus had been killed. She went to His tomb but His body was gone. She told the disciples, two of whom came to look for themselves. Then they went away. But she remained, weeping.

Angels asked why she was crying. She said because she didn't know where Jesus was. Then she turned and saw a man standing there, not knowing He was Jesus. . .until He called her name.

God is with you. Ask Him to reveal Himself, to startle you, to remind you He is always everywhere, within your life.

[The angels] say unto [Mary], Woman, why weepest thou?
She saith unto them, Because they have taken away my LORD,
and I know not where they have laid him. And when she had thus
said, she turned herself back, and saw Jesus standing, and knew not
that it was Jesus. Jesus saith unto her, Woman, why weepest thou?
whom seekest thou? She, supposing him to be the gardener, saith unto
him, Sir, if thou have borne him hence, tell me where thou hast laid
him, and I will take him away. Jesus saith unto her, Mary.
JOHN 20:13–16

Lord, catch me off guard today. Surprise me with some
moment of beauty or pain so that for at least a moment
I may be startled into seeing that you are with me here in
all your splendor, always and everywhere, barely hidden,
beneath, beyond, within this life I breathe.

FREDERICK BUECHNER

DAY 352

It's one thing to know you're to trust the Lord. It's quite another to actually say, "In You, O Lord, I put my trust"—then believe it, and actually do it.

Today, admit you have such trust in God. Say it, pray it, and believe it. Then walk in the power, strength, and grace God so readily grants to those who trust in Him alone.

In thee, O LORD, do I put my trust. . . . I trusted in thee, O LORD: I said, Thou art my God. . . . The LORD preserveth the faithful, and plentifully rewardeth the proud doer. Be of good courage, and he shall strengthen your heart, all ye that hope in the LORD.

PSALM 31:1, 14, 23–24

O Lord God Almighty, Who givest power to the faint, and increasest strength to them that have no might! Without Thee I can do nothing, but by Thy gracious assistance I am enabled for the performance of every duty laid upon me. Lord of power and love, I come, trusting in Thine Almighty strength, and Thine infinite goodness, to beg from Thee what is wanting in myself, even that grace which shall help me such to be, and such to do, as Thou wouldest have me. O my God! let Thy grace be sufficient for me, and ever present with me, that I may do all things as I ought. I will trust in Thee, in Whom is everlasting strength.

BENJAMIN JENKS

DAY 353

When God looks upon you, His light vanquishes all the darkness within you. He fills you with His love and reveals treasures found in the wisdom of His Word.

Today, seek God's face. Allow Him to open you up to all He has to offer. Ask Him to bring to fruition the seeds of desire He's already sown in you. Permit His Spirit to awaken what you are to pray for.

Do all these things knowing God will satisfy all your longings and fill your hungry soul with His goodness (Psalm 107:9), leading to perfect peace.

One thing have I desired of the LORD, that will I seek after; that I may dwell in the house of the LORD all the days of my life, to behold the beauty of the LORD, and to enquire in his temple. . . . When thou saidst, Seek ye my face; my heart said unto thee, Thy face, LORD, will I seek.

PSALM 27:4, 8

Look upon us, O Lord,
and let all the darkness of our souls
vanish before the beams of thy brightness.
Fill us with holy love,
and open to us the treasures of thy wisdom.
All our desire is known unto thee,
therefore perfect what thou hast begun,
and what thy Spirit has awakened us to ask in prayer.
We seek thy face, turn thy face unto us and show us thy glory.
Then shall our longing be satisfied,
and our peace shall be perfect.

SAINT AUGUSTINE

DAY 354

Hoarders hate to have visitors. Although their home may look great on the outside, on the inside it's a cluttered mess. A nightmare. The last thing they want is to open their door to someone else's comments, surprise, disgust, pity, or worse.

You may not be a physical hoarder, but you may have some spiritual clutter you need to deal with. Today is your day!

Go to God with all the mess you have within your heart. Clear it of bitterness, hatred, fear, doubt, wrong desires, past missteps, and whatever else that's blocking the door to Jesus. Have a heart that He's glad to enter in when you open it from your side.

Behold, I stand at the door, and knock: if any man hear my voice, and open the door, I will come in to him, and will sup with him, and he with me. To him that overcometh will I grant to sit with me in my throne, even as I also overcame, and am set down with my Father in his throne. He that hath an ear, let him hear what the Spirit saith.
REVELATION 3:20–22

Let us have clean hearts ready inside us for the Lord Jesus, so that he will be glad to come in, gratefully accepting the hospitality of those worlds, our hearts: he whose glory and power will endure throughout the ages. Amen.

ORIGEN

DAY 355

Parents don't like when kids whine. And Father God is no exception.

When the Israelites were between the Egyptian army and the Red Sea, they cried out to God then complained to Moses. He told them to be quiet, not fear, stand firm, and God would fight for them.

That's good advice for all believers. Know that amid the direst circumstances, God's with you. He'll give you courage to stand firm and accept your situation, knowing victory is His—and yours.

The children of Israel. . .were sore afraid. . . And they said unto Moses, Because there were no graves in Egypt, hast thou taken us away to die in the wilderness? wherefore hast thou dealt thus with us, to carry us forth out of Egypt? . . . And Moses said unto the people, Fear ye not, stand still, and see the salvation of the LORD. . . . The LORD shall fight for you, and ye shall hold your peace.
EXODUS 14:10–11, 13–14

O Father, who hast ordained that we be set within a scheme of circumstance, and that in stern conflict we should find our strength and triumph over all; withhold not from us the courage by which we alone can conquer. Still our tongues of their weak complainings, steel our hearts against all fear, and in joyfully accepting the conditions of our earthly pilgrimage may we come to possess our souls and achieve our purposed destiny.
WILLIAM EDWIN ORCHARD

Your conscience is considered your "spirit" in the verse below. It's the candle given to you by God, searching every secret place, bringing to light that which needs to be seen. But *God's* Spirit is an even brighter candle, going even deeper within your being.

Today's prayer invites the Spirit's candle within you, to illuminate the very hidden things, the things your conscience may just be breezing by. It shines upon the things in your dreams, the forgotten memories, the past hurts you've suffered. Then the Spirit's candle goes even deeper, telling you who you truly are, revealing the seed God has planted within you from before the foundation of the world.

Use today's prayer to go deep with God. Allow Him to lighten you within so you can see the road without.

The spirit of man is the candle of the LORD,
searching all the inward parts of the belly.
PROVERBS 20:27

Give me a candle of the Spirit, O God, as I go down into the deeps of my being. Show me the hidden things, the creatures of my dreams, the storehouse of forgotten memories and hurts. Take me down to the spring of my life, and tell me my nature and my name. Give me freedom to grow, so that I may become that self, the seed of which You planted in me at my making. Out of the depths I cry to You.

GEORGE APPLETON

DAY 357

Think about your blessings, past and present, and those still to come. Then use today's prayer to thank God for all of them. And ask for one more thing: a grateful heart. Not just for the big things—but for all things.

To start you off, thank God for Jesus. For His love for you. For His mercy and compassion that never fail. Thank God for His Word that explores His wisdom, tells stories of prior faith walkers, and reveals His plan for you.

Renew your passion for thanking God by daily writing down something new for which you can praise Him. In so doing, you'll begin developing a heart whose pulse is one of praise.

Rejoice the soul of thy servant: for unto thee, O Lord, do I lift up my soul. For thou, Lord, art good, and ready to forgive; and plenteous in mercy unto all them that call upon thee. . . . Among the gods there is none like unto thee, O Lord; neither are there any works like unto thy works. . . . For thou art great, and doest wondrous things. . . . I will praise thee, O Lord my God, with all my heart.
PSALM 86:4–5, 8, 10, 12

Thou has given much to me;
Give one thing more—a grateful heart.
Not thankful when it pleaseth me,
As if thy blessings had spare days,
But such a heart whose pulse may be
Thy praise.
GEORGE HERBERT

DAY 358

Many paths and choices lie before you. But God wants you to take the road He's paved for you, to choose what He would have you choose.

Today, ask God for the desire, wisdom, and resources to take the path He's already surveyed and prepared for you. Ask Him to open you up to His voice so you'll know for certain the route He would have you take and not be swayed to go another way, one less pleasing to Him. Ask Him to give you the knowledge, passion, and ability to do all He's required you to do so your pathway to Him will be safe and smooth to the end.

But the path of the just is as the shining light, that shineth more and more unto the perfect day. . . . Let thine eyes look right on, and let thine eyelids look straight before thee. Ponder the path of thy feet, and let all thy ways be established.
PROVERBS 4:18, 25–26

Grant me, I beseech Thee, Almighty and most merciful God, fervently to desire, wisely to search out, and perfectly to fulfil, all that is well-pleasing unto Thee. Order Thou my worldly condition to the glory of Thy name; and, of all that Thou requirest me to do, grant me the knowledge, the desire, and the ability, that I may so fulfil it as I ought, and may my path to Thee, I pray, be safe, straightforward, and perfect to the end.
SAINT THOMAS AQUINAS

DAY 359

When focused on the darkness of the world, it's a short way down to the depths of despair. But there's a solution—found in Jesus and the Word, God and His Spirit.

To stay above the fray, to find the light that saves, remember the words of Jesus. Build yourself up in faith by delving into the Word. Pray in the Spirit. And keep yourself in God's love. For He, the Giver and Sustainer of life and light, will lift you up out of the dark valley of despair, setting you down upon the mountain of hope.

Beloved, remember ye the words which were spoken before of the apostles of our Lord Jesus Christ. . . . Ye, beloved, building up yourselves on your most holy faith, praying in the Holy Ghost, keep yourselves in the love of God, looking for the mercy of our Lord Jesus Christ unto eternal life. And of some have compassion, making a difference. . . . Now unto him that is able to keep you from falling, and to present you faultless before the presence of his glory with exceeding joy, to the only wise God our Saviour. . .
JUDE 1:17, 20–22, 24–25

And now unto him who is able to keep us from falling and lift us from the dark valley of despair to the mountains of hope, from the midnight of desperation to the daybreak of joy; to him be power and authority for ever and ever. Amen.
MARTIN LUTHER KING JR.

Goudge, Elizabeth, 1900–1984; English author.

Grey, Lady Jane [a.k.a. Lady Jane Dudley or the Nine-Day Queen], 1536/1537–1554; English noblewoman and committed Protestant.

Grou, Jean Nicholas, 1731–1803; French Roman Catholic author.

Guyon, Jeanne [a.k.a. Jeanne-Marie Bouvier de la Motte-Guyon, Madam Guyon], 1648–1717; French mystic and writer.

Hallesby, Ole, 1879–1961; Norwegian theologian, author, and educator.

Hammarskjöld, Dag, 1905–1961; Swedish diplomat, author, and second secretary-general of the United Nations.

Hare, Maria [a.k.a. Twtaria Lycester/Mrs. Augustus Hare], 1798–1870; English writer.

Hatch, Edwin, 1835–1889; English theologian and composer.

Herbert, George, 1593–1633; Welsh poet, speaker, and priest.

Hickes, George, 1642–1715; English rector, chaplain, and writer.

Houselander, Caryll, 1901–1954; English writer, artist, and poet.

Hunter, Leslie, 1890–1983; bishop of Sheffield and author.

Jarrett, Bede, 1881–1934; English Dominican friar, Catholic priest, and author.

Jenks, Benjamin, 1646–1724; English curate and author.

Johnson, Samuel, 1709–1784; English author, poet, and moralist.

Jowett, John Henry, 1863–1923; British Protestant preacher and author.

Julian of Norwich, c. 1342–c. 1416; English author and theologian.

Kelly, Blanche Mary, 1881–1966; American journalist and writer.

Kempis, Thomas à, 1380–1471; Dutch author of *The Imitation of Christ*.

Kierkegaard, Søren, 1813–1855; Danish poet, philosopher, theologian, and author.

King, Martin Luther, Jr., 1929–1968; American preacher, activist, humanitarian, and leader of the African American civil rights movement in the US.

Lewis, C. S. [Clive Staples], 1898–1963; British writer of fiction and nonfiction, teacher, poet, speaker, and theologian.

Livingstone, David, 1813–1873; Scottish doctor, missionary, and explorer of Africa.

Luther, Martin, 1483–1546; German professor, composer, monk, and leader of the Protestant Reformation.

MacDonald, George, 1824–1905; Scottish author, poet, and minister.

Mansfield, Katherine, 1888–1923; New Zealand short story writer.

Marshall, Catherine, 1914–1983; American writer and wife of minister Peter Marshall.

Marshall, Peter, 1902–1949; Scottish American preacher, pastor, and chaplain of the US Senate.

Martineau, James, 1805–1900; Unitarian minister, philosopher, theologian, and writer.

Matheson, George, 1842–1906; Scottish clergyman, writer, and hymn writer.

McComb, Samuel, 1864–1938; Irish-born, Oxford-educated Canadian professor, and American minister, writer, and speaker.

Mechthild of Magdeburg, c. 1207–1282/1294; German mystic and poet.

Merton, Thomas, 1915–1968; American monk and writer.

Meyer, F. B. [Frederick Brotherton], 1847–1929; Baptist preacher and writer.

Miller, J. R. [James Russel], 1840–1912; American author and pastor.

Milner-White, Eric, 1884–1963; English priest, soldier, and Dean of York in the Church of England.

Moody, D. L. [a.k.a. Dwight L. Moody], 1837–1899; American evangelist, publisher, and author.

More, Sir Thomas, 1478–1535; English author, statesman, lawyer, and Roman Catholic saint.

Mother Teresa [born Anjezë Gonxha Bojaxhiu], 1910–1997; Roman Catholic nun, missionary, and saint.

Muggeridge, Malcolm, 1903–1990; British author and agnostic who became Christian.

Murray, Andrew, 1828–1917; South African–born Scotsman, author, and pastor.

Nayler, James, 1616–1660; English Quaker leader, evangelist, minister, and writer.

Newman, John Henry, 1801–1890; English Roman Catholic cardinal.

Niebuhr, Reinhold, 1892–1971; American minister, theologian, ethicist, seminary professor, and writer.

Oldham, John, 1653–1683; English poet and educator.

Oosterhuis, Huub, 1933– ; Dutch theologian and poet.

Orchard, William Edwin, 1877–1955; minister, priest, writer, and pacifist.

Origen, c. 184–253; early Christian theologian.

Oxenden, Ashton, 1808–1892; English clergyman, author, and bishop of Montreal.

Patrick, Simon, 1626–1707; English theologian, bishop, and writer.

Penn, William, 1644–1718; English Quaker, philosopher, and founder of Pennsylvania.

Pope, Alexander, 1688–1744; English poet.

Pusey, Edward B., 1800–1882; English churchman, professor, and author.

Quoist, Michel, 1918–1997; French Catholic priest and writer.

Rahner, Karl, 1904–1984; German Jesuit priest and writer.

Rauschenbusch, Walter, 1861–1918; American theologian and pastor.

Rice, Helen Steiner, 1900–1981; American writer and poet.

Roberts, Evan, 1878–1951; Welsh revivalist, poet, and speaker.

Rossetti, Christina, 1830–1894; English poet.

Sailer, Michael [a.k.a. Johann Michael Sailer], 1751–1832; German professor and bishop.

Saint Anatolius, 449–458; Greek patriarch of Constantinople.

Saint Anselm, 1033–1109; monk, abbot, and philosopher.

Saint Augustine [a.k.a. Augustine of Hippo], 354–430; theologian, philosopher, and writer.

Saint Basil the Great, c. 329–379; Greek bishop, theologian, and writer.

Saint Bede the Venerable, 672/673–735; English monk, scholar, and author.

Saint Benedict of Nursia, c. 480–543 or 547; saint.

Saint Bernard [a.k.a. Bernard of Clairvaux], 1091–1153; French abbot, author, and "doctor of the church."

Saint Clement of Rome, died AD 99; bishop of Rome.

Saint Columba of Iona, 521–597; Irish abbot and missionary.

Saint Columbanus, 543–615; Irish-born founder of monasteries, preacher, and poet.

Saint Francis of Assisi [born Giovanni di Pietro di Bernardone], 1181/1182–1226; Italian Roman Catholic friar, preacher, writer, and poet.

Saint Francis de Sales, 1567–1622; bishop of Geneva, author, and Roman Catholic saint.

Saint Gregory of Nazianzus, c. 329–390; archbishop of Constantinople, theologian, and philosopher.

Saint Ignatius of Loyola, 1491–1556; Spanish knight, hermit, and priest.

Saint Jerome, 347–420; priest and theologian; translated most of the Bible into Latin.

Saint Patrick, 5th century; Romano-British Christian missionary, bishop, and saint of Ireland.

Saint Peter Claver, 1580–1654; Spanish priest and missionary.

Saint Richard of Chichester [a.k.a. Richard de Wych], 1197–1253; bishop.

Saint Symeon, 949–1022; Byzantine Christian monk and poet.

Saint Teresa of Ávila, 1515–1582; Spanish nun and author.

Saint Thérèse of Lisieux [a.k.a. Marie Francoise-Thérèse Martin], 1873–1897; French nun.

Saint Thomas Aquinas [a.k.a. Tommaso d'Aquino], 1225–1274; Italian friar, Roman Catholic priest, philosopher, and writer.

Sanford, Agnes, c. 1897–1982; American author.

Shakespeare, William, 1564–1616; English poet, actor, and playwright.

Sherman, Frank Dempster, 1860–1916; American poet and professor.

Smith, Hannah Whitall, 1832–1911; American Quaker, speaker, and author.

Snowden, Rita, 1907–1999; New Zealand missionary and author.

Solzhenitsyn, Aleksandr, 1918–2008; Russian novelist, historian, dramatist, and short story writer.

Spurgeon, Charles, 1834–1892; British preacher and writer.

Starck, Johann Friedrich [a.k.a. John Frederick Stark], 1680–1756; German pastor, author, and hymn writer.

Stevenson, Robert Louis, 1850–1894; Scottish novelist, poet, and essayist.

Steward, Mary, American high school principal, women's club member, and writer.

Stowe, Harriet Beecher, 1811–1896; author and abolitionist.

Taylor, Jeremy, 1613–1667; English author and cleric.

Temple, William, 1881–1944; English bishop, archbishop, teacher, preacher, and writer.

ten Boom, Corrie, 1892–1983; Dutch Christian and author.

Tersteegen, Gerhard, 1697–1769; German reformed religious writer, speaker, poet, and hymn writer.

Torrey, R. A. [Ruben Archer], 1856–1928; American pastor and writer.

Tozer, A. W. [Aiden Wilson], 1897–1963; American preacher, author, and editor.

Underhill, Evelyn, 1875–1941; English writer and pacifist.

van Dyke, Henry, 1852–1933; American clergyman, educator, and author.

Wells, H. G. [Herbert George], 1866–1946; English writer of novels, history, and textbooks.

Wesley, Charles, 1707–1788; English preacher and hymn writer.

Wesley, John, 1703–1791; English preacher and writer.

Westcott, Brooke Foss, 1825–1901; British bishop, scholar, and writer.

Whittier, John Greenleaf, 1807–1892; American Quaker, poet, and abolitionist.

Wilberforce, William, 1759–1833; English politician and abolitionist.

Wilcox, Ella Wheeler, 1850–1919; poet.

William of Saint-Thierry, 1085–1148; monk, theologian, mystic, and abbot.

Williams, Rowland, 1817–1870; British priest, vicar, and professor.

Wilson, Thomas, 1663–1755; English Anglican bishop.

Woolman, John, 1720–1772; North American merchant, essayist, journalist, and Quaker preacher.

SUBJECT INDEX

If You Liked This Book,
You'll Want to Take a Look at. . .

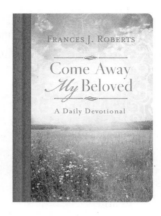

Come Away My Beloved Daily Devotional

Author Frances J. Roberts started a quiet phenomenon with her book *Come Away My Beloved*, and now excerpts from her beloved writings—including *Come Away*, *Dialogues with God*, *Progress of Another Pilgrim*, and *On the Highroad of Surrender*—are available in a beautiful, printed hardcover package. Features the New King James Version of scripture.

Hardback / 978-1-68322-482-2 / $16.99